BAKING
with the
BRASS SISTERS

Also by the Brass Sisters

Also by the Brass Sisters

Heirloom Baking
with the Brass Sisters

Heirloom Cooking
with the Brass Sisters

Baking
with the
BRASS SISTERS

Over 125 Recipes for Classic Cakes,
Pies, Cookies, Breads, Desserts, and Savories
from America's Favorite Home Bakers

MARILYNN BRASS AND SHEILA BRASS

Photography by Andy Ryan

ST. MARTIN'S GRIFFIN
New York

Food styling by Marilynn and Sheila Brass.
Props from the collection of Marilynn and Sheila Brass.

www.stmartins.com

Designed by Kathryn Parise

LIBRARY OF CONGRESS CATALOGING-IN-PUBLICATION DATA

Brass, Marilynn.

Baking with the Brass sisters : over 125 recipes for classic cakes, pies, cookies, breads, desserts, and savories from America's favorite home bakers / Marilynn Brass and Sheila Brass; photography by Andy Ryan.—First edition.

pages cm

ISBN 978-1-250-06435-6 (paper over board)

ISBN 978-1-4668-7004-8 (e-book)

1. Baking. 2. Desserts. I. Brass, Sheila. II. Ryan, Andy. III. Title.

TX765.B729 2015

641.81'5—dc23

2015019390

First Edition: October 2015

10 9 8 7 6 5 4 3 2 1

To Our Father, Harry Brass,

and to Daniel "Dad" Carey (Honorary),

with Love

CONTENTS

LIST OF CONTRIBUTORS OF RECIPES

A Lady From North Carolina

Nanall Gertrude Brubaker Alleman

Aunt Eller

Aunt Ida

Rachel W. Banks

Karen Barrs

Bernice

Bertha Bohlman

Kristina Bracciale

Dorothy Katziff Brass

Harry Brass

Shirley Broner

Evelyn Cardozo

Mother Carleton

Nana May Cleary

Fran Da Costa

Edith

Edna

P. Finelli

Mandy Timney Finizio

Mrs. Finkelstein

Big Mama Ethel Johnson Geer

Amelia George

Grandma Celia Goldberg

Julia Greevsky

Shivani Grover

Harry's Mother

Ann E. Herzog

Harriet Hodges

Joe

Joyce

June

Alison Kennedy

Lawrence and Louise Kimball

Myrna and Chester Langlois

Mrs. Melania Marassi

Marie

Mary Frances

Anna Regina (Hughes) McLaughlin

Grandmother Meinhold

Mary Messer

Merry

Jack Milan

Mom

Maria O'Brien

Jeni Oliver

Mama Ruth Mozley O'Shields

Mary and Ralph Perlovsky

Grandma Mary Agnes Sader Rometo

Arline Ryan

Aunt Grace Schleiger

Aunt Minnie Schleiger

Nana Rose Schraffa

Gertrude Smith

Palma Snarskis

Gloria Schleiger Story

Sue Truax

Helen Varsamis

Muriel Weaver

Grace and Steven Williams

Jayne and Dana Williams

Mrs. Carl Winchenbach

Grandma Rowena Pollard Woodward

Lise Zimmer

ACKNOWLEDGMENTS

Once again, two roundish ladies from Cambridge, Massachusetts, have embarked on a new culinary adventure with the presentation of *Baking with the Brass Sisters*.

We're back to join you in baking the classic cakes, pies, cookies, breads, desserts, and savories that our mothers, grandmothers, and aunts baked for us. We've dipped into our collection of handwritten manuscript cookbooks, and talked with family and friends, and continue to be the stewards and interpreters of newly discovered treasured recipes.

No book is ever written alone. Someone had to recognize our vision, and Claudia Cross of Folio Literary Management was that person. From the moment she told us that we had a beautiful voice, to the actual conception and development of our new baking book, she has guided us graciously and knowledgeably. Her assistant, and our honorary nephew, Michael Sterling, was instrumental in helping us prepare the manuscript for delivery, and we still remember that weekend in November when we worked together to meet our deadline, he in New York and we in Cambridge.

We are fortunate to have an elegant, sophisticated, literary man in our editor, Michael Flamini, to guide us through the joyful journey that was writing *Baking with the Brass Sisters*.

Associate editor Vicki Lame was always available to provide the right answers to our questions, make the right decisions, and graciously slice tea cakes for our launch. Her invaluable literary and management skills helped us achieve our goal of producing our new baking book.

The rest of our team at St. Martin's Press were fun to work with, and we celebrate their creativity and professionalism.

Our thanks to Lisa Marie Pompilio, for the cover design, and Kathryn Parise for the interior design. Leah Stewart performed nobly as copyeditor but, more important, brought her baking experience to the manuscript. Thanks to Samantha Miller for a great index.

Elizabeth Curione and Cathy Turiano guided us through production and were ever ready to answer our questions.

We also thank Jessica Preeg, Tracy Guest, Jeanne-Marie Hudson, Annie Hulkower, Brant Janeway, Jeff Dodes, and Marie Estrada, for publicity and marketing. Our gratitude for setting us on the right track and helping us to start the numerous dialogues needed to launch *Baking with the Brass Sisters*.

Andy Ryan, our gifted photographer, made our photo shoots "a party of three." Andy, who has traveled the world to photograph the famous, often found himself ironing tablecloths and napkins to get just the right background for the classic photographs of what we baked and styled.

A special thank-you to Lisa Ekus, who has always been a source of good advice. We forgive you for hiding that spoon when we took your course.

Everything you told us that could happen, did, and we were ready for it.

Danese Carey, our beloved "third sister," provided vitamins for the soul with her telephone conversations and good advice, especially when we found ourselves living in almost the North Pole last winter as the Massachusetts snowfall reached a record level. The entire Carey, McCoy, Collins, and Bordenca families created an atmosphere of love and support, as they tasted, lovingly criticized, and praised what we baked.

Thank you to Lois and Norman Katziff, Joan and Neal Kline, and Flo Tedeschi, who always said we could do it, and continue to lavish us with love and support.

A special thanks to our cheering section, Naomi Yang, Damon Krukowsky, Ira Silverberg, and Bob Morris, who made this happen.

To Sue Truax, who provided several of her family's recipes for our cookbook, thank you for your contributions, your good baking sense, your generosity, and your friendship.

Finally, special thanks to three friends from New York City: classically trained baker and chef Nick Malgieri, who inspired us to write cookbooks, Bonnie Slotnick, who always found countless handwritten recipes for us to interpret and bake, and majestically talented cookbook author Rick Rodgers, who makes us feel so young by referring to us as "les girls."

The following people generously gave us the encouragement and support, personal as well as professional, that made it possible for us to write *Baking with the Brass Sisters*: Andy and Linda Abelman, Mark Alpert, Thea Anderson, Bonnie Asselin, Steve Axelrod, Judy and Allen Azer, Loretta and Richard Band, Cynthia Broner, the Belmont Post Office, the Broudreau Branch of the Cambridge Public Library, Hilary Finkel Buxton, Maria and Carol Cardozo, Lynn Chase, Barbara Davidson, Margaret Drain, Todd English, Pat and Michael Enwright, Rachel Falino, Deb and Bill Fantasia, Jay Fialkov, Mandy and Fran Finizio, Bobby Flay, the crew at the Fresh Pond Market, Leslie Gaydos, Amy Geer, Annemarie Geldart, Mary and George Geuras, Melissa Gray, Phil Greenough, Olga Greevsky, Tim Grimes, Ishan and Valerie Gurdel, Bill Gustat, Barbara and Herb Haber, Sandy Hyman-Mahaffey, Michael Jenike, Karen Johnson, April Jones, Lee Joseph, Sherri and Jerry Kaplow, Roger and Jan Kulz, Jan Langone, David Lima, Jim, Maria, Zack, and Nicole Levine, Dorothy Lopes, John Lopes, Jenna Lucke, Hilary and Peter McGhee, James McLaughlin, Mary Ann McLaughlin Messick, Richard Muto, Alexandra Myles, Meredith Nierman, Dennis O'Reilly, Lance Ozier, Catherine Pappas, Jamie Parker, Josie Parker, Mary and Eddie Poirer, Esther and Chris Pullman, Jeri Quinzio, Phoebe Ramler, Sally and Kathleen, our Chocolate Angels, Lisa Ann Schraffa, Susan Sherman, Ken Shulman, Linda Smith, Ronn Smith, Mike Kelly and the team at Staples, Donna and Eric Taub, Maureen Timmons, Rick Tompkins, Glenn Truax, Ming Tsai, the WGBH Educational Foundation, Kathy and Nicki Walsh, Barbara Wheaton, Margaret Yarranton, and Nancy Venti Yonge.

Quick Oatmeal Bread, Honey Molasses Bread (Weetabix), and Salt and Pepper Potato Bread

Baking with the Brass Sisters is about the past, the present, and the future.

Because we are ladies in our seventh decades with 128 years of combined home baking experience, we realize that our roles in the kitchen have evolved. We no longer consider ourselves simply the guardians of the precious handwritten recipes we continue to collect. We have assumed a new role as their interpreters. We have found that we not only want to share the recipes we have discovered, but we also want to share the way we bake, translate, and enjoy them. We acknowledge that there is much to be learned from them.

Sometimes we bake the recipes as we find them, but other times we find it necessary to make adjustments in ingredients, baking techniques, temperatures, or timing. Often they inspire us to try them in new and different ways. The lessons we have learned in the several kitchens in which we have baked—the kosher kitchen of our childhood, our first apartment kitchens in Cambridge, the kitchens of family and friends, and even the few commercial kitchens into which we have ventured—have all served to lovingly educate us as home bakers.

Although we continue to present these living recipes from handwritten and oral sources with respect and dignity, we have found that we have come to look at them through the filter of our own experience—what we have tasted or baked ourselves. We also have learned that when we explore variations of a recipe and make adjustments, the results can be even more interesting and appealing. We have come to realize that these fragile scraps were an important step in our becoming innovative home bakers.

We have found that we often rely on the memories of the cakes, tarts, breads, and cookies we ate decades ago—the rich chocolate *Sachertorte* with its apricot and chocolate glaze we enjoyed at The Window Shop in Harvard Square in the 1960s, the light and lively Lemon Chiffon Pie served at the MIT Faculty Club, and the ice cream sundaes with their wealth of velvety hot fudge sauce from Bailey's on West Street in Boston in the 1970s.

There are also times when we are tempted to replicate a pie or a cake we sampled years ago, relying on our ability to remember how they tasted—the Brandy Alexander and the Lemon Rio Pies, which we served to the select group of marriageable hopefuls who courted us. Often we find ourselves involved in the excitement of creating a new recipe using what we have learned through our years of home baking. We decide to reinterpret the flavor of Brandy Alexander Pie as a cheesecake. We savor these experiences. We treasure the ability to add new recipes to our baking repertoire, but what continues to inspire us when we bake these recipes is that we can share them with you.

At some time in our lives, we, like so many home bakers, were challenged to make something from nothing, and we found that baking a simple cake or a pie or a cookie that tastes wonderful and costs little is the recipe that often held our family or friends together. In times of strife or celebration, what we baked in our home kitchens and shared with others defined the meaning of friendship.

We continue to believe that there is nothing that tastes as good as something baked by someone who loves us, unless it is something we have baked and shared with someone we love. Times change, and more and more, we are all faced with greater challenges to re-create and preserve the nurturing, comforting presence of the home kitchen.

We acknowledge those who came before us, who lived by the seasons and respected the land. We believe they not only endured, but flourished, because of their skill in the field and in the kitchen. These earlier generations of home bakers enjoyed the cycle of foods that were available to them, and, most important, they knew that a kitchen with the scent of homemade bread or baking cookies was what really defined a land of milk and honey.

One of our goals is to honor those who came before us, but we also want to enlist the present generation of home bakers to join us in sharing the knowledge and enjoyment they derive from baking with those who will become the next generation of home bakers.

Our Web site continues to be a rich source of stories, recipes, and new friends. We are thrilled with the response to it from people all over the country. This book includes many of their recipes and stories, and those of their families and friends, in addition to the many older ones from our collection and new ones we've created, and so *Baking*

with the Brass Sisters is really about both old and new.

You may recognize some of these recipes as similar to ones prepared by your own mothers, grandmothers, sisters, and aunts. How fortunate we are that bakers all over the country—from recent immigrants to those with deep roots in this part of the world—have shared them with one another and with us.

The recipes in this book are as diverse in their sources as their American home bakers' countries of origin and cultures—Russian, Greek, Jewish, Ukrainian, German, French, Armenian, Italian, English, Irish, Czechoslovakian, Norwegian, and South American—after all, most of us came from somewhere else.

Baking with the Brass Sisters is a cookbook for the twenty-first century. Even though we are women of a certain age, we do not hesitate to enjoy the culinary opportunities that are now available to us. We encourage you to contact us through our Web site, www.thebrasssisters.com, and to consult our blog, *Comfort Food & Joy*. We plan to keep you updated on our activities on Facebook. As part of our extended family of home bakers, we want you to feel that we are available to answer any baking questions that may arise in your own kitchens.

We admit to including much of ourselves in *Baking with the Brass Sisters*—our curiosity, our spirit of adventure, and our satisfaction when we see the dough for Almond Jam Clothespin Cookies come together, when we smell a Pumpkin Tea Cake baking, or when we taste the creamy texture of our Black and White Cheese Pie. We've had fun testing and baking these recipes in our kitchen, and we encourage you to bake them in yours. Each of the recipes is a gift from us to you, and when you bake them, it is a gift to us. We invite you to join us in celebrating the culinary past, in baking with us today, and in creating the future of home baking.

BAKING
with the
BRASS SISTERS

Introduction

Some Thoughts on Home Baking

I t's hard for us to believe that it has been sixty-six years since Sheila started baking at our mother Dorothy's side, and it is sixty years since Marilynn wielded her own child-size wooden rolling pin in the second-floor kitchen of our house on Sea Foam Avenue in Winthrop, Massachusetts.

What we remember is how much fun those times were. We were learning a new skill, we loved spending time with our mother, and whatever we made tasted delicious, perhaps more so because we had baked it ourselves.

We have memories of the large family kitchen with its adjoining pantry stocked with all manner of ingredients. For years the color scheme was 1930s cream and pale green, highlighted by the shining pots and pans that Mama scrubbed diligently after each baking and cooking session.

We grew to know our stove, that large black cast-iron presence, with its green enamel trim, which challenged us every time we placed a loaf of challah or one of Mama's apple pies into its unpredictable oven.

We remember the cousins who came to our seaside home for the summer, fighting over which piece of chocolate cake they were served because Mama had camouflaged a slightly uneven top with extra chocolate frosting. Because we understood that the kitchen floor, with its cheerful flowered linoleum, was slightly slanted, we always entered that variable into our equation for successful baking.

Home baking challenged us when we were young, and it still does today. As it did then, it allows us to feed the people we love, and it makes us appreciate the successful outcome of a Chocolate Chess Pie or a Passover Sponge Cake. Home baking also allows us to feel adventurous and inventive, and at peace with the world.

With 128 years of combined baking experience, we find that we are considered experienced home bakers. We are excited to learn that more and more people are watching us bake on television, and enjoying the recipes and stories we presented in our books *Heirloom Baking* and *Heirloom Cooking*.

For *Baking with the Brass Sisters* we have once again consulted our collection of manuscript cookbooks, but in a different way. We carefully paged through these notebooks, which have been so earnestly inscribed with the personal recipes and stories of home bakers. We like to call them "living recipes" because they are as vibrant and compelling to us today as they were years, or even decades, ago when they were first baked in home kitchens. We have found that we can translate those recipes for cakes, pies, breads, and cookies served in home kitchens years ago into modern versions. Often, they become the jumping-off point when we venture into our own home kitchen and interpret them with present-day ingredients and techniques. For us, it becomes a celebration, not only of those who baked decades before us, but for us, because we find ourselves creating new recipes from the old. We have learned to treasure the words, "variation" and "adaptation."

Not only do we search for these tangible pieces of baking wisdom, but we sometimes have the chance to do a gentle interrogation of their previous owners, who are grateful that these bits of culinary documentation have come under our stewardship. They are happy that we test the recipes, and that someone once again bakes the cakes, pies, breads, and cookies from their family's past. They are pleased that so many home bakers will have the chance to taste Aunt Edna's Feather Gingerbread, or sample a slice of Mrs. Finkelstein's Chocolate Marble Cake.

Because we found that baking these older recipes also preserved the stories of their originators, we discovered that we enjoy being storytellers, and because everyone has a story, we realized that we wanted to tell our own stories, too—how we learned to bake; how we explored the cafés, restaurants, and patisseries of Cambridge, Boston, New York, London, and Copenhagen. We found that we could replicate the biscotti of Boston's Italian North End and the tender tea cakes of London's Borough Market. The flaky pastries of Denmark, with fillings of chocolate, jam, or marzipan, were not so different from those we tasted in New York's Greenwich Village and Soho. We learned from everything we tasted, and then baked them ourselves. This is our story, and we want to share every buttery mouthful with other home bakers.

We carried our culinary childhood memories of baking with Mama into the exciting 1960s and 1970s, when we used to refer to ourselves as "Sweet Young Things." At that time, we were experiencing the joy of our first apartments and the baking of quiches and flourless chocolate cakes, and yet it seems not so long ago. No longer did we have to use the unpredictable, rather daunting home oven of our childhood. Although we had the opportunity to use a modern apartment stove, we understood that the rules for home baking that we had learned when we could barely reach the kitchen table never changed. They were the constants when we entered our small galley kitchens.

We still always read a recipe at least twice before we begin to bake. We still have all our ingredients at hand, and lay out the utensils and pans we will need. We always measure accurately. We check temperatures and baking times and know instinctively when to cover a pie with a tent of aluminum foil because the crust is browning too quickly.

We employ these constants when we test the heirloom recipes we find in our manuscript cookbooks, or when we create new recipes in our home kitchen. Ingredients may vary slightly—the texture of the flour, the amount of moisture or salt in the butter. We might have to work with inconsistent oven temperatures or measurements originally in the irregular proportions of teacups or tumblers, but the way we test old or new recipes remains the same. Because we have done this so many times, we have had the courage to reinterpret recipes or create them using modern, now readily available, ingredients and utensils. When we are whisking ingredients in our kitchen in Cambridge, we remember the old teacup that our mother kept in her flour canister in Winthrop so many years ago. Now, we use standard measuring cups in our modern home kitchen.

The experience of taking loaves of Honey Molasses Bread or a Brown Soda Bread with Dried Cherries, hot and fragrant from the oven, is our reward. We are the richer for the experience. Not only is there satisfaction when a recipe turns out right, but there is the gratitude we feel for the opportunity to be creative and inventive in the kitchen.

Sometimes we add toasted walnuts to the soda bread, and sometimes we sprinkle a cake that originally called for frosting with confectioners' sugar. Sometimes, we are able to bake the recipe just the way it is presented, and we know that the Honey Cake in our oven smells just like the one Grandma Goldberg baked almost 100 years ago, even if it took an afternoon of e-mails between her two granddaughters and us to decipher her notes.

We encourage home bakers to use their culinary memory banks when reading recipes, and when a recipe for Husband's Cake, for example, calls for cinnamon and nutmeg, we hope they will be able to imagine what the addition of a touch of cloves would do to enhance the flavor. We did, and it made a difference in the final recipe.

Baking with the Brass Sisters contains chapters on breakfast, cakes, cookies, breads, pies, family gatherings, teatimes, coffee hours, the joys of summertime treats, and the indulgence of chocolate, and is filled with the recipes and stories of the (mostly) women who created and baked them years ago. There are even recipes for Rhubarb-Walnut Conserve and Vidalia Onion Relish. We encourage you to try these recipes and find out that the past is delicious! However, we also invite you to bake the recipes we have replicated from our own culinary past or created during our culinary present, to discover that the present can be just as delicious as the past.

There is nothing we like better than hearing from you about your experiences with the recipes we have tested and presented. We love meeting with you in airports and sharing the recipe for an oatmeal or butter cookie, or having you explain the best way to make your grandmother's Sand Tarts.

We love to enter the always exciting realm of the Internet to learn that a home baker who lives in British Columbia is sending us a recipe for shortbread, or a gentleman from the Midwest wants to share his mother's recipe for raisin cookies. Once someone e-mailed us from Georgia to say that her whole African American family was sitting around the kitchen table reading our cookbooks and pledging to try some of the heirloom recipes we've rescued.

All of this amazing communication has broadened our world, but so much remains the same since those exciting times when we wrote our first cookbook, *Heirloom Baking*. We still live in Cambridge, Massachusetts. Marilynn still believes that the epicenter of the world is Huron Avenue, with its Fresh Pond Market and Formaggio Kitchen. Sheila still loves sampling the pretzels from the Clear Flour Bakery in Brookline.

Sometimes, it doesn't seem so long ago that we were two hopeful young girls walking the sands of Winthrop Beach, sharing our dreams of the cakes, cookies, breads, and pies we looked forward to baking for family and friends.

Thank you for allowing us to share our story of how we learned to bake. We hope you will share your baking questions, challenges, triumphs, and recipes with us. You have become a part of our extended home baking family, and we will always be your two old friends in the kitchen.

How to Use This Book

Sweet Talk from Two Old Friends

Writing this book has been a joy! It has given us the chance to visit with you in your home kitchen. We've written *Baking with the Brass Sisters* as a tribute to all of the home bakers we've known and the ones we'd like to meet. Too often, the section in cookbooks that tries to tell the reader how to use the book is overly long and contains countless lists of the numerous utensils and ingredients that should be found in the home kitchen.

We decided to do things differently in this book. We wanted to talk with you—home baker to home baker. We also want to make you aware of the variables that arise in any home kitchen, so we have included sidebars throughout the book. We've also used italics when we want to remind you about an important ingredient or instruction in the recipe.

For some, baking is a chore and a challenge. For others, it is as simple as putting on an apron. We want to make baking simple for you, and, more important, we want to make baking fun! When we were starting out in our own apartment kitchens in Cambridge, Massachusetts, we bought all of our pots, and pans at yard sales. Because Cambridge had a large student population, people were always moving and downsizing. We rarely paid more than fifty cents or a dollar for tube pans, cookie sheets, and good-quality frying pans and saucepans. We are still using some of those pans forty-five years later. We suggest that you buy the best kitchen utensils you can afford. They will serve you well, and you will have them for a very long time.

In writing the recipes for *Baking with the Brass Sisters*, we were sure to tell you just what ingredients and what baking equipment are needed. Nearly all of the ingredients in our book are those found in most home pantries or kitchens. You won't have to make a trip to your local gourmet food store. We also tested the recipes with store brands as well as brand name ingredients.

Before You Begin Baking

- Read each recipe several times to make sure you understand the directions and know what ingredients are needed.
- Adjust the oven racks before turning on the oven.
- Have all the ingredients at room temperature, unless otherwise stated.
- Prepare the baking pans and set out racks for cooling.
- Assemble your ingredients and utensils.

It Is Useful To

- Combine ingredients in the order they are listed.

- Set a timer after the recipe is in the oven.
- Allow baked cakes, pies, and cookies to cool completely, unless otherwise noted.
- Store baked items in appropriate containers or refrigerate.

Kitchen Safety

Being two old friends in the kitchen, we are quick to point out possible safety concerns:

- We always have fun in the kitchen, but we suggest that you be rested and focused when baking. Do not take phone calls in the middle of baking, especially when working with hot fluids or sugar syrup.
- Baking with children requires a different, more stringent, set of safety rules. Do not leave a child unattended in the middle of baking.
- Do not leave handles of pots and pans sticking out from the top of stove.
- Do not pick up a hot baking pan with *wet* pot holders or *wet* oven mitts.
- When working with a hot sugar syrup, keep a large bowl full of ice and cold water close to where you are working.
- Turn off a stand mixer before removing ingredients from the bowl. We always unplug the mixer when we're done putting the batter together and we are ready to transfer the batter to the prepared baking pan.
- Turn off the food processor and unplug it before removing the contents. You are working with sharp blades.

- We caution you to refrigerate recipes containing eggs or custard, such as Lemon Curd, Lemon Rio Pie, Kahlúa Pie, Chocolate Guinness Bread Pudding, and others.
- *We give safety instructions in italics in the body of the recipes so that you will be prepared when handling hot liquids.*

Utensils, Stoves, and Appliances

BAKING PANS

Each recipe notes the size and material of bakeware we use. We always use standard sizes that are available in most kitchenware stores. Manufacturers of glass baking products often suggest a lower temperature when using their products. We suggest that you follow the instructions that come with any product you use. When you buy bakeware, we suggest that you explore all the options, buy brand names, and keep copies of warranties and instructions on how to use them in a handy file folder. It is also very important to handle the bakeware and utensils you want to buy to see if they feel comfortable in your hand.

MIXERS AND FOOD PROCESSORS

Once again, buy brand names. We used a Kitchen Aid stand mixer for most of the recipes because one of our goals was to save home bakers as much time as possible. A stand mixer usually can sustain the speed and duration of beating ingredients for long periods of time. A handheld mixer will work for many of the recipes, as will a wooden spoon or a whisk.

We used a 7-cup Cuisinart food processor

usually fitted with the metal blade. Using a food processor for mixing pastry or cookie dough or chopping nuts or coconut is a big help for the home baker.

STOVES, OVENS, AND MICROWAVES

We used a gas stove and oven to test the recipes. Since every appliance is different, we suggest that you learn to work with your own stove. Use an oven thermometer. We usually bake one sheet of cookies at a time, but if you do multiples, switch the baking sheets from rack to rack, and turn them front to back halfway through the baking, especially if your oven doesn't bake evenly. A microwave oven is also helpful to melt butter and chocolate: be sure to use the lowest setting and microwave in small increments of time. Never use metal utensils, containers, or foil in a microwave oven.

BAKING AIDS

There are some baking aids that we would take with us if we were running away from home.

- Offset spatula to smooth batter and frost cakes and cookies
- Microplane for grating zest
- Oven thermometer
- Instant-read thermometer to test water temperature for proofing yeast
- Scale for weighing ingredients or batter
- Disposable gloves and disposable piping bags
- Strainers for sifting, removing seeds from citrus juices, removing nut husks and nut "dust" from chopped nuts, and dusting cakes with confectioners' sugar
- Silpat or silicone liners

- Wax paper and parchment paper
- Standard measuring cups and standard measuring spoons
- Glass measuring cups for measuring liquid ingredients

Quick Guide to Ingredients

ALCOHOL

Use good-quality brandy, whiskey, rum, or wine to plump raisins and dried fruit, and to flavor recipes.

BUTTER

Use unsalted, or sweet, butter, softened at room temperature unless otherwise noted such as cold or melted.

CHOCOLATE AND COCOA

We were diligent in stating the type of chocolate used in the recipes. Baking, or bitter, chocolate is just that: unsweetened chocolate used for baking. The use of semisweet or bittersweet chocolate is noted. Once again, especially when using white chocolate, use the best you can obtain.

CITRUS JUICE AND ZEST

We use medium lemons and oranges with firm, unblemished skins. We used a Microplane to grate the rinds of the fruit to remove the zest; avoid the bitter white pith. We roll the fruit on a flat surface to break up the juice pockets before juicing them on a reamer. Strain the juice to remove the seeds. *A lemon weighing 4½ ounces yields approximately 2 teaspoons of grated zest and 3 tablespoons of lemon juice.*

An orange weighing 6¼ ounces yields approximately 2 tablespoons of grated zest and 4 tablespoons of orange juice.

COFFEE AND TEA

We sometimes use orange pekoe tea when plumping raisins.

We use instant coffee or espresso powder in the recipes.

DAIRY PRODUCTS

We use homogenized whole milk in the recipes. We do not use skim milk. We use cultured buttermilk or sweet milk soured with one tablespoon of lemon juice or white vinegar. We use heavy or whipping cream, not half-and-half.

EGGS

We use only U.S. graded large eggs. Unless otherwise noted, the eggs should be at room temperature. Some recipes call for beating the eggs before adding them to the recipes. Egg whites should be at room temperature before being beaten. Egg whites should be beaten to either soft or firm peaks. Do not overbeat egg whites or they will be dry. If egg whites are used for part of the leavening in a recipe, do not tap the filled pan before placing it in the oven. This will cause the bubbles to burst and will prevent the cake from reaching its full height. Sometimes, eggs are mixed with part of the other ingredients to temper them so they won't be "cooked" by the temperature of the hot ingredients. We tell you how to do this in the recipes.

EXTRACTS, PASTES, AND PURE FLAVORED OILS

Use only pure extracts, and avoid using flavorings. Pure citrus and anise oils substituted for extracts also provide true flavors. Follow the directions on the bottle. The black walnut extract called for in Mother Carleton's Black Walnut Bundt Cake is elusive. If black walnut extract is not readily available, we suggest that you substitute either vanilla or almond extract. *Be sure to buy black walnut extract that is used only to flavor cakes or cookies, and not for medicinal purposes.*

Vanilla paste can be substituted for vanilla extract in all of the recipes. Using vanilla paste is easier than using a vanilla bean. The paste provides those lovely little brown specks without your having to split and scrape a vanilla bean. Follow the directions for substitution on the bottle of vanilla paste. Most brands recommend substituting 1 teaspoon of vanilla paste for 1 teaspoon of vanilla extract.

FLOUR AND GRAINS

Use all-purpose bleached or unbleached flour unless the recipe calls for a specific type, such as cake flour. Some recipes require graham flour, and we found that Bob's Red Mill Graham Flour is the easiest to work with for the Graham Shingle Cookies. We use yellow cornmeal, but white cornmeal works as well.

Measure flour by scooping a cup of flour and leveling it with a knife. If a recipe calls for "1 cup sifted flour," sift the flour and then measure it. If a recipe calls for "1 cup flour, sifted," measure the flour first and then sift it.

FRESH, DRIED, AND CANDIED FRUIT

Use fresh fruit only in season. The quality will be high, and it will taste better. When baking with plums, peaches, or pears, use firm, rather than soft, fruit. Do not use green or unripe fruit. Purchase dried or candied fruit in small quantities and store in a cool place or in the refrigerator.

NUTS

Buy nuts in small quantities from stores with a large turnover. Store and date them in sealed plastic bags or covered plastic containers in the freezer to preserve their freshness. Bring the nuts to room temperature before using them if they have been stored in the freezer. Toasting the nuts gives a richer flavor.

OILS

We used good-quality light olive oil in the recipes, as well as good pure vegetable oil such as corn oil or canola oil. Always check to be sure the oil smells fresh, its color is true, and the "use by" date is current.

SPICES AND HERBS

Buy spices and herbs in small amounts and store in a cool dry place. Do not keep spices near the stove or in the refrigerator. Date containers of spices and herbs to keep track of how old they are. Try mixing spices to achieve an enhanced flavor in the recipes.

SUGAR, MOLASSES, HONEY, AND MAPLE SYRUP

Use white granulated sugar unless a recipe calls for a specific type, such as light brown sugar, confectioners' sugar, or sanding sugar. We gener-

ally do not use dark brown sugar because we feel the flavor is too assertive for most of the recipes, but you may prefer it. When measuring molasses, honey, or syrups, coat the measuring spoon or measuring cup with vegetable oil spray before measuring. It is much easier to use everything in the spoon or cup. We used Grade A or Grade B maple syrup in the recipes, and bought them at our local grocery store.

YEAST

We used active dry yeast in recipes that called for a raised dough. We used quick-rising yeast only when we found that the recipe benefited from its use. We did not use cake yeast. We proofed our yeast in water that had been warmed to 115°F.

Food Styling

We did the food styling for all of the photographs for this book. We did not use any false ingredients or embellishments for the photographs of the pies, cakes, breads, and cookies we present in *Baking with the Brass Sisters*. We used nothing that cannot be consumed.

Because it is sometimes difficult to present recipes at their best when photographing them because of hot lights or varying light, there might be a temptation to use artificial means to replicate what a baked Cheddar Cheese Crust or the frosting on a Pink Velvet Cake looks like at its best. We have not given in to temptation. We have presented the recipes just as we have baked them. Often, we bake two of everything just in case a crust crumbles or a cake is sliced unevenly.

EMBELLISHMENTS

We do have some informal rules for making what we bake look its very best whether in a photograph or when you serve it.

We do not use jelly beans, gumdrops, or regular jimmies. We do use Callebaut chocolate vermicelli, available at Whole Foods Market or Sparrow Enterprises. We do not use dragées, those shiny silver, gold, or white inedible squares, triangles, or disks that say *for decorative use only* on their labels. These are fine for large cakes meant to be viewed, rather than eaten.

We do use chocolate curls, sanding sugar, coarse clear sanding sugar, chocolate-covered coffee beans, chocolate coffee beans, or the chocolate triangles found at Trader Joe's, and edible chocolate perles (pearls) available at Whole Foods Market. Jagged pieces of chocolate broken from bars can also be used on top of a cake, pie, or cookie. We use good-quality food coloring. We use edible gold or silver dust and fragments of edible gold or silver to decorate what we bake. It is expensive, but a little goes a long way.

Whipped cream, confectioners' sugar, and cocoa are three of our good friends. Using a stencil with confectioners' sugar or cocoa can simply and quickly turn a cake or pie into a masterpiece. Whipped cream either in rosettes or dollops can enhance the appearance and taste of something baked, and it can cover a multitude of unavoidable sins such as the tops of uneven cakes or pie.

We do not use candied violets, roses, or mint leaves because they are hard to eat. We do use fresh mint leaves on occasion. We use the tiny pink and yellow edible candy balls distributed by India House.

We make our own frosting flowers using a pastry bag and pastry tips. We do not use bought frosting or gum paste flowers, but if you prefer to do that, it is fine with us. We use Danish sugar (small jagged pieces) and Swedish pearl sugar (round pieces).

We hope that our conversation on home baking has been helpful and encouraging. We hope you will try the recipes and use them as a guide to developing your own creative approach to your time in the kitchen.

Marilynn and Sheila's Home Baking Tips

Bread

TEA BREADS AND QUICK BREADS

In England, a tea cake is a flat bun that can be split, buttered, and served with jam. In the United States, tea breads have a slightly firmer crumb than tea cakes and are usually baked in loaf or round cake pans. Tea cakes, with their more delicate crumb, are also baked either in loaf pans or round pans. They are usually denser and are baked with fruit or nuts or a combination of both. They are often referred to as quick breads. An example of a common quick bread is a banana bread.

DRIZZLE CAKE

A drizzle cake is a very British confection that calls for poking holes in the top of the baked cake and pouring a thick, flavored sugar syrup over it. An opaque glaze forms over the top and down the sides of the cake. Some of the sugar syrup is absorbed by the cake. Lemon Drizzle Cake seems to be the most common of the drizzle cakes we've encountered.

BAKING MORE THAN ONE SHEET AT A TIME

When baking two sheets of cookies at once, one sheet should go on the middle rack, and one sheet should go on the lower rack. Switch and reverse the sheets halfway through for even baking.

Butter

TO BRING BUTTER TO ROOM TEMPERATURE QUICKLY

Place a stick of cold butter, cut into 8 slices, in a glass bowl, cover with plastic wrap, and microwave for 10 seconds. Check and microwave for 10 additional seconds, and then another 10 seconds if necessary—three times in all.

CUTTING BUTTER INTO DICE

Always use *cold* butter when cutting diced butter for the tops of pies, bread puddings, and kugels. The dice should be ¼ -inch square.

Cakes

HOW TO PREVENT HOLES FROM FORMING IN CAKES

Tap cake pans filled with batter gently on the counter to break any bubbles in the batter. Do *not* do this with cakes containing whipped egg whites because the air beaten into the egg whites will be lost, and the cake won't rise.

HOW TO TELL WHEN A CAKE BAKED IN A BUNDT OR TUBE PAN IS DONE

The best way to determine when a cake baked in a Bundt or tube pan is completely baked is to insert a metal tester. If the tester comes out clean, the cake is done. However, with cakes baked in Bundt or tube pans, the cake will pull away from the center and sides when it is done.

HOW TO DIVIDE BATTER BETWEEN TWO PANS

Some of the recipes in *Baking with the Brass Sisters* should be divided and baked in two pans. One to enjoy and one to give away or freeze for later. There are three ways to divide the batter evenly.

- The easiest of all: Divide the batter by eye, place in the prepared pans, level, and insert a metal cake tester in each pan. The leveled batter in each pan should reach the same point on each cake tester.
- Measure the batter in cupfuls and place in the prepared pans.
- Weigh the batter and then divide and weigh it again before placing in the prepared pans

THE DIFFERENCE AMONG FROSTINGS, ICINGS, AND GLAZES

We've always thought of frosting as being more substantial than icings and glazes. Frosting can be used to thickly cover the top and sides of cakes, and is dense enough to fill a pastry bag for piping. It can be used as a filling between layers of cake because it seems to hold up better than icing.

Frosting and icing are often used interchangeably. It all depends where you live. Frosting seems the more popular term in home kitchens in the Northeastern part of the country. Icing seems more frequently used by Southern bakers.

Glazes are thinner, and they are often translucent. To us in Massachusetts, icing is what you put on doughnuts. The term *icing* also seems to be used more often by professional bakers, while *frosting*, to us, will always be a more down-home term.

Chocolate and Cocoa

BAKING CHOCOLATE VS. BITTER CHOCOLATE VS. BITTERSWEET CHOCOLATE

It is very important to use the correct chocolate when baking. Baking chocolate and bitter chocolate are the same. Baking chocolate is known as bitter chocolate in some parts of the United States. Both baking chocolate and bitter chocolate contain no sugar, and they are not eaten as you would a candy bar. Bittersweet chocolate should not be substituted for bitter chocolate. Not only does it contain sugar, but it also contains a different level of cocoa liquor. Bittersweet and semisweet chocolate can be used in the form of chips or chunks in baking, even though they may contain different amounts of sugar and cocoa butter.

"WHITE CHOCOLATE" VS. DARK OR MILK CHOCOLATE

White chocolate is really not chocolate. It is made without cocoa powder or solids. It is made from cocoa butter, milk, and sugar. It is used in candy, frostings, fillings, and sauces. Because of its high oil content, the amount of white chocolate in recipes and how it is treated has to be adjusted carefully. White chocolate cannot be substituted for equal amounts of dark or milk chocolate.

TO MEASURE COCOA NEATLY

When measuring cocoa, place a measuring cup on a sheet of wax paper or parchment paper so that any spills can be easily placed back in the tin.

Citrus

MEYER LEMONS

Meyer lemons are slightly sweeter and often smaller than conventional lemons. They are available for a short season in grocery stores. Adding the zest and juice of a conventional lime to that of a conventional lemon brings the flavor closer to that of the Meyer lemon.

HOW TO GRATE CITRUS ZEST

The best way to grate citrus zest is to use a Microplane grater. The shreds come out light and fluffy and are uniform in size and texture. It is better to grate citrus zest over a piece of plastic wrap rather than a piece of wax paper. The acid from the zest will not eat through the plastic, and it is easy to wrap and store the zest in the plastic wrap until ready to use. The newly designed Microplane graters are curved in shape to catch the grated zest, making it easy to transfer to a bowl.

LEMON AND ORANGE JUICE AND ZEST

We use medium lemons and oranges with firm, unblemished skins. Use a Microplane or a traditional grater to remove the zest or yellow or orange part of the rind, leaving behind the bitter white pith. To juice citrus, roll the fruit on a flat surface to break up the juice pockets first. Cut the fruit in half and juice it on a reamer. Strain the juice to remove any seeds. A lemon weighing 4½ ounces yields about 2 teaspoons grated zest and 3 tablespoons lemon juice. An orange weighing 6¼ ounces yields about 2 tablespoons grated zest and 4 tablespoons orange juice.

Coconut

BAKING WITH COCONUT

When baking cookies or bars containing coconut, it is helpful to shorten the shreds of shredded coconut in the bowl of a food processor fitted with the metal blade. The coconut should be pulsed until it reaches ¼ inch in length. Pulsing too many times could result in coconut "dust." It's much harder to cut cookies or bars after baking when the shreds of coconut are long. When covering a frosted cake with coconut, it is acceptable to use the longer shreds. Coconut is also available in large flakes, which are wonderful for "styling" cakes, cookies, and bars that have already been cooled and frosted.

Dairy—Milk and Cheese

TO WARM COLD MILK

Place cold milk in a glass bowl or glass measuring cup and microwave for 15 seconds. Check and warm in 10-second increments, if necessary, to achieve the desired temperature.

DRY CURD, FARMER'S, AND POT CHEESES

Farmer's cheese, or pot cheese, is less moist than cottage cheese or dry curd cottage cheese and works well as a filling for pastries, such as the Vatrushki on page 43.

Dried Fruit

HOW TO BAKE WITH DRIED FRUIT

To prevent raisins or other dried fruit from sinking to the bottom of cakes and breads, dust them first in 1 to 2 tablespoons of flour before adding them to the batter. Be sure to subtract the 2 tablespoons of flour from the rest of the flour used in the recipe. *The only exception to this rule is dried dates. If you dip cut dried dates in flour, they develop little white jackets of flour when baked.*

Eggs

TO WARM COLD EGGS IN SHELL

Place unshelled eggs in a bowl of lukewarm water for 5 minutes. Remove from the water, shell, and use.

TO SEPARATE EGGS MORE EASILY

It is easier to separate room-temperature eggs than ones taken directly from the refrigerator. Eggs break easier with a single tap when they are at room temperature.

When separating eggs, it is easier to break the whole egg into a small bowl and then separate the eggs into whites and yolks.

TO AVOID ADDING A SPOILED EGG TO A RECIPE

When using eggs, always break them individually into a small bowl before adding them to a batter or dough to prevent adding spoiled eggs to a recipe.

Extracts, Oils, and Pastes

VANILLA, LEMON, ORANGE, AND ALMOND EXTRACTS

Vanilla, lemon, orange, and almond extracts are the most popular flavors in many of the recipes we bake. We suggest that you use only pure extracts, rather than flavorings. Pure citrus oils are also good choices for baking, but you might have to use less than liquid extracts. Vanilla is available in liquid, paste, bean, and powder form.

BLACK WALNUT EXTRACT

Black walnut extract lends a unique flavor to Mother Carleton's Black Walnut Bundt Cake. Since we suggest that home bakers use extracts rather than flavors, if black walnut extract is not readily available, we suggest that you substitute either vanilla or almond extract. *Be sure to buy black walnut extract that is used only to flavor cakes or cookies, and not for medicinal purposes.*

MAPLE SYRUP

We found that the Grade A maple syrup called for in the New England Maple Walnut Cake and the Buttery Maple Walnut Pie has a subtle maple flavor. The maple syrup enhances the flavor of the other ingredients. If you wish, you can use maple extract to add a more pronounced maple flavor to those recipes.

Green Tomatoes

BAKING WITH GREEN TOMATOES

Tomatoes are actually a fruit, even though we think of them as a vegetable. The green tomatoes we use in baking are unripened tomatoes, not the heirloom green variety that are sweet enough to eat when green. For years, home bakers have made Green Tomato Pies and Green Tomato Mincemeat. Green tomatoes can bake into a moist chocolate cake. Recipes made with green tomatoes are seasonal and are a great way to use up those last field tomatoes between the end of summer and the beginning of autumn before they turn red. It is not unusual to bake with vegetables such as green tomatoes, zucchini, pumpkin, and sweet potatoes.

Hot Liquids

BRINGING LIQUIDS TO A ROLLING BOIL

A rolling boil describes a mixture placed over heat and brought to a boil—in which large bubbles form and "roll" across the surface of the mixture being heated.

Stand Mixer

WHEN TO ADJUST THE SPEED DIAL ON A STAND MIXER

When using a stand mixer, do not immediately move the speed dial to the highest setting. This could burn out the motor. Gradually accelerate the speed. When adding dry ingredients, such as flour or cocoa, use slow to moderate speed to prevent the dry ingredients from flying out of the bowl.

STAND MIXER SAFETY TIPS

Always insert beater attachments into stand mixer *before* plugging the cord into the wall outlet.

Always *turn off* the power and *remove* the plug from the wall outlet before removing the beater attachments.

Measuring

MEASURING LIQUIDS VS. SOLIDS

Always use the proper utensils for measuring liquids or solids. Always place measuring cups on a level surface. Glass measuring cups are used for measuring liquids. Metal measuring cups are used for measuring solids such as flour, sugar, brown sugar, cornstarch, grains, and tapioca.

MEASURING HONEY, MOLASSES, MAPLE, OR CORN SYRUP

To measure honey, molasses, maple, or corn syrup easily, coat the measuring cup or measuring spoon with vegetable oil spray.

MEASURING BROWN SUGAR

Brown sugar should always be firmly packed into a measuring cup for accurate measurement.

THE GREAT TEACUP DEBATE
(Measuring Dry Ingredients)

We have found that in translating old recipes so that they work in home kitchens, we have to be kitchen sleuths. When we first started baking from these heritage recipes, many of them handwritten on scraps of paper or compiled in notebooks, the recipes didn't work the way they should have. After reading the recipes over several times and combining the clues we found by talking with and e-mailing home bakers all over the country, we discovered that a cup of flour or sugar often meant a teacup of flour or sugar. Many home bakers told us that Grandma or Mama kept an old teacup, one usually missing a handle ("we never waste anything") in her flour or sugar bin. The actual capacity of the teacup differed significantly from a measuring cup. Sometimes the cup was smaller, sometimes the cup was larger, but the discrepancy was enough to throw off the success of the recipe. Once we made adjustments to the recipe, we were able to work with it to achieve the desired results. It was tricky, but we managed after several tries.

YIELDS ARE APPROXIMATE

Each yield for the recipes in *Baking with the Brass Sisters* is approximate. One home baker's heaping teaspoon is not the same as another's. Some bakers use a regular teaspoon, while others use a 1-teaspoon measuring spoon. There is a difference between a soupspoon, a tablespoon, and a 1-tablepoon measuring spoon. Using a small scoop to measure cookie dough when making drop cookies may also affect the yield. The number of slices provided from a cake or pie can vary by how wide a slice is cut. However, you will find that most of the yields are very close to the number of cookies or slices listed.

Nuts

HOW TO TOAST NUTS

Preheat the oven to 350°F. Spread nuts out on a foil-lined baking sheet, with the foil shiny side up. Toast the nuts for 5 minutes. Remove the baking

sheet from the oven. Shake the nuts to promote even toasting and return to the oven for another 5 minutes. Toast pine nuts for 3 minutes on each side. Cool on a rack. Store cooled toasted nuts in sealed plastic bags or covered plastic containers labeled with the name of the nuts, quantity, and date toasted. Store nuts in the freezer. Bring nuts to room temperature before using. Buy nuts in small quantities.

BAKING WITH SALTED NUTS

Take into account the amount of salt added to the recipe when using salted nuts. You might want to reduce the amount of salt in the recipe.

Ovens

After reading the handwritten recipes in our collection of manuscript cookbooks, we found that there was often no mention of how to cope with differing oven temperatures or baking times. The recipe would simply ask for a hot or quick or slow oven.

We suggest that you invest in an accurate oven thermometer. If you find that it takes a longer or shorter time for a cookie or pie or cake to brown, or to test done, when you bake in your own oven, go by your own guidelines. If you need to turn a sheet of cookies or brownies halfway through the baking process to be sure of even baking, do so. If you find the temperature that we suggest seems too high or too low to produce the desired finished result in your oven, adjust the recipe accordingly. No one knows your stove better than you do.

Piecrust

TO MAKE A SCALLOPED PIECRUST EDGE

To make a decorative scalloped piecrust edge, coat the pie pan with vegetable spray or butter. Place the piecrust in the pie pan. Using clean scissors, trim excess piecrust along the edges of the pie, leaving enough to form a decorative edge. To make a scalloped edge, place the knuckles of your index and third fingers together on the inside edge of the crust. Place the bottom of a wooden spoon handle between your two knuckles. Continue doing this until you go along the entire edge of the pie. If there is leftover piecrust, roll it between your hands to form a small rope. Cut the rope into four pieces each about 1¼ inch long and place on four equal sections of the piecrust edge. Pinch each piece to attach it to the bottom edge of the pie pan and the top edge of the crust. These are the "keepers." They will prevent the edge of the crust from falling into the center of the pie. They can be easily removed after the pie is baked and cooled.

Pie Tips

- Keep a pie pan lined with an unbaked bottom crust in the refrigerator while making the filling. Remove the piecrust from the refrigerator 10 minutes before filling and baking.
- Leftover piecrust can be used to patch the edges of a pie.

HOW TO ROLL OUT AND STORE PIECRUST AND COOKIE DOUGH

When rolling out a sheet of piecrust or cookie dough, place the unrolled dough inside a plastic bag, roll it to the desired length and thickness, and close. Store the dough in the refrigerator or freezer until ready to use.

Safety

WET HANDS AND POT HOLDERS DON'T MIX

Never use pot holders with wet or damp hands when handling hot pot handles or taking pans out of the oven. This is especially important when removing pans or bowls from a water bath or *bain-marie*. If pot holders become wet, dry them *thoroughly* before using.

Seeds

HOW TO TOAST SESAME SEEDS

Toasting white sesame seeds brings out their nutty sweet flavor. Place sesame seeds in a heavy frying pan and stir with a wooden spoon over medium heat. Sesame seeds, which contain a lot of natural oil, will begin to shine as they are toasted and will turn a golden brown. It should take 3 to 5 minutes to toast the seeds. Do not leave them in the pan unattended. Place the pan of toasted sesame seeds on a wire rack to cool.

TUXEDO SESAME SEEDS

Either black or white sesame seeds are a good way to decorate savory and cocktail crackers.

A mix of both black and white sesame seeds is known as "tuxedo" sesame seeds. If you can't find the blend, you can make your own by simply mixing the two types of sesame seeds. *Black sesame seeds should not be toasted.* They are used in Asian cooking, while white sesame seeds are preferred in the Middle East. If sesame seeds smell rancid or look dried out, do not use them. They are not fresh. Store sesame seeds in the refrigerator or freezer between uses.

NOTE TO READER

Consuming raw or undercooked eggs may increase your risk of food-borne illnesses. Recipes made with custard containing eggs should be kept refrigerated before and after serving.

1 *Rise and Shine*

THE RECIPES

W ith age comes wisdom, and we have come to regard breakfast as the most important and, perhaps, the most enjoyable meal of the day.

We've found that every family has its own breakfast tradition. Some talk lovingly about everyone gathered around a table laden with eggs, breakfast meats, and hearty breads and muffins, exchanging pleasantries and leisurely lingering over second cups of tea or coffee. Some of us, however, only have time to finish a cupful of cold cereal or, if we're lucky, a bowl of hot oatmeal before starting our day.

The history of the American breakfast also includes an unusual morning meal of slices of hearty mincemeat or apple pie and, in New England, a generous fragment of sharp cheddar cheese to go with that apple pie.

Growing up in the 1940s and 1950s, breakfast was most often eaten at home or occasionally at a Hayes-Bickford Cafeteria in Boston, where we ate bowls of hot oatmeal or small stacks of pancakes. On weekdays, we would have the traditional cold cereal, eaten mainly with the anticipation of foraging for a small metal toy in the half-empty carton, or for collecting the valuable box tops used to order a decoder ring or a crime fighter's badge.

Sometimes, we deigned to eat a bowl of hot farina or, begging a tardy awakening, would breakfast on a home-baked corn muffin or a piece of our mother's Cinnamon Coffee Cake.

The more elaborate breakfasts were saved for Saturday and Sunday mornings when our father was in charge of the kitchen, the stove, and the waffle maker. A pharmacist, he was precise in his measurements and his methods. Each buckwheat pancake, courtesy of Aunt Jemima, was perfect. Each waffle was splendid, glistening with a pat of butter and "maple" syrup—suitable for a spread in *Gourmet*. His omelets were fluffy, and his French toast divine. Weekend breakfasts with Daddy were priceless. It was when we all, like the sun, could rise and shine.

Our New England Baked Maple French Toast Casserole simplifies making French toast for a crowd, while the delicate Breakfast Corn Cake, Grandma Woodward's Whole Wheat Date Muffins, Cowboy Coffee Cake, and Sweet Potato Drop Scones with their orange glaze are perfect for a more intimate family meal or a solitary breakfast.

Quick Tips

- To prevent tough muffins, do not overbeat the batter.
- Make sure the griddle or pan is hot enough before frying the pancakes.
- When dividing batter for breakfast cakes between more than one pan, weigh the batter in the pans on a scale.
- Use clean kitchen scissors, coated with vegetable oil spray, to cut dried dates for Grandma Woodward's Whole Wheat Date Muffins.

A Little Girl's Blueberry Cake

*We found this recipe handwritten in the back of a 1932
copy of* Kitchen Fun, A Cook Book for Children,
*by Louise Price Bell. It looked so simple and good,
we decided to make a few adjustments and bake it as
two loaves of Blueberry Cake. It must have been a very
special recipe for the little girl who owned this cookbook.
We added the cinnamon and nutmeg and the coarse
sanding sugar on the top.*

CAKES

3 eggs, separated

2 cups blueberries, washed and dried

3½ cups flour

4 teaspoons baking powder

1 teaspoon salt

1 teaspoon cinnamon

1 teaspoon nutmeg

1 cup milk

2 teaspoons vanilla extract

¾ cup (1½ sticks) unsalted butter, at room
    temperature

1 cup granulated sugar

TOPPING

2 tablespoons coarse white sanding sugar

1. Set the oven rack in the middle position.
Preheat the oven to 350°F. Prepare two 9 by 5 by
3-inch loaf pans by coating them with vegetable oil
spray. Cover the bottoms and ends of each pan with
a single strip of wax paper. Coat the wax paper
liners with vegetable oil spray. Dust the pans with
flour and tap to remove the excess.

2. Add the egg whites to the bowl of a stand
mixer fitted with the whisk attachment and beat
until firm peaks form. If you have only one mixer

bowl, transfer the beaten egg whites to another
bowl and set aside.

3. Add the blueberries to a small bowl. Measure the flour into a large bowl and remove
2 tablespoons. Add the 2 tablespoons of flour to the
blueberries and mix together to coat. Set aside. Add
the baking powder, salt, cinnamon, and nutmeg to
the flour in the larger bowl and whisk to combine.
Set aside. Combine the milk and vanilla in a glass
measuring cup and set aside.

A Little Girl's Blueberry Cake

A Little Girl's Blueberry Cake

4. Add the butter and granulated sugar to the bowl of the stand mixer fitted with the paddle attachment and beat to combine. Beat in the egg yolks one at a time, making sure to scrape down the mixture from the bottom and sides of the bowl. Add the dry ingredients and the liquid ingredients alternately in three additions and continue beating. Fold in the whipped egg whites in three additions. Fold in the floured blueberries. Pour the batter into the prepared pans and sprinkle the tops with coarse sanding sugar. Bake the cakes for 45 minutes, or until a metal tester inserted into the center of each loaf comes out clean.

5. Cool the cakes on a wire rack for 20 minutes before removing from the pans. Run a butter knife around the edges of pans to loosen the cakes. Lift the cakes by the ends of the wax paper and remove from the pans. Place the cakes back on the rack, remove the wax paper, and allow to cool completely. Cut the cooled cakes with a sharp serrated knife. Store the cooled cakes, loosely wrapped in wax paper, at room temperature.

Yield: 2 loaves; 12 slices per loaf

SWEET TIP: Wash the blueberries and dry them thoroughly. Blueberries that are still damp will clump together when dipped in flour.

Breakfast Corn Cake

This recipe for a Breakfast Corn Cake came from the manuscript cookbook of Amelia George of Patterson, New Jersey. This is a corn "cake," not a cornbread, and it is made in a stand mixer. The original recipe never mentioned what type of pan in which to bake the Breakfast Corn Cake, so we decided on two loaf pans. This corn cake is great with strawberry jam and unsalted butter. A cornbread becomes a corn cake when beaten egg whites are used to help it rise.

3 eggs, separated

1 tablespoon cream of tartar

2 cups cornmeal

2 cups flour

4 teaspoons baking powder

½ teaspoon salt

1 teaspoon nutmeg

2 cups milk

1 teaspoon vanilla extract

¾ cup (1½ sticks) unsalted butter,
    melted and cooled

1 cup granulated sugar

Coarse clear sanding sugar for top (optional)

1. Set the oven rack in the middle position. Preheat the oven to 350°F. Prepare two 9 by 5 by 3-inch loaf pans by coating them with vegetable oil spray. Cover the bottom and ends of each pan with a single strip of wax paper. Coat the wax paper liners with vegetable oil spray. Dust the pans with flour and tap to remove excess flour.

2. Add the egg whites to the bowl of a stand mixer fitted with the whisk attachment and beat for 1 minute. Add the cream of tartar and continue beating until firm peaks form. If you have only one mixer bowl, transfer the beaten egg whites to another bowl and set aside.

3. Add the cornmeal, flour, baking powder, salt, and nutmeg to a separate bowl and whisk to combine. Set aside. Add the milk and vanilla to a glass measuring cup and set aside.

4. Add the butter and granulated sugar to the bowl of the stand mixer fitted with the paddle attachment and beat to combine. Beat in the egg yolks one at a time, making sure to scrape the mixture from the bottom and sides of the bowl. Add the dry ingredients and liquid ingredients alternately in three additions and continue beating until incorporated. Fold in the beaten egg whites in three additions. Pour the batter into the prepared pans. Sprinkle with coarse sanding sugar for a sweeter corn cake, if desired. Bake the corn cakes for 45 minutes, or until a metal tester inserted into the center of each loaf comes out clean.

5. Cool the corn cakes on a wire rack for 20 minutes. Run a butter knife around the edges of the pans to loosen the cakes. Lift the cakes by the ends of the wax paper to remove them from the pans. Remove the wax paper from the cakes. Let the cakes cool completely. Cut the cooled cakes with a sharp serrated knife. Store the cooled cakes, loosely wrapped in wax paper, at room temperature.

Yield: 2 loaves; 12 slices per loaf

NORTHERN CORNBREAD VS. SOUTHERN CORNBREAD

As ladies from Massachusetts, we are used to yellow cornmeal and sugar in our cornbread and corn cakes. However, all of the recipes we've found for cornbread from the Southern part of the country are made with white cornmeal, no sugar, and buttermilk. There is a difference in taste. We like to think of our sweet yellow cornbread from the North as almost a confection. The Southern cornbread we've experienced is a no-nonsense "bread," and when made with cracklings (rendered slivers of pork skin and pork fat), results in a rich bread.

Buckwheat Pancakes

We've tried to replicate the nutty-tasting buckwheat pancakes our father made for us on chilly Sunday mornings in our Winthrop kitchen. We must confess that Aunt Jemima and the Vermont Maid, she of "maple" syrup fame, were two honored guests at our table during the 1950s, but this recipe is made without a mix. Most recipes for buckwheat pancakes are very similar, but we added brown sugar and used beaten eggs whites for added leavening. As when making quick breads, the less beating and folding in, the better.

¾ cup buckwheat flour

¾ cup all-purpose flour

1 teaspoon baking powder

1 teaspoon baking soda

½ teaspoon salt

2 tablespoons firmly packed brown sugar

2 eggs, separated

3 tablespoons unsalted butter, melted and
　　cooled

2 cups buttermilk

Butter or vegetable oil, for frying the
　　pancakes

1. Add the buckwheat flour, all-purpose flour, baking powder, baking soda, salt, and brown sugar to a mixing bowl and whisk to combine. Set aside.

2. Beat the egg whites in the bowl of a stand mixer fitted with the whisk attachment until they form stiff peaks.

3. Whisk the egg yolks in another bowl. Add the butter and buttermilk to the egg yolks and whisk to combine. Add this wet mixture to the dry ingredients and combine: do not overmix. Gently fold the beaten egg whites into the pancake batter in two additions.

4. Coat the inside of a glass 2-cup liquid measuring cup with vegetable oil spray and fill with pancake batter. Heat a griddle or frying pan over medium-high heat and place 1 tablespoon of butter on top of the griddle or in the frying pan. Pour a teaspoon of batter onto the prepared griddle and wait until it begins to form. When the tiny test pancake is turned and done on both sides, remove it from the griddle. Pour enough batter onto the griddle to make four 4- to 5-inch pancakes (¼ cup of batter makes a 4-inch pancake). Lift the cup high when pouring the batter because it will help you control the flow. Cook the pancakes until bubbles form on the tops of the pancakes and around the edges. Lift one edge of each pancake to be sure it is formed and that the underside is brown. Turn and cook until the bottom side of each pancake is golden brown, 1½ to 2 minutes. Do not overcook. Serve the pancakes immediately, topped with maple syrup, sour cream, or melted butter. Add more butter to the griddle before making the rest of the pancakes.

Yield: 14 to 15 pancakes

SWEET TIPS: You can also coat the griddle with vegetable oil spray to prevent the pancakes from sticking.

• The pancakes should be eaten as soon as they are done. If this is not possible, keep the cooked pancakes warm on a baking sheet in an oven turned to a low setting, 250°F.

• A teaspoon of vegetable oil can be substituted for butter when frying Buckwheat Pancakes.

SOLVING THE MYSTERY OF
MAKING PANCAKES

There are some variables in making pancakes that should be addressed:

THE PAN: We found that making pancakes on a heavy flat griddle produced the best pancakes, thin and easy to turn. The griddle should be large enough so that you can comfortably turn the pancakes or move them around on the griddle.

THE STOVE: What is medium-high for one kitchen stove can sometimes be hot for another stove. The Calphalon griddle we used could take the fairly hot medium-high heat on our burner. You can always turn the heat down or up, as needed.

THE TIMING: Some pancakes will be ready in 1 to 2 minutes before turning. Lift an edge with a metal spatula to be sure the pancake is brown on the bottom before turning it over. It is easier to make thinner pancakes on a griddle than in a frying pan. If your pancakes are too thick, they will take longer to cook, and extra batter may leak onto the griddle when you turn them. Thin pancakes are easier to make than large thicker ones.

Chocolate Walnut Banana Muffins

This recipe reminds us of the luxurious muffins we used to eat at Bailey's on West Street in Boston in the 1960s and the 1970s. Rich and moist, paired with a cup of strong black coffee—pure heaven at ten in the morning. For those of you who don't know about Bailey's, they were famous for their candy and muffins, and for serving their ice cream sundaes in tall hotel silver dishes on large hotel silver saucers to catch the generous drips from the hot fudge sauce.

2 cups flour

½ teaspoon salt

1 teaspoon baking powder

½ teaspoon baking soda

1 cup firmly packed brown sugar

½ cup (1 stick) unsalted butter, melted and cooled

2 eggs, beaten

1 teaspoon vanilla extract

½ cup buttermilk

2 large ripe bananas, mashed (1 cup)

3 ounces bitter chocolate, melted and cooled

1 cup chopped walnuts or pecans

18 walnut or pecan halves

1. Set the oven rack in the middle position. Preheat the oven to 375°F. Coat the entire top surface and cups of a 12-cup muffin pan and a 6-cup muffin pan with vegetable oil spray. If using paper liners, spray the top surface of the pans before placing the paper liners in the openings. Muffin cups should have a diameter of 2½ inches across the top.

2. Add the flour, salt, baking powder, and baking soda to a large bowl and whisk to combine. Set aside.

3. In a separate bowl, whisk together the brown sugar, butter, eggs, vanilla, and buttermilk to combine. Add the wet mixture to the dry ingredients and whisk gently to incorporate. Fold in the mashed banana, cooled chocolate, and nuts.

4. Fill each prepared muffin cup with the batter, dividing the batter evenly among the pans. Add 1 walnut or pecan half to the top of each muffin. Bake for 18 to 20 minutes, or until a metal tester inserted into the center of a muffin comes out clean. Cool the muffins in the pan on a wire rack for 5 minutes before turning them out. Store the muffins, loosely wrapped in wax paper, at room temperature.

Yield: 18 muffins

SWEET TIP: Use a wire whisk or wooden spoon to prepare these muffins. Do not use an electric mixer because muffin batters should not be overmixed.

SWEET TOUCH: These muffins are wonderful with salted butter and apricot jam.

Cowboy Coffee Cake

We found this recipe handwritten in a copy of Laboratory Recipes. *Not satisfied with the original recipe, which called for buttermilk and cinnamon, we decided to substitute sour cream to enrich the texture, and our own blend of cardamom, mace, and ground cloves. This is a very easy "hands-on" recipe, but the instructions are a little bit out of the ordinary. Cowboy Coffee Cake is fun to make with the children in your family.*

2½ cups flour

2 cups firmly packed brown sugar

½ teaspoon salt

⅔ cup (10⅔ tablespoons) unsalted butter, at room temperature

1 teaspoon cinnamon

1 teaspoon cardamom

½ teaspoon mace

¼ teaspoon cloves

½ cup pecans, toasted and coarsely chopped

¼ cup coarse sanding sugar

2 teaspoons baking powder

½ teaspoon baking soda

2 eggs

1 cup sour cream

1 teaspoon vanilla extract

1. Set the oven rack in the middle position. Preheat the oven to 350°F. Line the bottom and four sides of a 9 by 13 by 2-inch metal pan with aluminum foil, shiny side up. Coat the foil with vegetable oil spray.

2. Add the flour, brown sugar, salt, butter, cinnamon, cardamom, mace, and cloves to a mixing bowl and combine with your fingers until crumbly. Transfer ½ cup of the crumb mixture to another bowl. Add the pecans and coarse sanding sugar to the ½ cup of crumb mixture and set aside for the topping. Add the baking powder and baking soda to the larger amount of the crumb mixture, and combine.

3. Add the eggs to bowl of a stand mixer fitted with the paddle attachment and beat until pale. Add the sour cream and vanilla and beat to combine. Add the larger crumb mixture and beat on *low* to break up any clumps in the batter. Add the batter to the prepared pan and smooth the top with an offset spatula. Sprinkle the pecan-and-sanding-sugar mixture on top of the cake. Bake the cake for 35 minutes, or until a metal tester inserted into the center comes out clean. The sides of the cake will pull away slightly from the sides of the pan. Transfer the cake to a wire rack and cool completely. When cool, remove the cake from the pan, using the sides of the foil as handles. Remove the foil from the coffee cake and cut the cake into squares. If you want to serve the cake sooner, place the pan in the refrigerator to cool. Leftover cake should be stored, loosely covered with wax paper, at room temperature.

Yield: one 9 by 13 by 2-inch cake; about twenty-four 2-inch squares

SWEET TIP: Using disposable gloves is helpful when making the crumb mixture.

SWEET TOUCH: Serve with softened vanilla ice cream or whipped cream.

Grandma Woodward's Whole Wheat Date Muffins

This recipe came from our friend Jeremy Woodward's, great-grandmother Rowena Pollard Woodward, a Maine matriarch who knew how to bake the hearty food that kept her family going through cold New England winters. The recipe for these muffins originally called for graham flour, but we tried them with whole wheat flour to lighten their texture. Graham flour gives them a nutty taste and a coarser crumb. These substantial muffins are easy to make and are best eaten the day they are made. The coarse sanding sugar melts into the muffin tops to form a sweet glaze.

1 cup all-purpose flour

6 ounces chopped dates or 1 cup firmly
    packed coarsely chopped dates

1 cup whole wheat or graham flour

2 teaspoons baking soda

½ teaspoon salt

1 teaspoon nutmeg

2 tablespoons granulated sugar

¼ cup (½ stick) unsalted butter, melted
    and cooled

1 tablespoon honey

2 eggs, beaten

2 cups buttermilk

1 teaspoon vanilla extract

2 tablespoons coarse clear sanding sugar

1. Set the oven rack in the middle position. Preheat the oven to 400°F. Coat the entire top surface and cups of a 12-cup muffin pan with vegetable oil spray.

2. Add the flour to a large bowl. Add either the whole wheat or graham flour, baking soda, salt, nutmeg, and granulated sugar to the flour in the larger bowl and whisk to combine. Set aside.

3. Add the butter, honey, eggs, buttermilk, and vanilla to a separate bowl and whisk to combine. Add this wet mixture to the dry ingredients and whisk gently to combine: do not overmix. Fold the dates into the batter with a spatula. Pour the batter into a 2-cup glass measuring cup with a pouring lip. Pour the batter into the cups of the prepared muffin pan, filling them to the top. Gently shake the muffin pan to evenly distribute the batter in the muffin cups. Smooth the tops of the muffins with an offset spatula. Sprinkle the tops with sanding sugar. Bake the muffins for 25 minutes, or until a metal tester inserted into the center of a muffin comes out clean.

4. Transfer the muffin pan to a wire rack and allow the muffins to cool for 5 minutes. Remove the muffins from the pan, place on a second rack, and continue to cool. If the tops of the muffins stick to the pan, run a butter knife around the tops of the muffins. The muffins may be eaten while still warm.

Yield: 1 dozen muffins

SWEET TIP: If buttermilk is not available, add 1 tablespoon lemon juice or vinegar to milk to sour it.

• A 4-cup glass measuring cup can be used to pour the batter into the muffin cups, but a 2-cup glass measuring cup is easier to use.

SWEET TOUCH: These muffins are wonderful served with salted butter or cream cheese.

Harriet's Bran Muffin Bread

We found this handwritten recipe in a cookbook belonging to Harriet Hodges. This annotated Southern cookbook from the 1890s highlighted the regional specialties of a lady who loved to bake for her family. This bran bread is sweetened with molasses, possibly New Orleans molasses, rather than New England molasses.

4 eggs

1¼ cups buttermilk

½ cup (1 stick) unsalted butter, melted and cooled

½ cup molasses

2 cups wheat bran

2 cups flour

1 teaspoon baking powder

1 teaspoon baking soda

1 teaspoon salt

½ teaspoon cinnamon

½ teaspoon nutmeg

1 cup golden raisins

1. Set the oven rack in the middle position. Preheat the oven to 350°F. Coat two 9 by 5 by 3-inch loaf pans with vegetable oil spray. Line the bottoms and ends of the pans with a single strip of wax paper and coat with vegetable oil spray. Dust the pans with flour and tap to remove the excess.

2. Add the eggs to large bowl and beat until the yolks and whites are well combined. Add the buttermilk, butter, molasses, and wheat bran to the eggs and gently mix. Let the mixture stand for 10 minutes.

3. In a separate bowl, whisk together the flour, baking powder, baking soda, salt, cinnamon, and nutmeg to combine.

4. Add the dry ingredients to the wheat bran mixture and stir just until combined. Using a spatula, fold in the raisins; do not overmix.

5. Divide the batter equally between the prepared loaf pans. Tap the pans gently once to remove any air bubbles. Using a spatula, make a line in the batter down the length of each pan. Bake the loaves for 60 minutes, or until a tester inserted into the center of each comes out clean. Transfer the pans to a wire rack to cool for 15 minutes. When cool, run a butter knife around the edges of the pans, then flip the loaves out onto the rack. Remove the wax paper liners. Flip again and allow to cool before cutting into slices with a sharp serrated knife. Store leftover bran bread, wrapped in wax paper, at room temperature.

Yield: 2 loaves;
nine 1-inch slices per loaf

SWEET TIPS: Use regular size raisins, not jumbo, because the bread will be easier to cut.
• Cut 1-inch slices because the bread may be crumbly.

SWEET TOUCH: Try toasting the bread and spreading the slices with butter or orange marmalade.

Irish Soda Bread

We found this simple recipe from the 1930s for old-fashioned Irish soda bread written on an index card. This soda bread has a cakelike texture, and the tea-soaked raisins raise it to another level. It bakes into a charming addition to breakfast or afternoon tea. A slice is good with salted butter and orange marmalade.

4 cups flour

1 cup sugar

1 teaspoon baking soda

1 teaspoon salt

¾ cup (1½ sticks) cold unsalted butter, cut into ¼-inch dice

1⅓ cups buttermilk

1 cup raisins, soaked in hot tea for ½ hour

2 teaspoons caraway seeds (optional)

1. Set the oven rack in the middle position. Preheat the oven to 350°F. Coat a 9-inch springform pan with vegetable oil spray. Dust with flour and tap the pan to remove the excess flour.

2. Combine the flour, sugar, baking soda, and salt in a large bowl. Add the butter to the dry ingredients in the bowl and, using your fingers or a fork, incorporate until the dough has the texture of cornmeal. Add the buttermilk to the dough and mix thoroughly, making sure to catch all of the dry ingredients at the bottom of the bowl. The dough will be a little loose.

3. Sprinkle the raisins and caraway seeds, if using, over the dough. Using a spatula or your hands, work the raisins and seeds gently into the dough until all have been distributed, about 1 minute. Using a spatula, transfer the dough to the prepared pan. Using an offset spatula, smooth the dough evenly into the pan, making a disk. Cut a cross on the top of the dough with a sharp knife. Bake the loaf for 55 to 60 minutes. The bread is done when the crust turns a golden brown and a metal tester inserted into the center of the bread comes out clean.

4. Transfer the pan to a wire rack and cool the bread for about 20 minutes. Remove the sides and bottom of the pan and allow the bread to cool completely before slicing. Brush any excess flour from the bread with a pastry brush. Store leftover soda bread, wrapped in wax paper, at room temperature.

Yield: 1 loaf; 10 to 12 slices

SWEET TIPS: Do not cut the bread until completely cool, to avoid crumbling.

• The bread can be successfully frozen.

• Allow frozen bread to come to room temperature before serving, or warm it in a 300°F oven for a few minutes to take off the chill.

Mango Corn Muffins

This handwritten recipe from the 1930s was originally for a breakfast corn cake, but we decided to bake it as corn muffins. We added the cream and the mango jam. Apricot jam or orange marmalade are also acceptable choices for the filling that coats the inside of the baked muffin and forms a sweet surprise at the bottom.

3 eggs, separated

1 teaspoon nutmeg

2½ cups cornmeal

1½ cups flour

½ teaspoon salt

1 teaspoon baking soda

1 tablespoon cream of tartar

¾ cup (1½ sticks) unsalted butter,
    melted and cooled

1 cup sugar

1½ cups milk

½ cup heavy cream

2 teaspoons vanilla extract

1 ½ cups mango jam

1. Set the oven rack in the middle position. Preheat the oven to 400°F. Coat the entire top surface and cups of two 12-cup muffin pans with vegetable oil spray. If using paper liners, spray the top surface of the pan before placing the liners in the openings of the muffin pans. Muffin cups should have a diameter of 2½ inches across the top.

2. Add the egg whites to the bowl of a stand mixer fitted with the whisk attachment and beat until soft peaks form. Set aside. Add the nutmeg, cornmeal, flour, salt, baking soda, and cream of tartar to a bowl and whisk to combine. Set aside.

3. In a small bowl, beat the egg yolks; set aside. In another larger bowl, whisk together the butter and sugar. Add the beaten egg yolks, milk, cream, and vanilla and whisk gently just until combined. Add the dry ingredients to the wet ingredients in three additions and stir to combine. Fold in the whipped egg whites in three additions.

4. Fill each muffin cup three-quarters full with the batter. Add a tablespoon of jam on top of the batter in each cup. Add the remaining batter until each cup is full. Spread and smooth the batter with the back of a tablespoon until the jam filling is completely covered. Bake the muffins for 20 to 25 minutes, or until slightly brown around edges.

5. Cool the muffins in the pan on a wire rack for at least 20 minutes. Using your fingers, carefully remove the muffins from the pan (don't tip the pan and dump the muffins out). *The muffins should be cool enough to handle, but the melted jam may be still hot.* Store the cooled muffins, loosely wrapped in wax paper, in a plastic container or cardboard box in the refrigerator. Warm the muffins to room temperature before serving.

Yield: 2 dozen muffins

SWEET TIPS: Add the jam to a small bowl before using. Add additional jam, if needed, to the original bowl containing the jam using a clean spoon to avoid cross contamination from the eggs in the batter already in the muffin cups. Save only jam that has remained in the jar.

Mary's Pumpkin Bread

Mary Perlovsky, she of Banana Bread fame, generously gave us her recipe for the Pumpkin Bread she gifts us with every Christmas. This is a very simple recipe, but it combines the flavor and texture of pumpkin with a quartet of spices: cinnamon, nutmeg, ginger, and cloves. This pumpkin bread can be made by hand or with a mixer. The uncomplicated loaf nicely reflects the hospitality of the New England holiday season.

1¾ cups flour

1 teaspoon baking soda

¼ teaspoon baking powder

1 teaspoon salt

½ teaspoon cinnamon

⅛ teaspoon nutmeg

⅛ teaspoon ginger

¼ teaspoon cloves

⅓ cup (5⅓ tablespoons) unsalted butter,
    at room temperature

1⅓ cups sugar

⅓ cup milk

2 eggs

1 cup canned pure pumpkin puree
    (see sidebar, page 37)

1. Set the oven rack in the middle position. Preheat the oven to 350°F. Coat a 9 by 5 by 3-inch loaf pan with vegetable oil spray. Cover the bottom and ends of the pan with a single strip of wax paper and coat with vegetable oil spray. Dust with flour and tap the pan to remove the excess flour.

2. Add the flour, baking soda, baking powder, salt, cinnamon, nutmeg, ginger, and cloves to a bowl and whisk together until well blended. Set aside.

3. Cream the butter and sugar in the bowl of a stand mixer fitted with the paddle attachment. With the mixer running, add the eggs one at a time. Add the pumpkin puree and mix to combine.

4. Add the dry ingredients and milk alternately to the creamed mixture until all of the ingredients have been incorporated. Pour the batter into the prepared pan and tap gently to remove any air bubbles. Bake for 65 minutes, or until the bread pulls away from the sides of the pan and a metal tester inserted into the center comes out clean.

5. Transfer the pan to a wire rack and cool the bread for 10 minutes. Run a butter knife around the edges. Turn the bread out onto the rack, remove the wax paper, and allow it to cool completely. Cut the cooled bread with a wide-bladed serrated knife. Store leftover pumpkin bread, covered with wax paper, at room temperature. The pumpkin bread can be frozen and reheated for a few minutes in a 300°F oven before serving.

Yield: 1 loaf; 12 to 14 slices

USING CANNED PUMPKIN

We used canned pure pumpkin puree when baking the recipes in this book because it is readily available, and the texture and moisture are more uniform than making your own pumpkin puree. Because cooked fresh pumpkin is different in water content and fiber, we suggest that you use canned pumpkin in the recipes. Canned squash can also be substituted for canned pumpkin. The flavor will be a bit more subtle when using squash.

New England Baked Maple French Toast Casserole

This recipe is very much like a bread pudding, but we don't make it in a water bath (bain-marie), and we don't trim the crusts from the brioche. We thought it would be fun to replicate in casserole form the French toast our father made for us so many Sundays ago on Sea Foam Avenue. We didn't use real maple syrup in those days, but the "Vermont Maid" was a frequent visitor in our kitchen.

BREAD LAYERS

2 tablespoons maple syrup

¼ teaspoon cinnamon

¼ teaspoon nutmeg

½ cup plus 2 tablespoons (1 stick plus 2 tablespoons) unsalted butter, melted and cooled

12 to 14 large pieces challah or brioche

CUSTARD

1½ cups milk

1 cup heavy cream

½ cup Grade A maple syrup

1 teaspoon vanilla extract

½ cup granulated sugar

½ cup firmly packed brown sugar

½ teaspoon salt

½ teaspoon cinnamon

½ teaspoon nutmeg

8 eggs, beaten

TOPPING

1½ cups walnuts, toasted and coarsely chopped

¾ cup firmly packed brown sugar

3 tablespoons unsalted butter, melted

1. Coat a 9 by 13-inch ovenproof glass baking dish with vegetable oil spray and set aside.

2. To prepare the bread layers: Add the maple syrup, cinnamon, and nutmeg to the melted butter. *Lightly* brush the melted maple butter on both sides of each brioche slice.

3. To make the custard: Add the milk, cream, maple syrup, vanilla, granulated sugar, brown sugar, salt, cinnamon, and nutmeg to a bowl and whisk to combine. Add the beaten eggs to the mixture and whisk to incorporate.

4. Pour a small amount of the custard into the bottom of the prepared baking dish. Tilt and swirl until the bottom is covered. Make a layer of the brioche on top of the custard. Fill in the spaces with extra brioche. Pour one-third of the remaining custard over the brioche. Add another layer of brioche on top of the custard in the same manner. Pour half of the remaining custard on top of the brioche. Add the remaining brioche on top of the custard. Pour the remaining custard mixture on top of the brioche.

5. Using a knife, cut ten slits through the layered brioche and custard. Cover the top of the casserole with plastic wrap and press down firmly with your palm until the custard rises to the top. Let stand for 10 minutes, then push down gently again on top of the French toast. Place the casserole in the refrigerator for at least 4 hours, or overnight if possible, pushing down one more time to distribute the custard.

6. To make the topping: Add the chopped walnuts to a strainer and shake over the sink to remove any walnut "dust." Add the walnuts and brown sugar to a bowl, whisk to combine, and set aside.

7. Set the oven rack in the middle position. Preheat the oven to 350°F. Remove the casserole from the refrigerator and wait 15 minutes before sprinkling with the walnuts-and-brown-sugar mixture. Pour the melted butter over the top, cover with aluminum foil, and place in the oven. *Optionally, the baking dish can be placed on a rimmed metal baking sheet lined with aluminum foil and coated with vegetable oil spray, to prevent the casserole from possibly dripping into the oven.* Bake for 60 minutes. Remove the foil after the first 20 minutes. The casserole is done when it begins to pull away from the sides of the dish and a metal tester inserted into the center comes out clean.

8. Remove the casserole from the oven and place on a wire rack. Allow to cool for 5 minutes. Serve with maple syrup and sour cream. Any leftover casserole should be covered with wax paper and stored in the refrigerator.

Yield: 8 servings

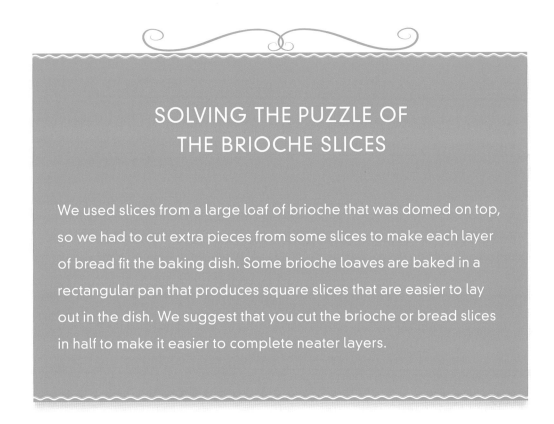

SOLVING THE PUZZLE OF THE BRIOCHE SLICES

We used slices from a large loaf of brioche that was domed on top, so we had to cut extra pieces from some slices to make each layer of bread fit the baking dish. Some brioche loaves are baked in a rectangular pan that produces square slices that are easier to lay out in the dish. We suggest that you cut the brioche or bread slices in half to make it easier to complete neater layers.

Sweet Potato Drop Scones

We've always been intrigued by sweet potatoes because they seem so irregular and bumpy on the outside, but when baked, their interiors are transformed into a velvety orange softness. We decided to carry this transformation one step further by making Sweet Potato Drop Scones. We tested them on a crew of house painters, and they received a thumbs-up in a medley of different hues of paint. The scones are best eaten the day they are made.

SCONES

2½ cups flour

1 tablespoon baking powder

¾ cup granulated sugar

½ teaspoon salt

1 teaspoon cinnamon

1 teaspoon ginger

½ teaspoon nutmeg

¼ cup (½ stick) cold unsalted butter, cut into
    4 slices

1 tablespoon grated orange zest

1 egg

1 cup mashed sweet potato

⅓ cup heavy cream

½ cup golden or dark raisins

½ cup pecans, toasted and coarsely
    chopped

GLAZE

1 cup confectioners' sugar

Pinch of salt

1 teaspoon grated orange zest

2 tablespoons orange juice

1. Set the oven rack in the middle position. Preheat the oven to 400°F. Use two silicone liners or cover two 14 by 16-inch baking sheets with aluminum foil, shiny side up. Coat the foil with vegetable oil spray.

2. To make the scones: Add the flour, baking powder, granulated sugar, salt, cinnamon, ginger, and nutmeg to the bowl of a food processor fitted with the metal blade attachment and pulse to combine. Add the butter and orange zest and pulse again to combine. Add the egg, sweet potato, and cream to a bowl and whisk to combine. Add to the dry ingredients in the processor and pulse until the dough pulls away from the blade and comes together. Transfer the dough to a mixing bowl. Fold in the raisins and pecans. The dough will be soft.

3. Drop the dough by ¼ cups onto the prepared baking sheets. Bake for 17 to 18 minutes, or until the tops are lightly brown and the bottoms are golden brown. Transfer the baking sheets to wire racks and let the scones cool for about 10 minutes.

4. To make the glaze: Sift together the confectioners' sugar and salt in a small bowl. Mix in the orange zest. Add 1 tablespoon of the orange juice, and whisk until smooth. Add the remaining orange juice, a teaspoon at a time, until you reach the desired consistency. Slip a sheet of wax paper under each rack to catch drips and place the scones on the rack. Using a teaspoon or fork, drizzle the glaze over the top of the scones and let set. Store, loosely covered with wax paper, at room temperature.

Yield: 1 dozen scones

SWEET TIP: We found that the batter for the sweet potato scones can be kept in the refrigerator overnight and baked the next day.

Sweet Potato Drop Scones

Vatrushki (Russian Cheese Pastries)

Vatrushki
(Russian Cheese Pastries)

We were looking through our collection of manuscript cookbooks when a slip of paper with a handwritten recipe for Vatrushki *fell out. We were intrigued when we read the recipe because it called for a filling made with farmer's or pot cheese, that dry curd cheese so popular in Eastern European baking and cooking. We were rewarded with a delicate dough and a creamy filling. These dear little pastries remind us of the sun, with their golden egg glaze and the "rays" formed with the tines of a fork. The half-moon is also a delightful variation. Vatrushki served with sour cream or honey make a breakfast or teatime a delight.*

FILLING

1 pound farmer's cheese

1 egg

2 tablespoons sugar

1 teaspoon vanilla extract

2 tablespoons flour

⅛ teaspoon salt

½ cup golden raisins

DOUGH

½ cup sugar

2 cups flour

1 teaspoon baking powder

⅛ teaspoon salt

1 cup (2 sticks) cold unsalted butter,
    cut into 1-inch slices

1 egg

1 teaspoon vanilla extract

EGG WASH

1 egg, beaten

1. To make the filling: Add the farmer's cheese, egg, sugar, and vanilla to the bowl of a stand mixer fitted with the paddle attachment and beat to combine. Add the flour and salt to mixture and beat to incorporate. Add the raisins to the filling and beat on low speed to distribute. *Keep the filling in the refrigerator until ready to make the vatrushki.*

2. To make the dough: Put the sugar, flour, baking powder, and salt in the bowl of the food processor fitted with the metal blade and pulse three times to mix. Add the butter and pulse until crumbly. Add the egg and vanilla and pulse until the mixture comes together.

3. Transfer the dough to a piece of wax paper, divide it in half, and shape each half into a disk. Unless your kitchen is very warm, you don't have to chill the dough before rolling it out.

4. Set the oven rack in the middle position. Preheat the oven to 350°F. Line a 14 by 16-inch baking sheet with a silicone liner or aluminum foil, shiny side up. Coat the foil with vegetable oil spray.

5. Before rolling out the dough, remove the filling from the refrigerator. Roll out each disk of dough between two sheets of floured wax or parchment paper to a ¼-inch thickness. With a cookie cutter dipped in flour, cut the dough into 4-inch circles. Place about 1 heaping tablespoon of the filling in the center of half of the circles. Place a second circle on top of the filling and crimp the edges with the tines of a fork dipped in flour. Place the pastries on the prepared baking sheet and brush with the egg wash. Bake for 25 minutes. The pastries will be a light golden brown when done.

6. To make half-moon Vatrushki: Take a 4-inch circle of dough and place a level tablespoon on one side of the circle, leaving a half-inch edge around the dough. Fold over the circle of dough into a half-moon shape and press the edges together

with the tines of a fork dipped in flour. Brush with the egg wash and bake for 25 minutes.

7. Transfer the baking sheet to a wire rack to cool. You may serve the Vatrushki while slightly warm, or at room temperature. Leftover Vatrushki should be wrapped in wax paper and *must* be stored in the refrigerator. Vatrushki are best eaten the day they are made, but they are still good reheated in a low oven the next day.

Yield: 18 round Vatrushki (takes about a half recipe of filling); 36 half-moon Vatrushki

SWEET TIPS: When making round pastries, any leftover filling can be used to fill omelets. *Leftover filling should not be eaten uncooked because it contains raw eggs. The filling should be cooked inside of omelets.*

• Fresh moist raisins do not have to be plumped because the liquid in the cheese will keep them moist when baked.

VATRUSHKI

Vatrushki are like individual cheese Danishes, but the dough is not a yeast dough. It is leavened with baking powder. Although we made ours round and enclosed the cheese filling in the pastry, some Vatrushki are made with a center of exposed filling. Some Eastern European bakers make the Vatrushki in half-moons folding over the circles of dough and crimping the edges over the filling. The cheese filling is traditional, but you can also fill the Vatrushki with jam. Vatrushki can be made with a savory filling of chopped meat or vegetables. Chopped wild mushrooms with fresh dill would make a superlative filling.

2 A Piece of Cake

THE RECIPES

We've always appreciated the infinite variety of cakes. There is nothing that surprises us when it comes to crumb, filling, or frosting. We love that cakes come in all sizes, shapes, flavors, and textures. We enjoy celebrating the layer cakes, cheesecakes, fruitcakes, pound cakes, coffee cakes, and nut cakes that come from the home kitchen.

Cakes were what we first baked as young girls, and since then, we've baked hundreds for family and friends. We've even baked some multitiered wedding cakes.

We like to think of our cake-baking experiences as our history, the story of how our personal and culinary lives were influenced and came together. Having a mother who was a gifted self-taught home baker, we were exposed to the best of home baking. We found that learning how to bake a cake wasn't difficult, and that it was the first step toward learning how to *create* a cake. We also discovered that it was acceptable to vary a recipe once you had learned how to bake it. We still remember a chocolate birthday cake decorated with chocolate roses and leaves that Sheila made, using a recipe for a vanilla cake, for Marilynn's sixteenth birthday, more than fifty years ago.

We still bake our mother's jelly roll, but at Christmas we make it as a chocolate *Bûche de Noël* for friends. We fill it with chocolate ganache and frost it with chocolate buttercream, but at its core it is still the recipe for our mother's jelly roll.

Everyone has a favorite cake, one that he or she requests for special occasions. Often, that requested and frequently baked cake becomes part of a family's culinary history, an intangible passed from generation to generation.

If you like layer cakes, you will love the recipes for the Pink Velvet Cake and Muriel's Banana Walnut Cake with Bourbon Frosting. One is a princess-perfect pink creation, baked with raspberry jam; the other, a culinary upgrade on a banana bread, but softer, lighter, and grown-up with its bourbon-laced frosting.

We confess we fell in love with the recipe for a delicate and airy Almond Chiffon Cake because it reminded us of the light summer dresses our aunts wore. Finished with a delicate almond glaze, a chiffon cake is a party in the making. The New England Maple Walnut Cake with its cream cheese frosting brings back memories of the scoops of maple walnut ice cream we consumed as children in our seaside neighborhood.

We never solved the mystery of Mother Carleton's Black Walnut Bundt Cake. Not only could we not find the true identity of Mother Carleton, but also her black walnut cake does not contain black walnuts. Although it is hard to describe the flavor of the cake when made with the elusive black walnut extract, it is both rich and substantial. The recipe also produces a very nice cake when made with vanilla extract.

Finally, in a salute to our younger days, we remember with pleasure a frozen Brandy Alexander pie made with crème de cacao and cognac and have translated it into a decadent cheesecake with a chocolate graham cracker crumb crust, with whipped cream and chocolate decorations on its top. Once you make it, you will find that home baking is just a piece of cake.

Quick Tips

- As instructed, allow the ingredients either to come to room temperature or be chilled before baking.
- Use correct measuring cups for measuring dry ingredients or liquids.
- Tap pans containing unbaked cake batter gently on the counter to remove air bubbles. Do *not* tap if the leavening of the batter relies on beaten egg whites.
- Level cake layers before frosting by slicing a thin sliver off the tops of the layers.

ABC Cake
(Apple, Banana, Coconut Cake)

This handwritten recipe called for all of the above ingredients, but we were inspired to experiment. We kept the three leading players—apple, banana, and coconut—but used large coconut flakes on the top. ABC Cake should be cooled and chilled before slicing into generous bars. This cake is sublime when all the flavors come together. We love the crispy flakes of coconut on the top.

2 cups Golden Delicious or Cortland apples, peeled and cut into ½-inch dice

1 cup pecans, toasted and chopped

1½ cups flour

1 teaspoon salt

1 teaspoon baking powder

¼ teaspoon cinnamon

1½ cups sugar

½ cup (1 stick) unsalted butter, melted and cooled

1 egg

1 large ripe banana, mashed (½ cup)

1 teaspoon vanilla extract

1 cup large coconut flakes or sweetened shredded coconut

1. Set the oven rack in the middle position. Preheat the oven to 350°F. Cover the bottom and sides of a 9 by 13 by 2-inch metal pan with aluminum foil, shiny side up. Coat the foil with butter or vegetable oil spray.

2. Mix the apples and pecans in a small bowl and set aside. Measure the flour into a larger bowl. Remove 2 tablespoons of the flour and add it to the apples and pecans and mix to coat. Set aside. Add the salt, baking powder, and cinnamon to the larger bowl with the remaining flour and whisk to combine. Set aside.

3. Add the sugar and butter to the bowl of a stand mixer fitted with the paddle attachment and cream until pale and fluffy. Beat in the egg. Add the mashed banana and vanilla and combine. Add the dry ingredients in three additions to the creamed mixture and combine. Fold in the apples and pecans. Spoon the batter into the prepared pan. Using an offset spatula, level the top of the batter. Sprinkle the coconut on top of the cake and press it gently into the batter with your hand. Bake the cake for 35 to 37 minutes, or until a metal tester inserted into the center comes out clean. The top should be a rich brown color.

4. Remove the cake from the oven and place on a wire rack to cool. When completely cool, place the pan in the refrigerator to chill. Remove the chilled cake from the pan, place on cutting surface or board, and carefully peel the foil from the cake. Using a wide-bladed knife, cut the cake into 3-inch squares. Any leftover ABC Cake should be loosely wrapped in wax paper and stored in the refrigerator.

Yield: one 9 by 13 by 2-inch cake; about 12 generous squares

SWEET TOUCHES: The cake can be warmed in a microwave for 7 to 10 seconds and served with unsweetened whipped cream.

• Nutmeg can be substituted for cinnamon, and walnuts can be substituted for pecans.

Almond Chiffon Cake

Almond Chiffon Cake

We almost gave up on this recipe—four tries, and a chiffon cake that fell in the center and stuck to the pan. We did our research and found that we had to bake the cake on the lower, rather than the middle, rack of the oven. The result was a light, almond-scented cake with a spongelike texture. We had to patiently wait for two hours for the cake to cool before removing it from the pan. Most chiffon cakes are made by hand, but this one can be made easily in a stand mixer.

CAKE

7 eggs, separated

½ teaspoon cream of tartar

2¼ cups flour

2 teaspoons baking powder

1 teaspoon salt

½ cup oil

½ cup milk

¼ cup water

1½ cups granulated sugar

1 teaspoon almond extract

ALMOND GLAZE

1 cup confectioners' sugar

Pinch of salt

¼ teaspoon almond extract

2 tablespoons water

2 tablespoons sliced almonds, toasted
    (optional)

Almond Chiffon Cake

1. Set the oven rack in the *lower* position. Preheat the oven to 325°F. Cut a sheet of parchment paper to fit the bottom of an 8-inch tube pan. *Do not grease the pan.*

2. To make the cake: Add the egg whites to the bowl of a stand mixer fitted with the whisk attachment and beat for 1 minute. Add the cream of tartar and continue beating until firm peaks form. If you only have one mixer bowl, transfer the beaten egg whites to another bowl and set aside.

3. Add the flour, baking powder, and salt to a separate bowl and whisk to combine. Set aside. Add the oil to a glass measuring cup and set aside. Combine the milk and water in another glass measuring cup and set aside.

4. Add the egg yolks to the bowl of the stand mixer fitted with the paddle attachment and beat for 1 minute to break up the yolks. Add the granulated sugar and almond extract to the egg yolks and continue to beat until well combined. Scrape down any egg yolk–sugar mixture sticking to the bottom and sides of the bowl and continue to beat.

Add the oil to the mixture and continue beating until completely combined. Add the dry ingredients alternately with the milk and water in three additions and beat until the batter is completely mixed.

5. Fold the egg whites into the batter in three additions. Pour the batter into the prepared pan. Place the pan on the lower rack of the oven and bake for 55 minutes. Increase the oven temperature to 350°F and continue to bake for 10 minutes, or until a metal tester inserted into the cake comes out clean. The cake will also spring back to the touch. Invert the cake on top of a wire rack and allow to cool for 2 hours. Turn the pan right side up and go around the edges and tube with a sharp knife to loosen the cake from the pan. Invert the cake onto the wire rack and allow to cool for another 20 minutes.

6. To make the almond glaze: Sift the confectioners' sugar into a small bowl. Add the salt and almond extract to the confectioners' sugar and mix to combine. Add the water and continue to whisk to combine. Add more water, a teaspoon at a time, if necessary to achieve the desired consistency. Slip a sheet of wax paper under the wire rack with the cake to catch drips. Using a teaspoon or fork, drizzle the glaze over the top of the cake. Sprinkle the almonds on top of the glaze, and press down gently

000with your hand to secure the almonds to the top of the cake. Alternatively, the top of the Almond Chiffon Cake can be dusted with sifted confectioners' sugar.

7. When the glaze has set, store the cake, loosely covered with wax paper, at room temperature, and insert six toothpicks evenly spaced into the top of the cake to prevent the wax paper from sticking to the glaze.

Yield: one 8-inch tube cake; 14 slices

SWEET TIP: If using a tube pan with a removable base, wrapping a piece of foil around the bottom of the pan will prevent any batter from leaking out during baking.

SWEET TOUCHES: This chiffon cake lends itself to many summertime desserts. It is delicious served with whipped cream and fruit such as strawberries, blueberries, or sliced peaches on the side.
• The cake can also be sliced horizontally and the center filled with crushed sweetened strawberries and whipped cream or Lemon Curd (page 185) in which case it should be kept refrigerated.

Almond Chiffon Cake

Aunt Ida's French Apple Cake

This recipe originally called for sliced canned apples. In a nod to culinary history, we tried the original version. We ended up with a flat cake oozing a rather pale applesauce. We baked the cake again, using sliced fresh Granny Smith apples, which we had sautéed in butter. What a difference! The resulting French Apple Cake was somewhere between a cake and a pie. The apples formed a magnificent thick layer of goodness reminding us of the Viennese Apple Slices we enjoyed in 1970s Cambridge at the Window Shop in Harvard Square. This cake takes more time than some recipes to prepare, but it's great for serving to company. Start this recipe early in the day.

FILLING

½ cup (1 stick) unsalted butter

8 large Granny Smith apples, peeled, cored, and cut into wedges (10 to 12 per apple)

2 teaspoons grated lemon zest

3 tablespoons lemon juice

¼ cup granulated sugar

2 tablespoons firmly packed brown sugar

1½ teaspoons cinnamon

1½ teaspoons nutmeg

¼ teaspoon salt

PASTRY

2 cups flour

1½ teaspoons baking powder

¼ teaspoon salt

1¼ cups granulated sugar

½ cup (1 stick) cold unsalted butter, cut into 8 slices

2 egg yolks, beaten

TOPPING

Reserved dough

½ teaspoon grated lemon zest

½ cup walnuts, toasted and coarsely chopped

2 tablespoons cold unsalted butter, cut into small dice

1. To make the filling: Melt the butter in two large heavy frying pans. Add the apples and sauté, turning several times with a wooden spoon, until light golden in color. (The apples can also be sautéed in one pan in two batches. *When both batches have been sautéed, return the first batch to the frying pan and continue with the recipe.*) Add the lemon zest, lemon juice, and both sugars and continue cooking, turning occasionally, until the apples are cooked but still a little firm, 7 to 10 minutes. Add the cinnamon, nutmeg, and salt. Bring the apples to a boil and cook until the liquid starts to thicken and caramelize, 1 to 2 minutes; do not let the apples stick to the surface of the pan. Remove the pan from the heat and allow the apples to cool.

2. To make the pastry: Place the flour, baking powder, salt, and granulated sugar in the bowl of a food processor fitted with the metal blade and pulse until the ingredients are combined. Add the slices of cold butter to the mixture and pulse to combine. Transfer the contents of the food processor to a mixing bowl. Add the beaten egg yolks to the dough and combine with your hands until you have a crumbly dough mixture. Remove 2 cups of the dough from the bowl and reserve for the topping.

3. Set the oven rack in the middle position. Preheat the oven to 375°F. Coat a 9-inch springform pan with vegetable oil spray or butter. Place two sheets of parchment paper on the bottom of

the pan. Coat the top piece of parchment with vegetable oil spray or butter. (This is a very heavy cake and having *two sheets of parchment paper on the bottom* helps to separate the cake from the bottom of the pan after the sides of the pan are removed.)

4. To make the topping: In a bowl, combine the reserved 2 cups dough with the lemon zest and walnuts.

5. Take the remaining dough and press it into the bottom and halfway up the sides of the prepared pan. Chill the dough–filled pan in the refrigerator for 30 minutes before adding the filling.

6. Once chilled, remove the pan from the refrigerator and carefully fill the unbaked shell with the cooled apple mixture. Smooth the top of the filling with an offset spatula. Sprinkle the topping on top of the apple filling and sprinkle the diced butter over the top of the crumbs. Wrap the bottom of the pan with aluminum foil and place on a baking sheet in the oven. Bake for 1 hour, or until the top is golden brown. Cool the cake on a wire rack for 5 minutes. Run a small pointed knife with a serrated edge carefully around the sides of the cake to loosen it from the pan. Cool for another 5 minutes, then remove the sides of the pan. Allow the cake to cool for 1 hour, then place in the refrigerator until cold.

7. If serving the cake at home, leave the cake on the bottom of the springform pan. *If transporting the cake to another location, carefully remove the cake from the bottom of the pan by inserting a large metal cake lifter between the two layers of parchment.* Transfer the cake to a flat heavy serving platter or heavy cardboard round. Any leftover cake should be stored, loosely covered with wax paper, in the refrigerator.

Yield: one 9-inch cake; 8 to 10 slices

SWEET TIP: Wide metal cake lifters are available in kitchenware stores. (See Sources page 287.)

SWEET TOUCH: This cake lends itself nicely to a dollop of whipped cream, a touch of crème fraîche, or a bit of sour cream. Vanilla ice cream is also wonderful as an accompaniment.

Brandy Alexander Cheesecake

When we were sweet young things in the 1960s and 1970s we used to serve a Brandy Alexander pie to family and friends. The pie was a sophisticated recipe because it was as rich as Warren Buffet, and used "spirits," which were not served in the Brass household unless someone fainted, announced an engagement, died, or celebrated the Jewish holidays with a tiny glass of Manischewitz grape wine. We decided to adapt the recipe by baking it as a Brandy Alexander Cheesecake, equally rich and creamy, and flavored with the requisite crème de cacoa and brandy. L'Chaim!

CHOCOLATE CRUMB CRUST

13 chocolate graham crackers, 2½ inches by
    5 inches each (1 sleeve from a 3-sleeve box)
¼ cup (½ stick) unsalted butter, melted and cooled
½ cup sugar

CHEESECAKE

Two 8-ounce packages cream cheese,
    at room temperature
1½ cups sugar
¼ cup cognac or brandy
¼ cup crème de cacao
1½ cups heavy cream
6 eggs
¼ cup plus 2 tablespoons flour
⅛ teaspoon salt

TOPPING

1 cup heavy cream
1 tablespoon crème de cacao
Chocolate coffee beans (confection)

1. Set the oven rack in the middle position. Preheat the oven to 350°F. Coat the bottom and sides of a 9-inch springform pan with vegetable oil spray. Cut a parchment paper or wax paper liner to fit the bottom of the pan. Insert the liner and coat with vegetable oil spray.

2. To make the crust: Place the graham crackers in the bowl of a food processor fitted with the metal blade and pulse to make crumbs the size of cornmeal (you should have about 1½ cups). Add the butter and sugar and pulse to combine. Press the crumbs over the bottom and 2 inches up the sides of the prepared pan. Wrap the outside bottom of the pan with aluminum foil.

3. To make the cheesecake: Put the cream cheese in the bowl of the stand mixer fitted with the paddle attachment and beat until smooth. Add the sugar and mix well. Add the brandy and crème de cacao and beat to incorporate. Add the cream and mix in. Add the eggs two at a time, mixing well after each addition. Add the flour and salt and and mix to combine.

4. Pour the batter into the crust in the springform pan. Bake for 1 hour 15 minutes. Turn off the oven and leave the oven door ajar by inserting a wooden spoon between the oven and door. After 45 minutes, remove the cheesecake from the oven and allow to cool thoroughly on a wire rack. Cover the cake, still in the baking pan, with plastic wrap and refrigerate overnight. If the top of the cheesecake cracks, don't worry; the top will be covered with whipped cream.

5. To make the topping: Add the cream to the bowl of the stand mixer fitted with the whisk attachment and beat until thick. Add the crème de cacao and whip to combine. Remove the cheesecake from the refrigerator. Spoon the whipped cream onto the top of the cheesecake. Using an offset spat-

ula, smooth the whipped cream over the top of the cheesecake. Pipe rosettes of whipped cream around the edge of the cheesecake, leaving room to place the chocolate coffee beans between the rosettes. Refrigerate until ready to serve.

6. Remove the cheesecake from the refrigerator 10 minutes before serving. Run a butter knife around the edge, remove the sides and bottom of springform pan, and place the cake on a serving plate. To store any leftover cheesecake, carefully cover with plastic wrap and refrigerate.

Yield: one 9-inch cheesecake; 16 slices

SWEET TOUCH: Chocolate decorations, such as stars, hearts, or chocolate coffee beans, can be used to decorate Brandy Alexander Cheesecake.

Edith's "Very Good" Orange Sponge Cake

This handwritten recipe was originally called an Orange Angel Food Cake, but it's really an Orange Sponge Cake because it uses both egg yolks and egg whites. We found this recipe in the manuscript cookbook of Amelia George of Patterson, New Jersey. Amelia's Aunt Edith was a prolific home baker. Some recipes have a notation of "Presbyterian Hospital" where Amelia may have been employed or done volunteer work. This is a luscious little sponge cake, very much like a Victoria sponge. The orange marmalade filling enhances the orange flavor.

CAKE

1½ cups cake flour
1 teaspoon baking powder
4 eggs, separated
Pinch of salt
1½ cups granulated sugar
1 tablespoon grated orange zest
½ cup orange juice

FILLING

1 cup orange marmalade or apricot jam

TOPPING

2 tablespoons confectioners' sugar
Whipped cream, for serving

1. Set the oven rack in the middle position. Preheat the oven to 350°F. Cut a parchment paper or wax paper liner to fit the bottom of an 8-inch tube pan and insert the liner.

2. To make the cake: Add the cake flour and baking powder to a small bowl and whisk to combine. Set aside.

3. Add the egg whites to the bowl of a stand mixer fitted with the whisk attachment. Place the yolks in a separate bowl, and set aside. Add the salt

to the whites and whisk until firm peaks form. If you don't have a second mixer bowl, transfer the egg whites to another bowl and set aside. The cake comes together quickly, so the beaten egg whites will not have time to deflate.

4. Add the egg yolks and the granulated sugar to the bowl of the stand mixer fitted with the paddle attachment and beat until combined. Add the orange zest and orange juice and continue to beat until combined. Add the cake flour mixture to the egg-sugar mixture in three additions and continue beating until incorporated.

5. Fold in the beaten egg whites in three additions until well distributed. Pour the batter into the prepared tube pan. Do *not* bang the pan to remove air bubbles; the bubbles are necessary for the cake to rise. Bake the cake for 40 to 45 minutes, or until a metal tester inserted into the center comes out clean. Invert the cake in the pan onto a wire rack and let cool for 30 minutes. Flip the cake right side up and cool completely. When the cake is cool, run a butter knife gently around the edges and tube of the pan and remove the cake from the pan.

6. To fill the cake: Slice the cake horizontally into two layers with a long serrated knife. Using a pastry brush, remove the loose crumbs from the cake. Spread the top of the bottom layer with marmalade or apricot jam. Place the top half of the cake on top of the marmalade. Sift the confectioners' sugar over the top of the cake. Serve with whipped cream, as you would a Victoria sponge.

Yield: one 8-inch tube cake; 12 slices

SWEET TIP: Add the marmalade to 1 cup whipped cream before frosting the top of the bottom layer.

Husband's Cake
(Tomato Soup Cake)

After we appeared in the Boston Globe *food pages, we received a note from Lawrence and Louise Kimball, who offered us a collection of family recipes. The recipe for Husband's Cake was one of them. We had heard of a tomato soup cake, but we had dismissed it as an oddity. Who would put tomato soup in a cake? We followed the recipe and made a few adjustments to the spices, and we were pleasantly surprised to see this beautiful reddish-brown spice cake come out of the oven. Our taste testers said they couldn't tell that there was tomato soup in the cake, but raved about its rich, spicy taste. Traditionally, this cake is finished with a cream cheese frosting (page 67)*

1 cup golden raisins

1 cup walnuts, toasted and coarsely chopped

3 cups flour

1 teaspoon salt

1 tablespoon baking powder

1 teaspoon baking soda

1 teaspoon cinnamon

1 teaspoon nutmeg

½ teaspoon cloves

¾ cup (1½ sticks) unsalted butter,
    at room temperature

1½ cups granulated sugar

1 teaspoon vanilla extract

¾ cup water

1 cup condensed tomato soup

Confectioners' sugar (optional)

1. Set the oven rack in the middle of the oven. Preheat the oven to 350°F. Coat the bottom and sides of an 8-cup Bundt pan or an 8-inch tube pan with vegetable oil spray and dust with flour. Tap the pan to remove excess flour.

2. Add the raisins and walnuts to a small bowl. Measure the flour and place in a large bowl. Remove 2 tablespoons of the flour and add it to the bowl containing the raisins and walnuts. Stir to coat the raisins and walnuts, and set aside. Add the salt, baking powder, baking soda, cinnamon, nutmeg, and cloves to the larger bowl containing the flour and whisk to combine. Set aside.

3. Add the butter and granulated sugar to the bowl of a stand mixer fitted with the paddle attachment and cream to combine. Add the vanilla and mix to incorporate. Add the water to the tomato soup in a 2-cup glass liquid measuring cup and whisk to combine. Add the flour mixture alternately with the water-soup mixture to the butter-sugar mixture in three additions. Add the floured raisins and walnuts and gently beat into the batter to distribute. Pour the batter into the prepared pan and bake for 55 to 60 minutes, or until a metal tester inserted into the center comes out clean. Transfer the cake to a wire rack and allow to cool for 30 minutes. Run a butter knife around the edges and center to loosen the cake from the pan, if necessary. Invert the cake onto another rack and then invert again onto the first rack. Allow to cool completely. Sift confectioners' sugar over the top of cake, if desired. Store the cake under a dome or loosely wrapped in wax paper at room temperature.

Yield: one 8-cup Bundt or 8-inch tube cake; 10 slices

Macaroon Cupcakes

We found this recipe mimeographed on a sheet of paper. It was credited to a P. Finelli. We adjusted the recipe a bit and found that we had baked some delightful little treats that were somewhere between a cupcake and a macaroon. A bit chewy, but still light, these confections are just the thing to serve at a party. They don't need frosting, so they are perfect for last-minute baking.

¾ cup flour

1⅓ cups sugar

½ teaspoon baking powder

½ teaspoon salt

1 cup coconut

6 egg whites

½ teaspoon cream of tartar

1 teaspoon vanilla extract

1. Set the oven rack in the middle position. Preheat the oven to 350°F. Coat the entire top surface and cups of two 12-cup muffin pans with vegetable oil spray. If using paper liners, spray the top surface of the pan before placing the paper liners in the openings of muffin pans. Muffin cups should have a diameter of 2½ inches across the top.

2. Add the flour, *1 cup* of the sugar, the baking powder, salt, and cocounut to a medium bowl and whisk to combine. Set aside.

3. Add the egg whites to the bowl of a stand mixer fitted with the whisk attachment and beat for 1 minute. Add the cream of tartar and continue beating until the egg whites are firm, but not dry. They should hold a peak. Fold in the remaining ⅓ cup sugar gradually. Fold in the vanilla. Gently fold the dry ingredients into the egg whites in three additions.

4. Divide the batter among the prepared cups and bake for 25 to 30 minutes, or until a metal tester inserted in the center of a cupcake comes out clean. Cool the cupcakes in the pan on a wire rack for 5 minutes before turning them out. Store the cupcakes, loosely wrapped in wax paper, at room temperature.

Yield: 2 dozen cupcakes

SWEET TIP: The sugar is divided into 1 cup for the batter and ⅓ cup to be folded into beaten egg whites.

Mama's Jelly Roll

This is the go-to recipe when we want to make a jelly roll. This is our mother Dorothy Katziff Brass's recipe. Marilynn was always fascinated by the rerolling of the sheet of sponge cake with the sugar-dusted damp dishtowel. We use this recipe for traditional sponge rolls filled with jam, or for that most daring of sponge rolls, chocolate with a filling of whipped cream. This jelly roll is the basis for our Chocolate Bûche de Noël covered with Chocolate Frosting, page 163.

JELLY ROLL

1 cup flour

¼ teaspoon salt

1 teaspoon baking powder

3 eggs, separated

1 ½ cups granulated sugar

¼ cup water

1 teaspoon vanilla extract

FILLING

1 cup jam of your choice: apricot, seedless
   raspberry, orange marmalade, ginger

TOPPING

2 tablespoons confectioners' sugar,
   sifted

1. Set the oven rack in the middle position. Preheat the oven to 375°F. Coat the bottom and sides of an 11 by 17 by 1-inch metal jelly roll pan with vegetable oil spray. Line the pan with parchment paper, and coat the parchment paper with vegetable oil spray. Because a jelly roll pan is so large, too much spray can accumulate. If so, remove the excess with a small piece of paper towel.

2. Add the flour, salt, and baking powder to a small bowl and whisk together. Set aside.

3. Add the egg whites to the bowl of a stand mixer fitted with the whisk attachment and beat until firm peaks form. If you don't have a second mixer bowl, transfer the beaten egg whites to another bowl and set aside.

4. Add the egg yolks, 1 cup of the granulated sugar, and water to the bowl of the stand mixer fitted with the paddle attachment and beat until pale yellow. Add the vanilla and beat to combine. Add the dry ingredients to the egg-sugar mixture in two additions and continue to beat until combined. Turn off the mixer, remove the bowl, and fold the beaten egg whites into the batter in three additions. Pour the batter into the prepared pan and level with an offset spatula. Bake for 20 minutes, or until the jelly roll springs back to the touch. Do not overbake, or the jelly roll may crack.

5. Moisten a dishtowel with water and dust generously with the remaining ½ cup granulated sugar. Turn the jelly roll out onto the prepared dishtowel and carefully peel the parchment paper from the bottom of the cake. Using the dishtowel, quickly roll up the jelly roll from one wide end and let rest for 10 minutes. Unroll the jelly roll and spread the jam over the entire surface with an offset spatula. Reroll the jelly roll and roll onto a sheet of wax paper longer than the jelly roll. Sift the confectioners' sugar on top of the jelly roll. Trim the ends of the jelly roll for a uniform appearance.

6. Transfer the jelly roll to a wire rack and allow to cool. When cool, transfer to a serving platter by picking it up from the wax paper sheet with a large metal cake lifter. Store the jelly roll in

the refrigerator until ready to serve. Remove the jelly roll from the refrigerator 10 minutes before serving. Slice with a serrated knife. Jelly roll is fragile and should be eaten the day it is baked.

Leftover jelly roll should be kept refrigerated if being used again, especially for trifle, because it is fragile, and sometimes contains an egg-based filling, such as lemon curd or custard.

Yield: 1 jelly roll; 10 slices

SWEET TIP: Leftover jelly roll can be used for making trifle.

Mother Carleton's Black Walnut Bundt Cake

We usually think of black walnuts as being somewhat exotic. Being native New Englanders, and, perhaps, a bit sheltered, we had never baked with them before. Our friend Karen Barrs gave us this recipe, which actually called for black walnut extract or flavoring. Karen recieved the recipe from her friend Jeni Oliver. Karen noted that she used the more readily available English walnuts, finely chopped, for her version of the cake. Black walnuts and black walnut extract can be obtained from gourmet food stores or from the Internet. This is a large cake, delightfully eggy and rich. We used a 12-cup Bundt pan when we baked it.

3 cups flour

1 teaspoon baking powder

⅛ teaspoon salt

1½ cups (3 sticks) unsalted butter, at room temperature

3 cups sugar

6 eggs

2 teaspoons black walnut extract or vanilla extract

1 cup milk

1 cup walnuts, toasted and finely chopped

1. Set the oven rack in the middle of the oven. Preheat the oven to 325°F. Coat a *12-cup Bundt pan* with vegetable oil spray. Dust the pan with flour and tap the pan to remove the excess flour. Set aside.

2. Add the flour, baking powder, and salt to a mixing bowl and whisk to combine. Set aside. Cream the butter and sugar in the bowl of a stand mixer fitted with the paddle attachment until pale and fluffy. With the mixer running, add the eggs one at a time, beating well after each addition. Add the black walnut or vanilla extract and beat to combine. Add the dry ingredients to the mixture in three additions alternately with the milk. Remove the bowl from the mixer and fold in the walnuts. Pour the batter into the prepared pan and place in the oven.

3. Bake the cake for 1 hour and 15 minutes, or until a metal tester inserted into the center comes out clean and the cake pulls away from the edges of the pan. Transfer the pan to a wire rack and cool the cake for 45 minutes. Gently go around the center of the Bundt pan with a sharp pointed knife to loosen if necessary. Turn out the cake onto second rack and allow to cool completely before slicing. Store any leftover cake, loosely wrapped in wax paper, at room temperature.

Yield: one 12-cup Bundt cake; 18 slices

SWEET TIPS: Vanilla extract can be substituted for the black walnut extract.
- We used hazelnut extract and finely chopped toasted hazelnuts for another version of this cake.

SWEET TOUCHES: Mother Carleton's cake can be dusted with sifted confectioners' sugar before serving, or served with whipped cream or vanilla ice cream.

USING BLACK WALNUT EXTRACT

We have found the flavor of black walnuts to be rather assertive, but the black walnut extract lends a unique flavor to Mother Carleton's Black Walnut Bundt Cake. We suggest that home bakers use extracts rather than flavors, but if black walnut extract is not readily available, black walnut flavoring can be used. *Be sure to buy black walnut extract or flavoring that is used only for cakes or cookies, and not for medicinal purposes.*

Muriel's Banana Walnut Cake with Bourbon Frosting

This is a banana cake from the 1930s, not a banana bread. The texture and taste of this cake is very different from a quick bread. We added the Bourbon Frosting, and we're not sorry. It just sets off the bananas and the toasted walnuts and makes a delectable filling for the three-layer cake. The finely chopped walnuts adorning the sides of the cake and the walnut halves on the top turn this cake into a special occasion cake.

CAKES

2 eggs, separated
2 cups flour
1 teaspoon baking powder
1 teaspoon baking soda
½ teaspoon salt
2 teaspoons vanilla extract
1 cup buttermilk
½ cup (1 stick) unsalted butter, at room
    temperature
1¼ cups granulated sugar
2 medium bananas, mashed (¾ cup)
1 cup walnuts, toasted and finely chopped

FROSTING

4 cups confectioners' sugar, sifted
1 cup (2 sticks) unsalted butter, at room
    temperature
⅛ teaspoon salt
2 tablespoons bourbon

1 cup walnuts, toasted and finely chopped
Toasted walnut halves (optional)

1. Set the oven rack in the middle position. Preheat the oven to 350°F. Coat the bottoms and sides of three 7-inch round cake pans with butter or vegetable oil spray. Line the bottoms of the cake pans with parchment paper or wax paper and coat with vegetable oil spray. Dust the pans with flour and tap the pan to remove excess flour. Set aside.

2. To make the cakes: Add the egg whites to the bowl of a stand mixer fitted with the whisk attachment and beat until firm but not dry; they should hold a peak. Set the beaten egg whites aside. If you don't have an additional bowl for your stand mixer, transfer the beaten egg whites to another bowl and set aside. The egg whites won't deflate while you put the cake together.

3. Place flour, baking powder, baking soda, and salt into a bowl and whisk to combine. Set aside. Combine the vanilla and buttermilk in a glass measuring cup and set aside.

4. Add the butter and granulated sugar to the bowl of the stand mixer fitted with the *paddle* attachment and cream together thoroughly. Add the egg yolks and combine. Add the mashed bananas and beat to combine.

5. Add the dry ingredients to the creamed mixture alternately with the vanilla-buttermilk mixture, ending with the dry ingredients. Remove the bowl from the mixer stand and fold in the walnuts. Mix one-third of the beaten egg whites into batter, then fold in the rest of the egg whites in two additions. Divide batter among the prepared pans and bake for 30 to 35 minutes. The cakes should be lightly brown and pull away from the edges slightly. A metal tester inserted into the center of the cakes should come out clean.

6. Cool the cakes in the pans for 15 to 20 minutes on wire racks. When the cakes have cooled, go around the edges of the cakes with a smooth butter knife to loosen the cakes. Turn the cakes out onto

Muriel's Banana Walnut Cake with Bourbon Frosting

wire racks and remove the liners. Turn the cakes right side up on the racks. Allow the cakes to cool completely, then wrap in paper towels and place in the refrigerator until ready to frost.

7. To make the frosting: Combine the confectioners' sugar, butter, salt, and bourbon in the bowl of the stand mixer fitted with the *whisk* attachment. Beat to combine and, if necessary, add water, 1 teaspoon at a time, to reach the desired spreading consistency. Continue to beat until the frosting comes together.

8. Carefully slice a thin layer off the top of each cake to level them, if necessary. Place the bottom layer of cake on a cake round, lined with four small pieces of wax paper, and spread the frosting over the top of this cake layer with an offset spatula. Frost only the tops of the bottom and middle layers. Add the third layer, and frost the top and sides of the entire cake. Immediately cover the sides of the cake with finely chopped toasted walnuts. A circle of walnut halves can be placed on the top of the cake, if desired. Allow the frosted cake to set for 30 minutes to 1 hour in the refrigerator before slicing. Store any leftover cake, covered with wax paper, in the refrigerator. Use toothpicks to keep the wax paper from sticking to the frosting. Allow the cake to come to room temperature before serving.

Yield: one 7-inch 3-layer cake; 8 slices

SWEET TIP: Sifting confectioners' sugar after measuring removes lumps.

SWEET TOUCHES: Vanilla extract can be substituted for bourbon in the frosting.
• To make all of the walnut halves on top of the cake uniform in color, add ¼ cup molasses to a small bowl and, using a pastry brush, coat the tops of the walnut halves with molasses. Allow the walnut halves to dry on a piece of wax paper or parchment paper, then place around the edge of the top layer of the frosted cake.

New England Maple Walnut Cake

We decided to dedicate this Maple Walnut Cake to the state of Vermont. The combination of maple syrup and finely chopped toasted walnuts make this cake sublime. The recipe for the cream cheese frosting comes from Myrna and Chester Langlois, the grandparents of our friend Maureen Timmons. We crowned the top of the cake with shards of Maple Spiced Nut Brittle.

CAKE

2 eggs, separated

½ cup walnuts, toasted and finely chopped

2 cups flour

2½ teaspoons baking powder

½ teaspoon salt

½ cup Grade A maple syrup

1 teaspoon vanilla extract

½ cup milk

¾ cup (1½ sticks) unsalted butter, at room temperature

1 cup firmly packed brown sugar

CREAM CHEESE FROSTING

3 cups confectioners' sugar

Pinch of salt

¼ cup (½ stick) unsalted butter, at room temperature

8 ounces cream cheese, at room temperature

⅓ cup heavy cream

1 teaspoon vanilla extract

MAPLE SPICED NUT BRITTLE

½ cup Grade A maple syrup

2 tablespoons unsalted butter, at room temperature

½ teaspoon salt

¼ teaspoon cinnamon

¼ teaspoon nutmeg

1 cup walnuts, toasted and coarsely chopped

1. Set the oven rack in the middle position. Preheat the oven to 350°F. Coat the bottoms and sides of three 7-inch round cake pans with butter or vegetable spray. Line the bottoms of the cake pans with parchment paper or wax paper and coat with vegetable oil spray. Dust the pans with flour and tap the pans to remove the excess flour.

2. To make the cake: Add the egg whites to the bowl of a stand mixer fitted with the whisk attachment and beat until firm, but not dry. They should hold a peak, but should not be stiff and heavy. If you don't have an additional bowl for your stand mixer, transfer the beaten egg whites to another bowl and set aside. The egg whites won't deflate while you put the cake together.

3. Add the nuts to a small bowl. Put the flour in a larger bowl, remove 1 tablespoon, and add to the nuts. Whisk the flour and nuts until the nuts are coated with flour. Add the baking powder and salt to the flour in the larger bowl and whisk to combine. Set aside. Combine the maple syrup, vanilla, and milk in a glass measuring cup and whisk together. Set aside.

4. Add the butter and brown sugar to the bowl of the stand mixer fitted with the paddle attachment and cream thoroughly. Add the egg yolks and beat to incorporate.

5. Add the sifted dry ingredients to the creamed mixture alternately with the milk mixture, ending with the dry ingredients. Turn off the mixer, remove the bowl from the mixer stand, and fold in the walnuts. Mix one-third of the egg whites into the batter, then fold in the rest of the egg whites in two additions.

6. Divide the batter among the prepared pans and bake for 35 to 40 minutes, or until a metal tester inserted into the center of the cakes comes out clean. The cakes should be golden brown and pull away from the edges slightly. Transfer the cakes to wire racks and allow to cool for 20 minutes. Run a butter knife gently around the edges to loosen the cakes. Invert the cakes and remove the liners. Set the cakes right side up on the racks. Allow the cakes to cool completely, then wrap in paper towels and place in the refrigerator until ready to frost.

7. To make the cream cheese frosting: Sift the confectioners' sugar and salt into a mixing bowl and whisk to combine. Set aside. Add the butter and cream cheese to the bowl of the stand mixer fitted with the paddle attachment and cream until combined. Add the confectioners' sugar and salt to the creamed ingredients in three additions and beat to incorporate. Add the cream and vanilla and continue to beat until well mixed and fluffy. Refrigerate the frosting and chill for 1 hour before using.

8. *For safety, keep a large bowl filled with cold water and ice cubes at hand when making the syrup.* To make the maple spiced nut brittle: Heat the maple syrup, butter, salt, cinnamon, nutmeg, and walnuts in a heavy frying pan over medium heat, stirring constantly with a wooden spoon, until the mixture begins to boil. Boil for 5 minutes, stirring constantly. Spread out the nut mixture on a baking sheet. Transfer the baking sheet to a wire rack to cool. When completely cool, break the brittle into shards and set aside until the cake is ready to be frosted.

9. When ready to frost the cake, remove the cake layers from the refrigerator. Carefully slice a thin layer off the top of each cake to level, if necessary. Place the bottom layer of cake on a cake round

lined with four small pieces of wax paper, and spread the frosting over the top of this cake layer with an offset spatula. Frost only the tops of the bottom and middle layers. Add the third layer, and frost the top and sides of the entire cake. Decorate the top of the frosted cake with shards of the brittle. Allow the frosted cake to set for 30 minutes to 1 hour in the refrigerator before slicing. Remove the cake from the refrigerator and allow to sit at room temperature for 10 to 15 minutes before serving. Store any leftover cake, covered with wax paper, in the refrigerator. Use toothpicks to keep the wax paper from sticking to the frosting.

Yield: one 7-inch 3-layer cake; 8 to 10 slices of Maple Walnut Cake; 3½ cups Cream Cheese Frosting; about 1 cup Maple Spiced Nut Brittle

SWEET TIP: We found that the maple syrup was sufficient to flavor the cake. We did not have to use maple extract.

SWEET TOUCH: Maple Spiced Nut Brittle can be placed in the bowl of a food processor fitted with the metal blade and pulsed to form walnut praline dust. The praline dust can be used to sprinkle on top of the cake instead of shards of the brittle.

NOTE: The recipe for Maple Spiced Nuts in *Heirloom Baking with the Brass Sisters*, published by Black Dog & Leventhal, was the forerunner of this nut brittle recipe.

Orange Pecan Olive Oil Cake

We had heard so much about olive oil cakes that we wanted to try one ourselves. We decided to be adventuresome, and experimented with using olive oil in conjunction with sour cream to create a moist cake with the richness of pecans, and a hint of orange flavor. This is an unassuming cake that satisfies. Our friends Mark and Bill, on tasting this cake, immediately asked for the recipe.

CAKE

2 cups flour

1 teaspoon baking powder

½ teaspoon salt

½ teaspoon finely ground black pepper

2 cups pecans, toasted and finely chopped

¾ cup light olive oil

2 cups granulated sugar

2 large eggs

1 cup sour cream

1 teaspoon orange extract

2 teaspoons grated orange zest

GLAZE

1 cup confectioners' sugar

Pinch of salt

1 teaspoon grated orange zest

2 tablespoons orange juice

1. Set the oven rack in the middle position. Preheat the oven to 350°F. Coat an 8-cup Bundt pan or an 8-inch tube pan with vegetable oil spray or butter and dust with flour. Tap the pan to remove the excess flour. Line the bottom of the pan with parchment paper.

2. To make the cake: Whisk together the flour, baking powder, salt, and pepper in a mixing bowl. Add the pecans and whisk to combine. Set aside.

3. Add the olive oil and granulated sugar to the bowl of a stand mixer fitted with the paddle attachment and mix to combine. Add the eggs one at a time, then the sour cream, and beat until well mixed. Add the orange extract and orange zest and mix in. Add the dry ingredients to the wet ingredients in three additions and beat until well combined.

4. Pour the batter into the prepared pan. Bake for 55 to 60 minutes, or until the cake pulls away from sides of pan, and a metal tester inserted into the center comes out clean. The cake might crack on top. Transfer the pan to a wire rack and cool the cake for about 20 minutes. Run a butter knife around the edges, if necessary. Turn out the cake onto the wire rack and allow to cool completely.

5. To make the glaze: Sift together the confectioners' sugar and salt into a small bowl. Mix in the orange zest. Add 1 tablespoon of the orange juice, and whisk to combine. Add the remaining orange juice, a teaspoon at a time, until the desired consistency is attained. Slip a sheet of wax paper under the wire rack with the cake to catch drips. Using a teaspoon or fork, drizzle the glaze over the top of the cake. After the glaze has set, store the cake, loosely covered with wax paper, at room temperature.

Yield: one 8-cup Bundt or 8-inch tube cake; 14 slices

SWEET TOUCH: The cake can be sprinkled with sifted confectioners' sugar instead of glazed.

Pink Velvet Cake

Pink Velvet Cake

We've always loved Red Velvet Cake, even making it into diminutive cupcakes, but we were looking for a very special cake for a young birthday girl, and we decided to bake a Pink Velvet Cake, just as delicious, but very "girly." We based this recipe on the Red Velvet Cake in Heirloom Cooking. *We admit that this cake, when frosted and decorated, reminds us a bit of those plastic doll cakes from the 1960s and 1970s, with their skirts made of cake. The Pink Velvet Cake relies on seedless raspberry jam for its pink color. We found that boys and men also enjoy a slice of this feminine cake.*

CAKE

2 cups cake flour

½ teaspoon salt

1 cup (2 sticks) unsalted butter, at room
temperature

1½ cups granulated sugar

2 eggs

¼ cup seedless raspberry jam

1 teaspoon vanilla extract

1 cup buttermilk

1 teaspoon baking soda

1 tablespoon apple cider vinegar

RASPBERRY FROSTING

4 cups confectioners' sugar, sifted

1 cup (2 sticks) unsalted butter, at room
temperature

⅛ teaspoon salt

½ cup seedless raspberry jam

2 tablespoons water, plus more if needed

TOPPING

1½ cups sweetened shredded coconut, lightly
toasted if desired

Pink candy dots (see Sources, page 287)

Pink Velvet Cake

1. Set the oven rack in the middle position. Preheat the oven to 350°F. Coat the bottoms and sides of three 7-inch round cake pans with butter or vegetable spray. Line the bottoms of the pans with parchment paper or wax paper and coat with vegetable oil spray. Dust the pans with flour and tap the pans to remove the excess flour. Set aside.

2. To make the cake: Add the cake flour and salt to a small bowl and whisk to combine. Set aside.

3. Cream the butter and granulated sugar in the bowl of a stand mixer fitted with the paddle attachment and beat until soft and fluffy. Add the eggs one at a time. Add the raspberry jam and beat to combine.

4. Combine the vanilla and buttermilk in a

glass measuring cup. Add the dry ingredients to the creamed mixture alternately with the buttermilk, beating well after each addition. Add the baking soda to the vinegar and fold into the batter.

5. Divide the batter among the prepared pans and bake for 35 to 40 minutes, or until a metal tester inserted into the center of the cakes comes out clean. Transfer the cakes to wire racks and allow to cool for 20 minutes. Run a smooth butter knife gently around the edges to loosen the cakes. Invert the cakes and remove the liners. Set the cakes right side up on the racks. Let cool completely.

6. To make the raspberry frosting: Add the confectioners' sugar, butter, salt, and jam to the bowl of the stand mixer fitted with the paddle attachment and beat to combine. Add 1 tablespoon of the water at a time and continue to beat until the frosting comes together. Add more water, one teaspoon at a time, if needed, to reach the desired consistency. The frosting should be a pale pink.

7. Carefully slice a thin layer off the top of each cake to level them, if necessary. Place the bottom layer of cake on a cake round lined with four small pieces of wax paper, and spread the frosting over the top of this cake layer with an offset spatula. Frost only the tops of the bottom and middle layers. Add the third layer and frost the top and the sides of the entire cake. Immediately cover the sides of the cake with shredded coconut. Pipe frosting flowers over the edge of the cake, using a #190 Ateco frosting tip. Place 1 pink candy dot in the center of each flower. Store the cake in the refrigerator. Remove the cake from the refrigerator 10 minutes before serving. Store any leftover cake in the refrigerator.

Yield: one 7-inch 3-layer cake; 8 slices

HOW TO TOAST COCONUT

Set the oven rack in the middle position. Preheat the oven to 350°F. Spread shredded or flaked coconut on a rimmed baking sheet. Toast in the oven for 5 to 7 minutes, stirring occasionally. Check to see that the coconut is not browning too quickly or burning. Remove the baking sheet from the oven and transfer to a wire rack to cool.

Shivani's Hazelnut Cake

This recipe is based on one from Shivani Grover, who first tasted it at her friend Adriana Pechanova's home. It is a Bohemian coffee cake known as a babovka. *Adriana passed on the recipe orally to Shivani, who made notes, but later misplaced them. Years later, Shivani experimented with a version, made from memory, to bake it again to honor her professor's wife, Mary Chandra, whose ancestors also came from Bohemia. The recipe became a treasured memory for the two women. The temperature may be a bit unusual, but the result is a moist, nutty cake. Our version uses nonalkalized cocoa and almond meal to capture the Bohemian flavor of this cake.*

2 cups flour
1 cup almond or hazelnut meal or flour
1 tablespoon baking powder
4 eggs, separated
⅛ teaspoon salt
1½ cups sugar
½ cup warm water
1 teaspoon almond or hazelnut extract
1 cup light olive oil or canola oil
¼ cup American natural nonalkalized cocoa, sifted

1. Set the oven rack in the middle of the oven. *Preheat the oven to 370°F.* Coat an 8-cup Bundt pan or 8-inch tube pan with vegetable oil spray and dust with flour. Tap the pan to remove the excess flour. *Note the baking temperature.*

2. Add the flour, almond or hazelnut meal, and baking powder to a mixing bowl and whisk to combine. Set aside.

3. Place the egg whites and salt in the bowl of a stand mixer fitted with the whisk attachment and beat until stiff, but not dry. The whites should be firm and massed inside the whisk. If you do not have a second mixer bowl, transfer the beaten egg whites to a separate bowl and set aside.

4. Add the egg yolks to the bowl of the stand mixer fitted with the paddle attachment and beat until the yolks break up and come together. Add the sugar and *1 teaspoon* of the *warm water* and beat on high speed until the sugar has dissolved and the mixture is pale yellow, 3 to 4 minutes. Add the almond or hazelnut extract, oil, and the *remaining* water and beat until frothy. Add the dry ingredients to the wet mixture in three additions and beat to combine.

5. Fold the beaten egg whites into the batter until incorporated. Pour two-thirds of the batter into the prepared pan. Add the cocoa to the remaining batter and beat gently to combine. Spoon the chocolate batter on top of the batter in the pan. Bake for 45 to 50 minutes, or until a metal tester inserted into the cake comes out clean. Cool on a wire rack for 20 minutes. The edges of the cake should pull away from the sides. If the center of the cake does not come away from the Bundt or tube pan, carefully go around the inside edges with a narrow, sharp pointed knife. Turn out the cake onto a second rack, and allow to cool completely before slicing. Store any leftover cake, loosely wrapped in wax paper, at room temperature.

Yield: one 8-cup Bundt or 8-inch tube cake; 16 slices

SWEET TIPS: Some recipes suggest beating egg whites just before adding them to a batter. We have found that beating the egg whites and setting them aside briefly before putting the rest of cake together does not cause them to deflate.

ALMOND MEAL AND HAZELNUT MEAL VS. ALMOND FLOUR AND HAZELNUT FLOUR

We found that the terms *almond meal* and *hazelnut meal* were used interchangeably with *almond flour* and *hazelnut flour*. We tried this cake with both almond meal (flour) as well as hazelnut meal (flour) and both versions were ethereal. Almond meal is made from both whole or blanched (skins removed) almonds, while almond flour is usually made with ground sweet almonds. Hazelnut meal or flour is made with ground hazelnuts. The texture of the meal or flour is what makes this cake special. Both meals should be kept refrigerated or frozen. The hazelnut meal from Bob's Red Mill is not blanched.

Worcester Pound Cake

We found this recipe for Worcester Pound Cake on a tattered slip of yellowed paper, like the "arithmetic paper" we used in grammar school. We were under the impression that a pound cake used a pound of flour, sugar, butter, and eggs, hence the name "pound cake." This is a slightly lighter version, and the mace, which is not usually the first choice for spicing a pound cake, turns this recipe into an exotic little gem. The mace becomes more evident the day after baking as the cake mellows. For those of you who want to know where Worcester, Massachusetts, is, it is located in the central part of the state, and it is the second largest city in the Commonwealth.

3 cups flour
½ teaspoon baking soda
1 teaspoon cream of tartar
¼ teaspoon salt
1½ teaspoons mace
4 eggs, separated

1 cup (2 sticks) unsalted butter, at room
   temperature
2 cups sugar
1 teaspoon vanilla extract
½ cup buttermilk

1. Set the oven rack in the middle position. Preheat the oven to 350°F. Coat a 10-inch standard tube pan with vegetable oil spray or butter. Line the bottom of the pan with wax paper or parchment and coat with vegetable oil spray. Dust the interior and bottom of the pan with flour, and tap the pan to remove the excess flour.

2. Add the flour, baking soda, cream of tartar, salt, and mace to a bowl and whisk to combine. Set aside.

3. Add the egg whites to the bowl of a stand mixer fitted with the whisk attachment and beat until they form soft peaks. If you don't have a second mixer bowl for the batter, transfer the egg

MACE AND NUTMEG

Mace is the outer membrane of the nutmeg. It has a sweet warm taste. Nutmeg has a sharper more pronounced taste. Nutmeg can be purchased whole and grated as needed. Both mace and nutmeg can be purchased in powdered form.

whites to another bowl and set aside. The pound cake comes together quickly so the beaten egg whites will not have time to deflate.

4. In the bowl of the stand mixer fitted with the paddle attachment, cream the butter and sugar until combined. With the mixer running, add the egg yolks one at a time, and mix well. Combine the vanilla and buttermilk in a glass measuring cup. Add the dry ingredients and liquid ingredients alternately to the creamed mixture and beat to combine.

5. Mix one-third of the egg whites into the batter, then fold in the rest of the egg whites in two additions. Spoon the batter into the prepared pan. Bake for 60 to 65 minutes, or until a metal tester inserted into the center of the cake comes out clean.

6. Transfer the pan to a wire rack and cool the cake for 20 minutes. Run a butter knife around the edges and tube of the pan and flip the cake to remove it from the pan. Turn the cake right side up onto the rack. Allow to cool completely before slicing. Any leftover cake can be covered with wax paper and stored at room temperature or stored in a cake keeper.

Yield: one 10-inch tube cake;
14 to 16 slices

SWEET TOUCH: This cake is sublime with a cloud of softly whipped cream flavored with a touch of vanilla, or dusted with confectioners' sugar.

3 The Cookie Exchange

THE RECIPES

W e titled this chapter "The Cookie Exchange" because we found that recipes for cookies seem to be those most often shared. Time and again, we've also found that bake sales, especially those at Thanksgiving and Christmas, are often referred to as "exchanges." We've learned of cookie exchanges that have been perpetuated by generations of congregants, club members, families, and friends. Cookies in decorated tins or ribbon-tied boxes are also anticipated and enjoyed gifts at the holidays.

We take a more personal view of cookies. We love them all—dropped, piped, shaped, fragile meringues, or substantial bar cookies. They have a personality of their own. They can be soft, delicate, or lacy; crispy or crumbly. Some cookies can be used to sandwich fillings of jam, frosting, or chocolate ganache.

A plate of cookies, glistening with sanding sugar, or a shiny glaze, or reinforced with nuggets of chocolate or nuts can make us feel loved and protected. It is the familiar taste and crackle of a favorite cookie that rewarded or comforted us as tearful children that sustains us when we face challenges later in life.

We acknowledge that a cookie can nourish us in more than one way.

Knowingly placed in a lunch box, a cookie is like a secret kiss between the giver and the recipient. We treasure the memory of the plates of cookies our own mother left us for when we returned home from school, always with a note signed, "Love, Mommy."

Cookies are usually the first recipe that young fingers and hands learn to bake. Each cookie becomes a canvas ready to be decorated by a young artist from a palette of sugars, glazes, and candies.

Baking and eating cookies such as Alison's Speculatius or Norwegian Spice Hearts can fill the home kitchen with the old world scents and tastes of foreign lands. Cookies can be piped with a guest's name to serve as a place card at gatherings, or even used creatively to construct spicy fairy-tale dwellings to delight young and old.

Since the cookie jar is kitchen central in most homes, family and friends often find themselves exploring its sweet contents. Home bakers seem to be perfectionists when it comes to cookie baking, because one that doesn't meet the standard is usually offered to and dispatched by eager children in the family until only crumbs remain.

Cookies do not necessarily require unusual ingredients and special equipment. Honey, molasses, jam, cornflakes, and other ingredients found on kitchen shelves or in pantries are pressed into service for the cookies we present. A small plastic bag with the corner snipped off can stand in for the more elusive piping bag when baking Lemon Clove Cookies.

We celebrate the old standards—the tried and true. Bernice's Irregular Cookies, Butterscotch Icebox Cookies, or Mom's Coconut Cornflake Cookies. Graham Shingles, Billy Goat Cookies, Cry Baby Cookies, and Vanilla Coat Buttons, along with their intriguing names, come with a history of their own. Finally, the bar cookies—Aunt Minnie's Date and Oat, and the fanciful Polka Dot Chocolate Bars, with their enhancement of both white and dark chocolate, are welcome additions to the overflowing plates of cookies we serve to family and friends.

We invite you to bake and enjoy the cookies and bars in this chapter, but we also encourage you to make the cookies you bake your own by varying their flavors, their shapes, and their decorations. A good cookie, like a good memory, should be treasured.

Quick Tips

- Do not place more than the suggested number of cookies on a baking sheet. Keep the spaces between cookies wide enough so that they will not spread together.
- Keep the size of unbaked cookies consistent.
- Check the bottoms of cookies to be sure they are a golden, not a dark brown. Dark cookie bottoms mean that cookies have been baked too long.
- Some cookies will firm up on cooling.
- Do not place hard candies or gold or silver dragées on cookies unless they are *not* meant to be eaten, but are to be used for decorative purposes, such as Christmas ornaments.

Alison's Speculatius

We've always been partial to a Christmas cookie with a history, and this is one from our friend Alison Kennedy. Alison's late mother, Joan, passed on this family recipe to all of her daughters. We love the fact that it is related to the German Spekulatius *and the old Dutch* Speculoos. *This dough was sometimes stamped with images and designs in years past, but this version is chilled, rolled out, and cut into shapes. Our kitchen smells very old world when we bake Alison and Joan's* Speculatius.

2 ¼ cups flour
½ teaspoon baking soda
⅛ teaspoon salt
1½ teaspoon cinnamon
½ teaspoon nutmeg
¼ teaspoon cloves
½ cup almonds, toasted and finely chopped in food processor
1 cup (2 sticks) unsalted butter, at room temperature
1 cup firmly packed brown sugar
¼ cup sour cream, at room temperature

1. Put the flour, baking soda, salt, cinnamon, nutmeg, cloves, and almonds in a bowl and whisk to combine. Set aside. Add the butter and brown sugar to the bowl of a stand mixer fitted with the paddle attachment and cream until smooth. Add the sour cream. Add the dry ingredients in two additions and continue to mix until the dough comes together.

2. Turn off the mixer, remove the dough from the bowl, and place it on a lightly floured sheet of wax paper. Lightly dust the dough with flour and form into a large ball. With a sharp knife, cut the dough into four equal portions. Lightly dust each portion with flour and form into four individual balls. Place three of the balls in a plastic bag and store in the refrigerator until ready to roll out and cut into shapes.

3. When ready to bake the cookies, set the oven rack in the middle position. Preheat the oven to 350°F. Line a 14 by 16-inch baking sheet with a silicone liner or aluminum foil, shiny side up. Coat the foil with vegetable oil spray.

4. Place the first portion of dough on a lightly floured sheet of wax paper. Sprinkle the dough with a small amount of flour, cover with another sheet of wax paper, and roll out into a circle or a rectangle, ¼ inch thick. Dip a 2½-inch round or square cookie cutter in flour each time you cut out the cookies. Place no more than 12 cookies on the prepared baking sheet. Using a pastry brush, remove any excess flour from the cookies. Bake for 12 minutes. Put any remaining scraps of dough in the refrigerator. Repeat the process with the remaining dough. When all of the dough has been rolled out at least once, put the scraps together and roll out again. The second rolling might produce cookies that are a little less tender.

5. Slide the foil or the silicone liner with the baked cookies onto a wire rack to cool. Remove the cooled cookies with a metal spatula and transfer to a second wire rack. The cookies will firm up as they cool. When cool, store between sheets of wax paper in a covered tin.

Yield: about 3½ dozen cookies

SWEET TIPS: *Speculatius* are even better the day after they are baked.
• The cookies can also be made with half butter and half lard, but they will have a slightly different texture.

Aunt Minnie's Date and Oat Bars

Aunt Minnie's Date and Oat Bars

This recipe is based on one that comes from our friend Sue Truax's Aunt Minnie, who made them throughout the 1950s and 1960s. They were a holiday special in the Schleiger and Story families. Sue remembers Aunt Minnie cutting her Date and Oat Bars and layering them in a large oatmeal cylinder between sheets of wax paper at Thanksgiving and Christmas. These bars are sweet and chewy, and they make a great holiday gift. We added the grated lemon zest and lemon juice to the date filling.

FILLING

1½ cups water

3 cups chopped pitted dates

¼ cup granulated sugar

Pinch of salt

2 teaspoons grated lemon zest

2 tablespoons lemon juice

BARS

1¾ cups flour

1 teaspoon salt

½ teaspoon baking soda

1½ cups rolled oats

¾ cup (1½ sticks) unsalted butter,
    at room temperature

1 cup firmly packed brown sugar

1 teaspoon vanilla extract

1. Set the oven rack in the middle position. Preheat the oven to 400°F. Cover the bottom and sides of a 9 by 13 by 2-inch metal pan with aluminum foil, shiny side up. Coat the foil with vegetable oil spray.

2. To make the filling: Add the water, dates, granulated sugar, salt, lemon zest, and lemon juice to a heavy-bottomed saucepan. Place the saucepan over medium-high heat and bring the date mixture to a boil, stirring constantly with a wooden spoon, until thickened. Cool the filling before spreading it over the oatmeal crust.

3. To make the bars: Add the flour, salt, and baking soda to a mixing bowl and whisk to combine. Set aside. Add the rolled oats to another bowl and set aside.

4. Add the butter, brown sugar, and vanilla to the bowl of a stand mixer fitted with the paddle attachment and beat until the ingredients are well mixed. Add the dry ingredients and beat to combine. Turn off the mixer, remove the bowl, and fold in the rolled oats. Press half of the flour-oat mixture into the prepared pan. Using an offset spatula, spread with the cooled date filling. Crumble the remaining flour-oat mixture evenly over the filling.

5. Bake the bars for 30 minutes, or until lightly browned. Remove from the oven, and transfer to a wire rack to cool. When completely cool, lift the pastry with the foil from the pan, place on a cutting board, and carefully remove the foil. Cut into 2-inch bars with a wide-bladed knife, wiping the blade with a damp paper towel between cuts. Store the bars between sheets of wax paper in a covered tin at room temperature.

Yield: 2 dozen 2-inch bars

BAKING WITH OATMEAL

Be sure to choose the right type of oats for baking. The size, shape, and texture of the oat grain may vary because of the amount of processing or rolling. Use old-fashioned or quick-cooking oats, not instant oatmeal, for oatmeal cookies or bars. Pinhead oats, also known as Irish, Scottish, or steel-cut oats, should be used for cooked cereals or hearty coarse-grained breads.

Oats may be added to toppings for crisps and crumbles. Their nutty taste enhances the flavor of baked fruit. The coarse texture of the oats prevents a topping from soaking up fruit juices and becoming soggy.

Bernice's Irregular Raisin Cookies

This recipe came from the McLaughlin family. It was handwritten in the back pages of their mother Anna Regina (Hughes) McLaughlin's favorite cookbook, where she recorded household tips and the baby formulas for her four children. The recipe came from a good friend named Bernice who may have grown up with Anna and her husband, James, in Oil City, Pennsylvania. We call these cookies "Irregular" because the raisins stick out through the cookie dough, but they regularly satisfy us when we feel like a good cookie.

1¾ cups flour

¾ teaspoon cream of tartar

¾ teaspoon baking soda

¼ teaspoon salt

2 teaspoons vanilla extract

1 tablespoon milk

½ cup (1 stick) unsalted butter, at room
    temperature

¾ cup sugar

1 egg

1 cup golden or dark raisins

1. Set the oven rack in the middle position. Preheat the oven to 350°F. Line a 14 by 16-inch baking sheet with a silicone liner or aluminum foil, shiny side up. Coat the foil with vegetable oil spray.

2. Add the flour, cream of tartar, baking soda, and salt to a mixing bowl. Whisk to combine, and set aside. Combine the vanilla and milk in a glass measuring cup.

3. Cream the butter and sugar in the bowl of a stand mixer fitted with the paddle attachment. Add the egg and continue to beat. Add the vanilla-milk mixture to the creamed mixture and beat to combine. Add the dry ingredients in three additions to the creamed mixture to form a dough. Fold in the raisins. Drop by heaping teaspoons, 12 to a baking sheet, and bake for 15 minutes. The cookies will be a light golden brown. Slide the foil or silicone liner with the baked cookies onto a wire rack to cool for 15 minutes. Remove the cooled cookies with a metal spatula and transfer to a second wire rack. The cookies will firm up when cool. Store the cookies between sheets of wax paper in a covered tin.

Yield: 3½ dozen cookies

SWEET TIP: We used golden raisins for one batch and dried dark cherries for another. When using the dried cherries, add 1 teaspoon of almond extract to the cookie dough instead of the vanilla extract.

Billy Goat Cookies

This recipe came from our friend Ronn Smith, who has fond memories of his mother, Gertrude, baking them. We've decided that these slightly lumpy cookies baked with sour cream and dates got their name because they look a little like billy goats. We found that these cookies are also referred to as "Kansas" cookies. Other recipes for Billy Goats include coconut and puffed rice cereal. The mix of cinnamon and cloves makes them fragrant and satisfying. Gertrude noted on her recipe card, "Real Good."

2 cups flour
2 teaspoons baking powder
¼ teaspoon baking soda
½ teaspoon salt
1 teaspoon cinnamon
¼ teaspoon cloves

2 eggs, separated
1 cup sugar
½ cup (1 stick) unsalted butter, at room temperature
½ cup sour cream
1 teaspoon vanilla extract
2 cups pitted dates, cut into small pieces

1. Set the oven rack in the middle position. Preheat the oven to 350°F. Cover a 14- by 16-inch baking sheet with a silicone liner or aluminum foil, shiny side up. Coat the foil with vegetable oil spray.

2. Add the flour, baking powder, baking soda, salt, cinnamon, and cloves to a mixing bowl and whisk to combine. Set aside.

3. Add the egg whites to the bowl of a stand mixer fitted with the whisk attachment and beat

HOW TO CUT DATES AND OTHER DRIED FRUIT

Sheila discovered that if she dedicated a clean pair of kitchen scissors to be used only with food, and lightly coated them with vegetable oil spray, it was easier to cut through the dried pitted dates for the Billy Goat Cookies. This is also a good way to cut up candied pineapple, orange or lemon peel, or candied cherries.

Tier One: Norwegian Spice Hearts and Billy Goat Cookies; Tier Two: Butterscotch Ice Box Cookies;
Tier Three: Cry Baby Cookies

until soft peaks form. If you only have one mixer bowl, transfer the beaten egg whites to another bowl and set aside.

4. Cream the sugar and butter in the bowl of the stand mixer fitted with the paddle attachment. Add the egg yolks and continue to beat until combined. Add the sour cream and vanilla and continue beating until incorporated. Add the dry ingredients in three additions to the creamed mixture to form a dough.

5. Add the dates and run the mixer for about 1 minute, or until the dates are distributed into the dough. Fold the beaten egg whites into the dough in two additions. Drop the dough by tablespoons, 12 to a baking sheet, and bake for 15 to 16 minutes. The cookies will be a light brown. Slide the foil or silicone liner with the baked cookies onto a wire rack to cool for 15 minutes. Remove the cooled cookies with a metal spatula and transfer to a second wire rack. Store the cookies, between sheets of wax paper, in a covered tin.

Yield: 4 dozen cookies

SWEET TOUCH: Sift confectioners' sugar over the tops of the cookies, if desired.

Butterscotch Icebox Cookies

This recipe comes from the era of iceboxes; those insulated heavy wood and metal pieces of kitchen furniture that graced most houses until the advent of electric refrigerators in the 1930s. Because nothing was ever thrown out before its time, iceboxes were still being used in the 1940s and 1950s for our summer rentals on Sea Foam Avenue. Iceboxes served a dual purpose. You got to know the man who delivered the ice, and you could chill your cookie dough so that you could bake a tray of these Butterscotch Icebox Cookies whenever you felt like it. Modern refrigerators serve the same purpose, and you don't have to empty a metal pan of water from under your refrigerator.

3 cups flour

1½ teaspoons baking powder

¼ teaspoon salt

1 cup (2 sticks) unsalted butter, at room temperature

2 cups firmly packed brown sugar

2 eggs, beaten

1 teaspoon vanilla extract

1 cup walnuts, toasted and coarsely chopped

1. Place the flour, baking powder, and salt in a bowl and whisk to combine. Set aside.

2. Add the butter and sugar to the bowl of a stand mixer fitted with the paddle attachment and beat to combine. Add the beaten eggs and vanilla and beat until combined. Add the dry ingredients in three additions to the creamed mixture and continue to beat until incorporated. Turn off the mixer, remove the bowl, and fold in the chopped walnuts.

3. Remove the cookie dough from the bowl and divide it into four equal pieces. Place each portion of cookie dough on a separate sheet of plastic wrap, form into a disk, seal with the plastic wrap, and chill in the refrigerator for at least 2 hours or overnight.

4. Set the oven rack in the middle position. Preheat the oven to 375° F. Line a 14- by 16-inch baking sheet with a silicone liner or aluminum foil, shiny side up. Coat the foil with vegetable oil spray. Prepare two baking sheets, if desired.

5. Remove one portion of the chilled dough from the refrigerator. Place the dough on a floured sheet of wax paper. Dust the dough lightly with flour and cover with another sheet of wax paper. Roll out the dough into a square or rectangle ¼ inch thick. Cut out cookies with a 2¼-inch round cookie cutter dipped in flour. Place the cookies 2 inches apart on the prepared baking sheet, putting on no more than 12 cookies per sheet. Bake for 17 minutes. Slide the foil or the silicone liner with the baked cookies onto a wire rack to cool. Remove the cooled cookies with a metal spatula and transfer to second wire rack. Cool until firm. Store the cookies, between sheets of wax paper, in a covered tin.

Yield: 8 dozen cookies

SWEET TIP: Always dip the cookie cutter in flour before cutting out Butterscotch Icebox Cookies.

Graham Shingles

Graham Shingles

This recipe came from a manuscript cookbook compiled by a young man who inscribed it "Merry Christmas to Mother, from Harry, 1941." The recipes are in one handwriting, probably Harry's, and are bound into a handmade book with an oilcloth cover illustrated with a stylized Scandinavian girl bearing a basket of apples, with a goose by her side. The recipes are probably earlier than 1941, and they show no indication of the rationing of sugar and butter. The original recipe suggested storing the cookies in a metal pail. Lard and peanut butter were sold in covered metal pails during the nineteenth and early twentieth centuries. These cookies have to be "docked," or pricked, to keep them from curling when baking.

SHINGLES

1 cup graham flour (Bob's Red Mill Whole Wheat Graham Flour—Whole Grain/Stone Ground)

1½ cups all-purpose flour

¾ cup granulated sugar

½ teaspoon salt

1 teaspoon baking soda

½ teaspoon cinnamon

½ cup (1 stick) cold unsalted butter, cut into ½-inch slices

2 tablespoons honey

1 teaspoon vanilla extract

¼ cup cold water

TOPPING (optional)

Coarse white sanding sugar

GLAZE ("PAINT" FOR SHINGLES) (optional)

1 cup confectioners' sugar, sifted

1 tablespoon vanilla extract

Pinch of salt

1 tablespoon water

1. To make the shingles: Place the graham flour, all-purpose flour, granulated sugar, salt, baking soda, and cinnamon in the bowl of a food processor fitted with the metal blade. Pulse two or three times until combined. Add the butter to the dry ingredients and pulse until the mixture looks like cornmeal. Add the honey, vanilla, and cold water and pulse until a soft dough forms. Remove the dough from the bowl of the food processor with a rubber spatula and divide into four portions. Place in 10 by 14-inch thin plastic bags, and roll out in the bags. Refrigerate for 1 to 2 hours until firm.

2. Remove one bag of dough from the refrigerator, remove the dough from the bag, and place on a lightly floured sheet of wax paper. Sprinkle flour lightly on top of the dough, cover with another sheet of wax paper, and roll out into a square or rectangle ¼ inch thick. Dip a 2½-inch square cookie cutter in flour each time you cut out a Graham Shingle. Shingles can be cut at the sides and at the bottom of the first cookie. Repeat down and across the rolled-out dough. With a fork dipped in flour, make three or four rows of pricks across each cookie. Using a pastry brush, remove excess flour from the shingles. Return any remaining scraps of dough to the refrigerator.

3. Set the oven rack in the middle position. Preheat the oven to 350°F. Line a 14-by 16-inch baking sheet with a silicone liner or aluminum foil, shiny side up. Coat the foil with vegetable oil spray.

4. Dip a 2½-inch metal spatula in flour and lift the Shingles from the wax paper and transfer to the prepared baking sheet, 12 cookies per sheet. Bake for 13 to 14 minutes. Cool the Shingles on a wire rack for 10 minutes before removing from the baking sheet with a 2-inch-wide spatula. The Shingles will become crisp when completely cool.

5. Remove each of the three remaining plastic bags from the refrigerator, one at a time, and repeat this procedure. Remove all the rechilled scraps of dough and roll them into a flat disk and cut into squares, following the directions above. Coarse sanding sugar may be sprinkled over the Shingles before baking for a sweeter cookie. If you prefer, you can glaze the cookies, following the instructions below.

6. To make the glaze: Mix together the confectioners' sugar, vanilla, and salt in a small bowl and stir in the water. Slip a sheet of wax paper under a wire rack to catch drips. Place the cookies on the rack. Using a teaspoon or fork, drizzle the glaze over the top of the Shingles. After the glaze has set, store the cookies between sheets of wax paper, in a covered tin, at room temperature.

Yield: 3 dozen cookies

SWEET TIP: Store unrolled dough in the refrigerator to keep it firm while cutting out the Shingles.

• Any size or shape cookie cutter may be used to cut the cookies, but the yield will be different.

Cry Baby Cookies

These cakelike cookies come from the recipe archive of a lady from the Midwest. Cry Baby Cookies have an appealing warm brown color and a compelling history that goes back to the mid-1800s. Several different stories about their origin and numerous variations have been found, but we like to think of it as an unpretentious American cookie. We like to think they were used to appease tearful children.

¾ cup shredded coconut

1 cup raisins

¾ cup walnuts, toasted and coarsely chopped

2¼ cups flour

1½ teaspoons baking powder

¾ teaspoon baking soda

¾ teaspoon salt

½ cup (1 stick) unsalted butter, at room temperature

½ cup sugar

1 egg

½ cup molasses

½ cup milk

1. Combine the coconut, raisins, and walnuts in a small bowl. Add the flour to a second larger bowl. Remove 2 tablespoons of the flour, add to the coconut, raisins, and walnuts, and mix until coated with flour. Set aside. Add the baking powder, baking soda, and salt to the remaining flour in the larger bowl and whisk to combine. Set aside.

2. Add the butter and sugar to the bowl of a stand mixer fitted with the paddle attachment and cream to combine. Add the egg and molasses and beat until combined. Add the dry ingredients, and the floured coconut, raisins, and walnuts to the creamed mixture alternately with the milk. Remove the cookie dough from the mixer bowl and divide into four pieces. Place each portion of cookie dough on a separate sheet of plastic wrap. Form into disk, seal with plastic wrap, and chill in the refrigerator for at least 2 hours or overnight.

3. When ready to bake the cookies, set the oven rack in the middle position. Preheat the oven to 350°F. Line a 14 by 16-inch baking sheet with a silicone liner or aluminum foil, shiny side up. Coat the foil with vegetable oil spray.

4. Remove one portion of the chilled dough from the refrigerator. Scoop out teaspoonsful of the cookie dough. Using wet hands or wearing disposable gloves, roll the dough into 1-inch balls. Work quickly before the dough becomes too soft to handle. Place the balls on the prepared baking sheet, 12 to a sheet, and bake for 13 minutes, or until golden brown. Do not overbake. Slide the foil or the silicone liner with the baked cookies onto a wire rack to cool. Remove the cooled cookies with a metal spatula and transfer to a second wire rack. Store the cooled cookies, between sheets of wax paper, in a covered tin at room temperature.

Yield: 7½ dozen cookies

Hazelnut Espresso Cookies

We've always loved the way chocolate becomes a team player when combined with other flavors. Adding espresso enhances the appeal of these cookies, and the taste and texture of coarsely chopped hazelnuts brings out their best. They may not be the prettiest of cookies, but they taste very cosmopolitan. A close cousin to Bernice's Irregular Raisin Cookies, they remind us of our youthful days, and nights spent in the coffeehouses and smoky cafes of Cambridge's Harvard Square and New York's Greenwich Village. This is a crisp cookie with a chewy center.

1½ cups flour

¼ cup American natural nonalkalized cocoa
    powder

2 tablespoons instant espresso or instant
    coffee

¾ teaspoon cream of tartar

¾ teaspoon baking soda

¼ teaspoon salt

1 teaspoon vanilla extract

1 tablespoon milk

½ cup (1 stick) unsalted butter, at room
    temperature

1 cup sugar

1 egg

1 cup hazelnuts, toasted, coarsely chopped,
    and shaken through a sieve to remove
    excess skin and small bits

1. Set the oven rack in the middle position. Preheat the oven to 350° F. Line a 14- by 16-inch baking sheet with a silicone liner or aluminum foil, shiny side up. Coat the foil with vegetable oil spray.

2. Add the flour, cocoa, espresso, cream of tartar, baking soda, and salt to a mixing bowl and whisk to combine. Set aside. Combine the vanilla and milk in a glass measuring cup.

3. Cream the butter and sugar in the bowl of a stand mixer fitted with the paddle attachment. Add the egg and continue to beat. Add the vanilla-milk mixture to the creamed mixture and combine. Add the dry ingredients in three additions to the creamed mixture to form a dough. Fold in the hazelnuts. Drop the dough by heaping tablespoons, 12 per sheet, onto the prepared sheet. Bake for 15 minutes. Slide the foil or the silicone liner with the baked cookies onto a wire rack to cool. Remove cooled cookies with a metal spatula and transfer to a second wire rack. The cookies will firm up when cool. Store the cookies, between sheets of wax paper, in a covered tin.

Yield: 3½ dozen cookies

Lemon Clove Cookies

These cookies are delightful. They have the delicate taste of lemon and cloves that go well together. The flavor is very subtle. Another plus is that they are a very crisp cookie. Thin and crunchy, they have a dainty browned edge. We found the recipe handwritten on a slip of paper titled "butter." No oven temperature or baking time was given. The original recipe called for cinnamon or cloves. We chose cloves, but you can try them with cinnamon.

2 cups flour

¼ teaspoon salt

½ teaspoon baking soda

¼ teaspoon cloves

½ cup (1 stick) unsalted butter, at room temperature

1 cup sugar

3 eggs

Grated zest of a large lemon

Juice of ½ large lemon

1. Set the oven rack in the middle position. Preheat the oven to 350°F. Line a 14 by 16-inch baking sheet with a silicone liner or aluminum foil, shiny side up. Coat the foil with vegetable oil spray.

2. Add the flour, salt, baking soda, and cloves to a mixing bowl and whisk to combine. Set aside.

3. Add the butter and sugar to the bowl of a stand mixer fitted with the paddle attachment and cream to combine. Add the eggs to the creamed mixture and continue to beat. Mix in the zest and lemon juice. Add the dry ingredients to the cookie dough in three additions and beat to incorporate.

4. Transfer the cookie dough to a piping bag with a ½-inch opening, or to a plastic bag with a corner snipped, and pipe the cookies onto the prepared baking sheet. The cookies should be about the size of a quarter, and there should be no more than 16 cookies to a baking sheet. Bake for 15 minutes. The cookies will be a pale brown with darker brown edges. Remove the cookies from the oven. Slide the foil or the silicone liner with the baked cookies onto a wire rack to cool. Remove the cooled cookies with a metal spatula and transfer to the second wire rack. When the cookies are cool, store them, between sheets of wax paper, in a covered tin at room temperature.

Yield: 7 dozen cookies

Mary Messer's Vanilla Coat Buttons

Mary Messer's Vanilla Coat Buttons

This charming little cookie from the 1930s looks just like a button with its two little holes. We discovered this recipe in a well-used wooden file box of recipes. The glaze makes these cookies look like mother of pearl buttons.

COOKIES

2½ cups flour

1 cup granulated sugar

¼ teaspoon salt

1½ teaspoons baking powder

½ cup (1 stick) cold unsalted butter

2 eggs

1½ teaspoons vanilla extract

¼ cup heavy cream

GLAZE

1 cup confectioners' sugar

Pinch of salt

1 tablespoon vanilla extract

1 tablespoon water

1. To make the cookies: Place the flour, granulated sugar, salt, and baking powder in the bowl of a food processor fitted with the metal blade and pulse two or three times until combined. Add the butter to the dry ingredients and pulse until crumbly. Add one egg and pulse to combine. Combine the vanilla and cream, then add to the processed mixture. Continue to pulse until all of the ingredients are combined and the dough comes together.

2. Remove the dough from the bowl of the food processor and place on a sheet of plastic wrap. Form into a disk, cover with plastic wrap, and chill the dough in the refrigerator for at least 1 hour or overnight.

3. When ready to bake the coat buttons, set the oven rack in the middle position. Preheat the oven to 350°F. Line a 14 by 16-inch baking sheet with a silicone liner or aluminum foil, shiny side up. Coat the foil with vegetable oil spray.

4. Divide the chilled dough into four portions. Roll out one portion of dough at a time. Keep the remaining dough chilled in the refrigerator until ready to roll out. Lightly dust a piece of wax paper with flour. Place a portion of dough on the wax paper, dust lightly with flour, and cover with another sheet of wax paper. Roll out the dough ¼ inch thick. Cut out cookies with a 2-inch round cookie or scalloped cutter dipped in flour. Place the cookies 2 inches apart on the prepared baking sheet, adding no more than 12 cookies per sheet. Beat the remaining egg. Brush the cookies with the beaten egg. Using the handle of a wooden spoon or the end of a plastic straw with a ⅜-inch opening, make two holes in the center of each coat button. Do *not* dip handle of the wooden spoon or end of the straw in flour before making holes in Coat Buttons; the flour will clog the holes. Bake the Coat Buttons for 20 minutes. Transfer the sheet of cookies to a wire rack and allow to cool for 5 minutes.

5. To make the glaze: Sift the confectioners' sugar and salt into a small bowl. Add the vanilla and water and whisk to combine. Add additional water to glaze by teaspoons, if necessary to achieve the desired consistency.

6. Place a sheet of wax paper under a second wire rack. While still warm, remove the cookies from the first rack and place on the second rack. Using a pastry brush, paint the cookies with the glaze. Allow to cool completely. Store the cookies, between sheets of wax paper, in a covered tin.

Yield: 3 dozen cookies

Cousin Helen's Greek Cookies
(Koulourakia)

This is a recipe we received from our friend George Geuras. It is based on his cousin Helen Varsamis's sesame seed cookies. The confectioners' sugar in the recipe gives the rolled, twisted cookies a unique texture. We brushed them with egg yolk and sprinkled them with sesame seeds before baking. We found that Koulourakia are also referred to as Greek Easter Cookies.

3½ cups flour

1½ teaspoons baking powder

½ teaspoon salt

½ teaspoon cinnamon

1½ cups confectioners' sugar

1 cup (2 sticks) unsalted butter, at room
    temperature

4 whole eggs

2 teaspoons vanilla extract

2 egg yolks

½ cup white sesame seeds

1. Add the flour, baking powder, salt, and cinnamon to a bowl and whisk to combine. Set aside. Sift the confectioners' sugar into a bowl and set aside.

2. Add the butter and confectioners' sugar to the bowl of a stand mixer fitted with the paddle attachment and beat for 5 minutes to combine. Add the 4 whole eggs to the butter-sugar mixture and beat for another 5 minutes to combine. Add 1½ teaspoons of the vanilla to the mixture and beat in. Add the flour to the mixture in three additions and continue to beat until the dough comes together. Turn off the mixer, remove the dough from the bowl, and place in a container. Cover the container with plastic wrap and place in refrigerator for at least 1 hour to chill, or until the dough can be rolled easily into balls.

3. Set the oven rack in the middle position. Preheat the oven to 350°F. Line a 14 by 16-inch baking sheet with a silicone liner or aluminum foil, shiny side up. Coat the foil with vegetable oil spray.

4. Remove the dough from the refrigerator. Add the egg yolks and the remaining ½ teaspoon vanilla to a small bowl and whisk to combine. Set the glaze aside.

5. Cut a piece of wax paper 10 by 12 inches in size. Draw two lines on the paper, with pencil or marker, 6 inches apart. Flip the wax paper over on the counter and tape it to the counter so that the lines are on the back of the sheet and the wax paper cannot move. Scoop a heaping teaspoon of dough from the container and roll it into a ball with your hands. Roll the ball between your palms until it forms a strand. Place the partially formed strand on the prepared sheet of wax paper, and continue to roll until the ends of the strand meet the two lines. The strands will be 6 inches in length. Carefully lift the strand, fold it in half, and twist twice to form a cookie.

6. Place the cookies approximately ½ inch apart on the prepared baking sheet. Do not place more than 15 cookies on the sheet. Brush the *Koulourakia* with the egg yolk glaze, and sprinkle the cookies with sesame seeds. Bake for 20 minutes, or until the cookies are golden brown.

7. Repeat with the remaining dough until all the dough is made into cookies.

8. Transfer the sheet of baked *Koulourakia* to a wire rack to cool. Allow to cool for 5 minutes before removing from the baking sheet and placing on a second wire rack. The cookies should be stored, between sheets of wax paper, in a covered tin.

Yield: about 5½ dozen cookies

Mom's Coconut Cornflake Cookies

This recipe from the 1940s, handwritten on an index card, credits "Mom." We don't know much about Mom, but she knew that coconut and cornflakes are a wonderful combination for a quick crunchy cookie. The index card was much handled and stained from use, so Mom's Coconut Cornflake Cookies were loved and made often. These are good when eaten with lemonade on a warm sunny day.

1 cup flour
½ teaspoon baking powder
½ teaspoon baking soda
½ teaspoon salt
½ cup (1 stick) unsalted butter, at room
    temperature
½ cup granulated sugar
½ cup firmly packed brown sugar
1 egg
1 teaspoon vanilla extract
¾ cup cornflakes
1 cup large coconut flakes or sweetened
    shredded coconut

1. Set the oven rack in the middle position. Preheat the oven to 350°F. Line a 14 by 16-inch baking sheet with a silicone liner or aluminum foil, shiny side up. Coat the foil with vegetable oil spray.

2. Add the flour, baking powder, baking soda, and salt to a mixing bowl and whisk to combine.

3. Add the butter and sugars to the bowl of a stand mixer fitted with the paddle attachment and cream to combine. Add the egg and vanilla to creamed ingredients and beat until combined. Add the dry ingredients and beat to incorporate.

4. Turn off the mixer, remove the bowl from the stand, and fold in the cornflakes and then the coconut. Drop the batter by heaping teaspoons onto the prepared baking sheet, no more than 12 cookies to a sheet. Bake for 12 minutes. Transfer the sheet of baked cookies to a wire rack to cool. After 5 minutes, remove the cookies from the baking sheet with a metal spatula and transfer to a second wire rack. The cookies will firm up as they cool. Store the cookies between sheets of wax paper in a covered tin.

Yield: 3 dozen

SWEET TIP: The larger flaked coconut gave more of a crunch to the cookies.

SWEET TOUCH: For a sweeter cookie, fold in ½ cup dark or white chocolate chips.

Norwegian Spice Hearts

We originally found a recipe for a sugar cookie that looked good on a tattered handout from an extension course. We labored mightily, but we were unable to bake a respectable cookie using the ingredients and directions. It happens. After several tries, we came up with an entirely different but delicious "Scandinavian" cookie, which uses a mix of four different spices, including the exotic, to us, cardamom.

2 ¾ cups flour

1 cup sugar

½ teaspoon salt

2 teaspoons baking powder

1 teaspoon ground cardamom

½ teaspoon cinnamon

½ teaspoon cloves

¼ teaspoon mace

½ cup (1 stick) cold unsalted butter

¼ cup milk

1 egg

1 teaspoon vanilla extract

1. Place the flour, sugar, salt, baking powder, cardamom, cinnamon, cloves, and mace in the bowl of a food processor fitted with the metal blade and pulse until well mixed. Add the butter and pulse until crumbly. Add the milk, egg, and vanilla to a 1-cup glass measuring cup and mix well. Add to the bowl of the food processor and pulse until the dough comes together. You may have to pat the dough together a bit. (The dough may be a little dry.)

2. Remove the dough from the bowl of the food processor and place on sheet of wax paper or plastic wrap. Form into four disks. Cover each disk with plastic wrap and chill in the refrigerator for at least 2 hours, or overnight.

3. Set the oven rack in the middle position. Preheat the oven to 400° F. Line two 14 by 16-inch baking sheets with a silicone liner or aluminum foil, shiny side up, and coat the foil with vegetable oil spray.

4. Remove one portion of the chilled dough from the refrigerator, and roll between two pieces of lightly floured wax paper to ¼ inch thick. Cut out cookies with a 2½-inch heart-shaped cookie cutter dipped in flour. Place 2 inches apart on the prepared baking sheets, adding no more than 12 cookies per sheet. Repeat this process with the rest of the dough, working with a quarter of the dough at a time. Bake the cookies for 10 minutes. Cool the cookies on the baking sheet on a wire rack. Using a spatula, transfer the cooled cookies to a second rack. The cookies will become firm when cool. Store the cookies between sheets of wax paper in a covered tin.

Yield: 4½ dozen

SWEET TIPS: Refrigerate the scraps after rolling out the dough twice, repeating with the rest of dough. Combine the refrigerated scraps, roll the scraps into a sheet of dough, and roll out more cookies until the cookie scrap dough is used up. Cookies baked from scraps may be a little less tender because of being reworked, but are none the less delicious.

Norwegian Spice Hearts and Billy Goat Cookies

Polka Dot Chocolate Bars

Polka Dot Chocolate Bars

We found this recipe handwritten on the back of a Naumkeag Trust Company deposit slip. It is definitely from the twentieth century because the line for the date starts with 19. The bank is located in Salem, Massachusetts. We added a simple linear pattern of white and dark chocolate chips on the top of the bars. Alternatively, white and dark chocolate chips can be melted and drizzled on top of the bars.

BARS

¾ cup dark chocolate chips

¾ cup white chocolate chips

1¼ cups walnuts, toasted and coarsely
    chopped

2 cups flour

½ teaspoon baking soda

½ teaspoon salt

2 cups firmly packed brown sugar

1 cup (2 sticks) unsalted butter, at room
    temperature

3 eggs

2 teaspoons vanilla extract

3 ounces bitter (baking) chocolate,
    melted and cooled

TOPPING

30 white chocolate chips

25 dark chocolate chips

ALTERNATIVE TOPPING

¼ cup dark chocolate chips, melted

¼ cup white chocolate chips, melted

1. Set the oven rack in the middle position. Preheat the oven to 350°F. Cover the bottom and sides of a 9 by 13 by 2-inch metal pan with aluminum foil, shiny side up. Coat the foil with butter or vegetable oil spray.

2. To make the bars: Place the chocolate chips, white chocolate chips, and walnuts in a bowl and set aside. Add the flour, baking soda, and salt to a separate bowl, whisk to combine, and set aside.

3. Add the sugar and butter to the bowl of a stand mixer fitted with the paddle attachment and cream until combined. Add the eggs one at a time, beating well after each addition. Add the vanilla and cooled chocolate to the creamed mixture and combine. Add the dry ingredients in three additions, beating slowly until thoroughly combined. Add the chocolate chips and walnuts and combine.

4. Turn the batter into the prepared pan and distribute it evenly, smoothing the top with an offset spatula. Bake for 40 minutes, or until a metal tester inserted into the center comes out clean.

5. Remove the pan from the oven and place on a wire rack. *Do not turn off the oven.* Carefully place 6 white chips evenly spaced across the 13-inch side of the bars. Place 5 white chips evenly spaced down the 9-inch side of bars. Place 5 dark chocolate chips between the white chips across 13-inch side. Place 5 dark chocolate chips evenly spaced down between white chips on 9-inch side. Return the pan to the oven for 2 minutes, then place on a wire rack to cool to room temperature. Remove the uncut bars from pan with the foil and place on a cutting board. Carefully slide the foil from under the bars. Cut into 2-inch bars with a wide-bladed knife, wiping the blade between cuts.

6. Alternatively, top the bars with melted chocolate. Using a fork and holding it high over the bars, drizzle melted dark chocolate at an angle over top of bars. Drizzle melted white chocolate over the

surface of the bars. Both chocolate drizzles may overlap.

7. Place the pan of chocolate-drizzled bars in the refrigerator until the chocolate becomes firm. Remove the cooled bars from the refrigerator, and place on the cutting board. Cut into 2-inch bars with a wide-bladed knife, wiping the blade between cuts. Place the bars in a covered tin between sheets of wax paper. Polka Dot Chocolate Bars can be successfully frozen and served at a later date.

Yield: about 2 dozen 2-inch bars

4 Filling the Bread Basket

THE RECIPES

*T*he smell of baking bread still means home to most people. We refer to a companion as someone with whom we share bread. To us, bread is holy, not just because it is symbolic in many of the world's religions, but also because it sustains life, and each slice is like a love letter to the person who consumes it. When we think of home bakers, we often describe them as the bakers of bread, those who know how to hold a family together no matter what challenges life presents.

The story of bread runs through most families. There is always someone who is known as "the bread baker." Usually, it is a grandmother, a mother, an aunt, or a sister who is honored with this title. Sometimes, it is a wife, a daughter, or a daughter-in-law who inherits the culinary legacy of the family and, through her home-baking skills, preserves and perpetuates the family's history of home baking.

We first started baking bread with our mother in our large family kitchen on Sea Foam Avenue where, supplied with our own child-size rolling pins, we shared a portion of our mother's wooden pastry board as we learned the basics of home baking. We diligently braided scraps of dough and brushed

them with beaten egg to produce our own minia-ture, burnished, Sabbath challahs in tiny loaf pans.

Just as we treasure the story of our own family's bread baking, we have found, time after time, that the home bakers we meet have precious stories of relatives or friends who learned to bake bread as children, and continued to bake bread to nourish their families and friends, even into their final years.

Our friend Maude O'Neill, who was born in Nova Scotia and learned to bake at an early age, soon found herself, as a young girl, cooking and serving meals accompanied by her own bread to two hundred patients and staff at her local hospital.

Maude lived most of her life in the United States, and in her late nineties, still vital and living in a nursing home, she missed her kitchen and baking bread. When she was granted permission to bake her bread in the residence kitchen, she baked loaf after loaf of bread for the staff and residents using the recipe she had created and committed to memory as a young girl in rural Canada. Maude baked her bread at the residence until she died at the age of ninety-eight.

Nana May Cleary, a lifelong Dorchester, Mas-sachusetts, resident, learned how to bake bread in her Irish mother's kitchen. Several years ago, her granddaughter, Mary Rita, submitted her grand-mother's recipe for her Irish Yeast Bread with Raisins to a baking competition sponsored by the *Boston Globe*. Nana May's recipe easily won first prize. Mary Rita, a Sister of St. Joseph, baked her grandmother's bread at the convent for many years, carrying on the Cleary Family's bread-baking tradition.

During a hot afternoon in Austin at the Texas Book Festival, we met a young woman who told us a miraculous story about bread. Her grandmother had been the bread baker in the family, and she had produced fragrant crusty loaves for years, but somehow no one had written down her recipe.

Heartbroken, one of the young woman's aunts dreamed that she was baking bread with her mother. She awakened the next morning and found that she remembered the recipe they had baked together in her dream. The cherished family recipe for baking bread had been reclaimed, and could now be shared with all of the home bakers in the family.

"Filling the Bread Basket" encompasses the whole spectrum of bread baking—yeast breads, batter breads, soda breads, and quick breads. There is nothing like baking Aunt Minnie Schleiger's tender Butterhorns, Lise's delicate Sweet Banana Yeast Bread, a nontraditional Brown Soda Bread with Dried Cherries and Toasted Walnuts, and a sweet Coconut Banana Bread to fill your own bread basket.

Quick Tips

- The temperature of water used for proofing yeast should not be higher than that called for in the recipe.
- Overkneading bread dough will toughen it.
- Use the correct size and shape pan for baking bread.
- Do not slice bread while it is still warm; it may fall apart.

Aunt Minnie's Butterhorn Dinner Rolls

Our good friend Sue Truax gave us this recipe for But-
terhorn Dinner Rolls from her Aunt Minnie Schleiger.
Mildred "Minnie" Schleiger baked fabulous desserts
when she was growing up in Sutton, Nebraska. Minnie
used a wood- or coal-burning stove for her baking, and
she never used a thermometer, so she had to judge the
temperature of her oven. These dinner rolls are extraor-
dinary! Light and fluffy, they lend themselves to all
manner of toppings such as sea salt, poppy seeds, or
dill.

ROLLS

½ cup milk

½ cup (1 stick) unsalted butter, melted and
    cooled, plus 3 tablespoons unsalted butter,
    melted, for rolling

½ cup plus 1 tablespoon sugar

1 teaspoon salt

One 1¼-ounce package active dry yeast

¼ cup water, warmed to 115°F

3 eggs

5 cups flour

TOPPING

2 eggs, beaten

Sea salt, poppy seeds, dill (optional)

1. Line two or three 14 by 16-inch baking sheets
with a silicone liner or aluminum foil, shiny side up.
Coat the foil with vegetable oil spray.

2. Add the milk to a heavy-bottomed saucepan
and scald over medium heat. Small bubbles will
form around the edges of the pan when the milk is
scalded. Remove the pan from the heat and add the
½ cup butter, ½ cup sugar, and salt. Mix to combine. Set aside, and cool to approximately 115°F.

3. Dissolve the yeast and remaining 1 tablespoon sugar in the warm water. Set aside and allow
to proof for 10 minutes.

4. In the bowl of a stand mixer fitted with the
paddle attachment, beat the eggs well. Add the
milk and the proofed yeast mixture and combine.
Stir in the flour, 1 cup at a time, until incorporated.
Change to the dough hook and knead for 5 minutes, or until the dough comes together.

5. *Preheat the oven to 175°F.* Coat a medium bowl
with butter or vegetable oil spray. Place the dough
in the greased bowl and swirl to coat. Cover the
bowl with plastic wrap or a clean dish towel. Place
the bowl on the back of the stove or in a warm
place and allow to rise for 1 hour, or until doubled
in size.

6. Punch down the risen dough and turn out
onto a piece of parchment paper 14 inches long.
Sprinkle with a little flour, and hand knead for
1 or 2 minutes to form into a smooth silky round.
Cut the dough into 4 portions and roll into 4 balls.
Place one ball on a lightly floured piece of parchment paper. Place another piece of parchment paper
on top of the ball. Roll out the dough into a 12-inch
circle. Cut dough into 8 wedges, and brush wedges
with the melted butter. Roll up the wedges starting at the outside edge and place on the prepared
baking sheets, slightly curling both ends to form a
crescent. Let rise in a warm place until doubled in
size, 30 to 45 minutes. Using a pastry brush, brush
the Butterhorns with the beaten eggs. Add any
topping at this time, if desired, such as sea salt,
poppy seeds, or dill. Repeat the process with the
remaining 3 balls of dough.

7. Place the oven rack in the middle position.
Raise the oven temperature to 350°F. Place the baking

sheet in the oven and bake for 20 minutes, or until golden brown. Transfer to a wire rack to cool. Repeat to bake the remaining rolls.

Yield: 32 butterhorn rolls

SWEET TIP: If you don't have parchment paper, and since the rounds of dough are 12 inches in diameter, use double sheets of wax paper overlapped or a wooden pastry board to roll out the rounds of dough.

Butterhorns

Brown Soda Bread with Dried Cherries
and Toasted Walnuts and Aunt Grace's
Rhubarb-Walnut Conserve

Brown Soda Bread with Dried Cherries and Toasted Walnuts

This version of a brown soda bread is a fun baking project. The dough is soft, and it needs a patient hand. The disk of dough will form a round loaf when baked and the kitchen will smell like "a little bit of Ireland." Toast and butter slices of this bread for a real treat.

2½ cups whole wheat flour

1½ cups all-purpose flour

½ cup sugar

1½ teaspoons baking soda

1 teaspoon salt

1 cup (2 sticks) cold unsalted butter, cut into
    ¼-inch dice

1⅔ cups buttermilk

1 cup dried cherries or raisins

1 cup walnuts, toasted and finely chopped

1. Set the oven rack in the middle position. Preheat the oven to 450°F. Coat a 9-inch springform pan with vegetable oil spray. Dust the pan with flour and tap the pan to remove the excess flour.

2. Put the flours, sugar, baking soda, and salt into the bowl of a food processor fitted with the metal blade. Pulse two or three times until combined. Add the butter to the dry ingredients and pulse until the mixture looks like cornmeal. Add the buttermilk and pulse until a dough forms; the dough will be loose. Turn off the mixer. Remove the dough from the bowl of the food processor with a rubber spatula and place it in a mixing bowl coated with vegetable oil spray.

3. Sprinkle the cherries and walnuts on top of the dough. Work them into the dough until all the fruit and nuts have been incorporated. Using a spatula or floured hands, transfer the dough to the prepared pan. Using an offset spatula, smooth the dough evenly into the pan. Cut a cross on top of the dough with a sharp knife. Bake for 15 minutes. *Reduce the oven temperature to 400°F* and bake for 30 minutes more. Check the bread at 30 minutes. The bread is done when a metal tester inserted into the center comes out clean. If not done, bake for another 5 minutes, or 50 minutes in all.

4. Transfer the pan to a wire rack and cool for about 20 minutes. Remove the sides and bottom of the pan and allow the bread to cool completely before slicing. Use a wide-bladed serrated knife to slice the bread. Store leftover bread, wrapped in waxed paper, at room temperature.

Yield: one 9-inch loaf;
10 to 12 slices

SWEET TIPS: Dried cranberries can be substituted for the cherries or raisins.

• Do not cut the bread until completely cool to avoid crumbling.

• The bread can be successfully frozen. Allow to come to room temperature before serving, or warm in a 300°F oven for a few minutes to take off the chill.

Chocolate Walnut Yeast Bread

We've seen a lot of recipes for chocolate breads, but most of them are quick breads. This Chocolate Walnut Bread is made with yeast and uses chocolate chips and cocoa. The texture is more substantial than a quick bread, and the recipe makes a slice that becomes ethereal when spread with salted butter or tangy cream cheese.

YEAST SPONGE

One 1¼-ounce package active dry yeast

¼ cup water, warmed to 115°F

1 tablespoon sugar

DOUGH

1 cup milk

½ cup (1 stick) unsalted butter, at room
    temperature

1½ teaspoons salt

½ cup firmly packed brown sugar

3½ cups flour

½ cup American natural nonalkalized cocoa
    powder, sifted

2 eggs, beaten

1 cup bittersweet chocolate chips

1 cup walnuts, toasted and coarsely
    chopped

1 cup dried cherries

1. To make the yeast sponge: Dissolve the yeast in the water. Add the sugar. Let stand, uncovered, in a warm place to proof, for about 10 minutes. Set aside.

2. To make the dough: Scald the milk in a heavy-bottomed saucepan over medium heat, stirring, until small bubbles form around the edges of the pan. This scalding process can happen quickly (see sidebar page 117). Whisk in the butter to melt.

Add the salt and brown sugar and mix well; adding the sugar will bring down the temperature quickly.

3. Add the flour and cocoa to a bowl and whisk together to combine. Set aside.

4. Combine the milk-and-butter mixture, proofed yeast, and eggs in the bowl of a stand mixer fitted with the paddle attachment. Add the flour-and-cocoa mixture and combine. Add the chocolate chips, walnuts, and cherries and beat to make a soft dough.

5. *Preheat the oven to 175°F.* Coat a medium bowl with butter or vegetable oil spray. Place the dough in the greased bowl and swirl to coat. Cover the bowl with plastic wrap or a clean dish towel. Place the bowl on the back of the stove or in a warm place and allow to rise for 1 hour, or until doubled in size.

6. Coat the bottom and sides of two 9 by 5 by 3-inch loaf pans with vegetable oil spray or butter. Divide the dough in half with a spatula or knife and transfer to the prepared pans. Smooth the top of the dough in each pan with an offset spatula dipped in water. Cover the loaf pans with plastic wrap or dish towels and allow to rise in a warm place for 1 hour, or until doubled in size. Remove wraps.

7. Place the oven rack in the middle position. *Raise the oven temperature to 350°F.* Bake the breads for 35 to 40 minutes, or until they pull away from the sides slightly. Remove the pans from the oven. Turn the breads out of the pans immediately onto a wire rack. The breads are done when they make a hollow sound when tapped on the bottom. Cool the breads completely before cutting. Store Chocolate Walnut Yeast Bread, wrapped in wax paper, at room temperature.

Yield: 2 loaves; 10 to 12 slices each

SWEET TOUCH: Chocolate Walnut Yeast Bread should *not* be toasted in a toaster because the chocolate chips will melt.

• Slices of this bread can be heated in a toaster oven, or spread with butter and pan-toasted in a frying pan.

SCALDING LIQUIDS

It is important to know how to scald milk or cream correctly. Add the milk or cream to a heavy-bottomed saucepan and place it over medium heat. Using a wooden spoon, stir until small bubbles form around the edges of the pan. This process can happen quickly. Scalded liquids are *not* brought to a rolling boil.

Honey Molasses Bread (Weetabix)
(Yeast Batter Bread)

We found this handwritten recipe on a lined index card. It is a golden brown treasure of a bread, not too heavy, not too crunchy, but with a hearty wheaten flavor. We had heard of Weetabix whole-grain cereal, but had never tried it before we baked this bread. Honey Molasses Bread is delicious toasted and spread with butter and orange marmalade. Weetabix originated in Africa and was later distributed by a company in Great Britain. It is now manufactured and distributed in the United States. The cereal is formed into large oval cushions and is crushed into a bowl before being eaten with milk. Weetabix is what gives this bread its distinctive texture.

6¾ cups flour

Two 1¼-ounce packages active dry yeast

1 tablespoon salt

1½ cups water

1 cup milk

⅓ cup molasses

½ cup honey

¼ cup (½ stick) unsalted butter, at room temperature

2 eggs

2 cups crushed Weetabix

1. In the bowl of a stand mixer fitted with the paddle attachment, combine 3 cups of the flour, the yeast, and the salt.

2. Combine the water, milk, molasses, honey, and butter in a saucepan, and heat until warm, about 115°F on a cooking theromometer. Add to the dry ingredients in the bowl and combine. Add the eggs and blend at low speed. Add the crushed Weetabix and mix. Add the remaining 3¾ cups flour and beat at low speed to combine. Change

to the dough hook and knead the dough for 6 to 8 minutes, or until it comes together and is smooth; the finished dough will be loose.

3. *Preheat the oven to 175°F.* Coat a medium bowl with butter or vegetable oil spray. Place the dough into the greased bowl and swirl to coat. Cover the bowl with plastic wrap or a clean dish towel. Place the bowl on the back of the stove or in a warm place and allow to rise for 1 hour, or until doubled in size.

4. Coat the bottom and sides of two 9 by 5 by 3-inch loaf pans with vegetable oil spray or butter. Divide the dough in half with a rubber spatula and transfer each half to the prepared pans. Smooth the top of dough with an offset spatula. Cover the loaf pans with plastic wrap or dish towels and allow to rise in a warm place for 1 hour, or until doubled in size. Remove wraps.

5. Place the oven rack in the middle position. *Raise the oven temperature to 375°F.*

6. Bake the breads until crusty, about 30 minutes. Cover the breads with a tent made of aluminum foil after 20 minutes if the tops are browning too quickly. Continue to bake for the remaining 10 minutes. Turn the breads out of the pans immediately onto a wire rack. The breads are done when they make a hollow sound when tapped on the bottom. Cool the breads completely before cutting. Store the breads, loosely wrapped in wax paper, at room temperature. Honey Molasses Bread freezes well.

Yield: 2 loaves; 10 to 12 slices each

Oatmeal Bread, Banana Yeast Bread, Honey Molasses Bread (Weetabix), and sheaves of wheat butter

Coconut Banana Bread

Sometimes the simplest things are the best. This recipe for banana bread came from our friend Ralph Perlovsky's wife, Mary, who uses walnuts in her recipe, but we decided to use shredded coconut instead. We added the pumpkin pie spice and the vanilla and topped it with roasted coconut chips. Before we knew it, guests were fighting over this Coconut Banana Bread. We know one couple who almost had to go into counseling because they fought so fiercely over the last piece. This recipe makes two loaves, one to enjoy and one to give away.

2½ cups flour

1 teaspoon baking powder

1 teaspoon baking soda

½ teaspoon salt

1 teaspoon pumpkin pie spice

½ cup (1 stick) unsalted butter, at room temperature

1 cup sugar

2 eggs

1 cup mashed ripe bananas (about 2 large bananas)

1 teaspoon vanilla extract

½ cup milk

1 cup sweetened shredded coconut

¼ cup large coconut chips

1. Set the oven rack in the middle position. Preheat the oven to 350°F. Coat two 9 by 5 by 3-inch loaf pans with vegetable oil spray. Cover the bottom and ends of each pan with a single strip of wax paper. Coat the wax paper liners with vegetable oil spray. Dust the pans with flour and tap the pans to remove the excess flour.

2. Add the flour, baking powder, baking soda, salt, and pumpkin pie spice to a bowl, whisk together until well blended, and set aside.

3. Cream the butter and sugar in the bowl of a stand mixer fitted with the paddle attachment. With the mixer running, add the eggs one at a time. Add the mashed bananas and vanilla to the batter and combine.

4. Add the whisked dry ingredients and milk alternately until all of the ingredients have been added. Add the shredded coconut and mix on low until evenly distributed. Pour the batter into the prepared pans and tap gently to remove any air bubbles.

5. Scatter the coconut chips over the tops of the breads, and press down gently on the topping with the palm of your hand. Bake for 45 to 50 minutes, or until the breads pull away from the sides of the pans and a metal tester inserted into the center of each loaf comes out clean. Do not overbake.

6. Transfer the pans to a wire rack and cool the loaves for 20 minutes. Run a butter knife around the edges. Turn out the breads onto the rack, and remove the wax paper. Allow to cool completely. Cut the cooled breads with a wide-bladed serrated knife. Store leftover banana bread, covered with wax paper, at room temperature. The banana bread can be frozen, defrosted, and reheated for a few minutes in a 300°F oven before serving.

Yield: 2 loaves; 12 slices each

Lise Zimmer's Sweet Banana Yeast Bread

We found this recipe from the 1950s while rummaging through a box of living recipes at our friend Bonnie Slotnick's cookbook store. Lise Zimmer notes that this yeast bread is good toasted or plain with sweet butter. She also recommends it thinly sliced for tea sandwiches. This is very much like a Portuguese Sweet Bread with a hint of banana flavor.

Two 1¼-ounce packages active dry yeast

6 cups flour

¾ cup milk

½ cup sugar

1 teaspoon salt

½ cup (1 stick) cold unsalted butter, cut into
    6 to 8 slices

2 whole eggs

1 cup mashed ripe bananas (about 2 large
    bananas)

1 cup golden raisins

1 egg white

1 teaspoon water

1. Combine the yeast and 2 cups of the flour in the bowl of a stand mixer fitted with the paddle attachment.

2. In a small heavy-bottomed saucepan, mix the milk, sugar, salt, and butter with a wooden spoon cooking over low heat until the mixture registers 115°F on a cooking thermometer. If the mixture gets too hot, pour it into a glass measuring cup and place in the refrigerator for a few minutes until it registers the proper temperature.

3. Add the milk mixture to the yeast and flour in the mixer bowl and combine. Add the eggs, mashed bananas, and raisins and combine. Beat on low speed for about 1 minute. Add the remaining 4 cups flour gradually and mix thoroughly to in-

corporate. Replace the paddle attachment with the dough hook and knead on medium speed for 3 to 4 minutes.

4. *Preheat the oven to 175°F.* Coat a medium bowl with butter or vegetable oil spray. Remove the dough from the mixer bowl, place in the greased bowl, and swirl to coat. Cover the bowl with plastic wrap or a clean dish towel. Place the bowl on the back of the stove or in a warm place and allow to rise for 1 hour, or until doubled in size. Punch down the dough, cover, and let rest for 10 minutes.

5. Coat the bottom and sides of two 9 by 5 by 3-inch loaf pans with vegetable oil spray or butter. On a sheet of lightly floured wax paper, divide the dough in half with a spatula or a knife, shape into two loaves, and place in the prepared pans. Make ⅛-inch-deep cuts on top of loaves at ¾-inch intervals. Beat the egg white with water and brush over the surfaces of the loaves. Loosely cover the loaf pans with plastic wrap or clean dish towels, and allow to rise again until doubled in size, about 1 hour.

6. Set the oven rack in the middle postion. *Raise the oven temperature to 375°F.* Bake the loaves for 25 to 30 minutes or until they are golden brown. Turn the breads out the pans onto a wire rack. The breads are done when they make a hollow sound when tapped on their bottoms. Cool the breads completely before cutting. Store the breads, loosely wrapped in wax paper, at room temperature. Sweet Banana Yeast Bread freezes well.

Yield: 2 loaves; 10 to 12 slices each

SWEET TIP: If kneading by hand, reserve a couple of tablespoons of flour. Sprinkle on the work surface and knead for 5 to 8 minutes.

Nana May's Irish Yeast Bread

The recipe for this Irish yeast bread with raisins comes from our friends Dana and Steven, who own Neon Williams in Somerville, Massachusetts. Our friendship goes back twenty-three years to when Sheila commissioned a "Café Marilynn" neon sign for Marilynn's fiftieth birthday. Both brothers told us about their Nana May, a Dorchester, Massachusetts, native whose granddaughter, Mary Rita, entered her recipe for an Irish yeast bread in a contest sponsored by The Boston Globe. *Nana May's recipe won hands down. This is our own version of Nana's recipe using golden raisins.*

BREAD

One 1¼-ounce package active dry yeast

1 tablespoon sugar

1½ cups water, warmed to 115°F

¼ cup (½ stick) unsalted butter,
   at room temperature

4 cups flour

1½ teaspoons salt

1 cup raisins

TOPPING

1 tablespoon unsalted butter, melted

1. Dissolve the yeast and sugar in the warm water, and set aside for 15 minutes to proof.

2. Add the proofed yeast mixture to the bowl of a stand mixer fitted with the paddle attachment. Gradually add the butter, then add the flour, salt, and raisins to the bowl, beating on low until combined. Increase the speed gradually until the dough comes away from the sides of the bowl and becomes smooth.

3. *Preheat the oven to 175°F.* Coat a medium bowl with butter or vegetable oil spray. Place the dough in the greased bowl and swirl to coat. Cover the bowl with plastic wrap or a clean dish towel. Place the bowl on the back of the stove or in a warm place and allow to rise for 1 hour, or until doubled in size.

4. Coat the bottom and sides of a 9-inch springform pan with vegetable oil spray or butter. Cut out a parchment paper circle to fit the bottom of the pan. Place the parchment on the bottom of the pan. Using a spatula, transfer the dough to the prepared pan. Smooth the top of dough with an offset spatula. Cover the pan with plastic wrap or a dish towel and allow to rise in a warm place for 1 hour, or until doubled in size.

5. Place the oven rack in the middle position. *Raise the oven temperature to 350°F.* Remove the covering from the risen dough and place in the oven. Bake for 35 minutes. Remove from the oven and brush with the melted butter. Return to the oven for 5 to 6 minutes, or until the crust is a golden brown. Transfer the pan to a wire rack. Using pot holders, remove the sides of the springform pan. Slide the bread off the bottom of the pan onto the rack. Remove the parchment circle. The bread is done when it makes a hollow sound when tapped on the bottom. Cool the bread completely before cutting. Store the bread, loosely wrapped in wax paper, at room temperature. Nana May's Irish Yeast Bread freezes well.

Yield: one 9-inch round loaf; 10 slices

SWEET TIP: We used golden raisins.

Quick Oatmeal Bread
(Yeast Batter Bread)

These golden brown loaves have a slightly coarse texture and a nutty taste. Most of the time we like to think of batter breads as breads using baking powder or baking soda combined with sour milk or buttermilk as leavening, but the dough for this bread is soft and loose like a batter rather than the traditional substantial yeast dough we were used to working with.

1 cup old-fashioned rolled oats or quick oats

1 tablespoon salt

½ cup molasses

⅓ cup (5⅓ tablespoons) unsalted butter, melted

2 cups boiling water

Two 1¼-ounce packages active dry yeast

2 eggs, beaten

5 cups flour

1. Add the oats, salt, molasses, butter, and boiling water to a large heatproof bowl and whisk to combine. Set aside to cool to lukewarm, about 115°F.

2. Add the cooled mixture to the bowl of a stand mixer fitted with the paddle attachment. Add the yeast to the beaten eggs, add to the cooled mixture, and beat to combine. Add the flour in four additions, and continue to beat until the mixture forms a batter.

3. *Preheat the oven to 175°F.* Coat a medium bowl with butter or vegetable oil spray. Place the dough in the greased bowl and, using a rubber spatula, turn the batter so that the whole mixture is thinly coated with the vegetable oil spray or butter. Cover the bowl with plastic wrap or a clean dish towel. Place the bowl on the back of the stove or in a warm place and allow to rise for 1 hour, or

until doubled in size. Punch down the dough with a spatula.

4. Coat the bottom and sides of two 9 by 5 by 3-inch loaf pans with vegetable oil spray or butter. Divide the dough in half with a spatula dipped in water and transfer to the prepared pans. Smooth the top of the dough with an offset spatula. Cover the loaf pans with plastic wrap or dish towels and allow to rise in a warm place for 1 hour, or until doubled in size.

5. Place the oven rack in the middle position. *Raise the oven temperature to 350°F.* Remove the covering from the loaves and place in the oven. Bake for 45 minutes, or until the crust is a golden brown. Turn the breads out of the pans onto a wire rack. The breads are done when they make a hollow sound when tapped on their bottoms. Cool the bread completely before cutting. Store the bread, loosely wrapped in wax paper, at room temperature. Quick Oatmeal Bread freezes well.

Yield: 2 loaves; 12 to 14 slices each

SWEET TIP: We used old-fashioned or quick-cooking oatmeal for this bread because we were not seeking a hearty, coarse-grained bread.

Orange Pecan Yeast Breads

Orange Pecan Yeast Bread

This is one of those recipes we re-created from memory. We first tasted the Lemon Bread at Formaggio Kitchen, in Cambridge, Massachusetts, twenty years ago, and we never forgot that fragrant, nut-filled bread. Using our memory bank of flavors, we embarked on a quest to replicate that treasured bread. We admit it's not exactly the same, but we came pretty close. This bread is wonderful spread with salted butter and orange marmalade.

BREAD

¼ cup water, warmed to 115°F

One 1¼-ounce package active dry yeast

3 tablespoons sugar

4½ cups flour

1½ teaspoons salt

¼ cup (½ stick) unsalted butter, melted

2 eggs

1 tablespoon orange zest

1 cup orange juice

1 cup pecans, toasted and coarsely chopped

GLAZE

1 egg, beaten

TOPPING

12 pecan halves, toasted

1. Combine the warm water, yeast, and 1 tablespoon of the sugar in a glass measuring cup, and set aside for 10 minutes to proof.

2. Add the flour and salt to a bowl, whisk to combine, and set aside.

3. To the bowl of a stand mixer fitted with the paddle attachment, add the proofed yeast mixture, the remaining 2 tablespoons sugar, and the melted butter and combine. Add the eggs, orange zest, and orange juice and beat to combine. Add the flour mixture, 1 cup at a time, to the liquid mixture in the bowl, beating well after each addition. Change to the dough hook and knead for 5 minutes at medium speed. Add the chopped pecans to the dough, and knead with the dough hook for another 2 to 3 minutes until the nuts are evenly distributed in the dough.

4. *Preheat the oven to 175°F.* Coat a medium bowl with butter or vegetable oil spray. Place the dough in the greased bowl and swirl to coat. Cover the bowl with plastic wrap or a clean dish towel. Place the bowl on the back of the stove or in a warm place and allow to rise for 1 hour, or until doubled in size. Punch down the dough.

5. Coat the bottom and sides of two 9 by 5 by 3-inch loaf pans with vegetable oil spray or butter. Divide the dough in half with a spatula or a knife, and transfer to the prepared pans. Smooth the top of each loaf with an offset spatula. Brush lightly with the beaten egg. Place 6 pecans on top of each loaf, lengthwise, and press down gently on the pecans. Loosely cover the loaf pans with plastic wrap or clean dish towels and allow to rise in a warm place for 1 hour, or until doubled in size.

6. Place the oven rack in the middle position. *Raise the oven temperature 350°F.* Remove the covering, and place the loaves in the oven. Bake for 40 to 45 minutes, or until the crust is a golden brown. Turn the breads out of the pans onto a wire rack. The breads are done when the loaves make a hollow sound when tapped on their bottoms. Cool the breads completely before cutting. Store the breads, loosely wrapped in wax paper, at room temperature. Orange Pecan Yeast Bread freezes well.

Yield: 2 loaves; 10 to 12 slices each

Aunt Eller's Apple Nut Bread

We don't know who Aunt Eller was, but she was obviously beloved by her family. This recipe, from the 1920s, was typed onto a recipe card, and the much-handled and stained card produced this delicious, unpretentious quick bread. The texture of this Apple Nut Bread is substantial. The bread is even better the second day.

BREAD

1 cup whole wheat flour

1 cup all-purpose flour

1 teaspoon baking powder

1 teaspoon baking soda

½ teaspoon salt

½ teaspoon cinnamon

½ teaspoon nutmeg

½ teaspoon ginger

1 cup (2 sticks) unsalted butter, at room temperature

⅔ cup firmly packed brown sugar

2 eggs

3 tablespoons honey

1 teaspoon vanilla extract

1½ cups unpeeled, cored Granny Smith apples, finely chopped

1 cup walnuts, toasted and finely chopped

TOPPING

2 tablespoons firmly packed brown sugar

2 tablespoons walnuts, toasted and finely chopped

1. Set the oven rack in the middle position. Preheat the oven to 350°F. Coat a 9 by 5 by 3-inch loaf pan with vegetable oil spray. Line the bottom and ends of the pan with a single strip of wax paper and coat with vegetable oil spray. Dust the pan with flour and tap the pan to remove the excess flour.

2. To make the bread: Add both flours, the baking powder, baking soda, salt, cinnamon, nutmeg, and ginger to a large bowl and whisk to combine. Set aside.

3. In the bowl of a stand mixer fitted with the paddle attachment, cream the butter and brown sugar until combined. Add the eggs one at a time, and continue to beat, scraping down the sides and bottom of the bowl. Add the honey and vanilla and continue to beat until combined. Add the dry ingredients in three additions. The batter will be stiff.

4. Remove the bowl from the mixer and fold in the chopped apples and then the chopped walnuts. Spoon the batter into the prepared pan and smooth the top of the bread with an offset spatula. Do *not* bang the pan to remove air bubbles because the nuts and apples might fall to bottom of pan.

5. To make the topping: Mix the brown sugar and chopped walnuts together and sprinkle on top of the dough. Gently press the topping into the dough with your hand.

6. Bake the bread for 55 to 60 minutes, or until a metal tester inserted into the center of the loaf comes out dry. The bread should start to pull away a little from the sides of the pan. Transfer the bread, in the pan, to a wire rack and allow to cool for at least 20 minutes. Go around the edges of the pan with a butter knife and remove the bread from the pan, lifting it by the wax paper flaps at each end: this prevents losing any of the sugar and walnut topping. Return the bread to the rack and cool completely before cutting with a serrated knife. Store the bread, wrapperd in wax paper, at room temperature.

Yield: 1 loaf: nine 1-inch slices

SWEET TIP: We used Granny Smith apples, but any firm baking apple will do.

SWEET TOUCH: You can always add a small amount of chopped candied ginger to Aunt Eller's recipe for a more pronounced ginger taste.

HOW TO CHOP APPLES FOR AUNT ELLER'S APPLE NUT BREAD

This recipe calls for cored, unpeeled apples chopped fairly fine. We suggest that you cut each unpeeled and cored baking apple in half and then into 8 wedges. Place the wedges in the bowl of a food processor and pulse three times; the apples should be finely chopped, but not mushy. The liquid for this recipe will come from the chopped apples. *Do not overprocess the apples.* If there are any larger pieces of apple left in the bowl of the food processor, chop them by hand. We found that 1 large Granny Smith apple yielded 1½ cups of chopped apple.

Salt and Pepper Potato Bread

We found this recipe handwritten on a slip of paper with the letterhead of the American Red Cross, Eighth Roll Call, Department of Wards, Philadelphia, Pennsylvania. The original recipe called for 1 cup of lard, but we exchanged butter for the lard, and we were not disappointed with the result. All the ingredients should be at room temperature.

BREAD

One 1¼-ounce package active dry yeast

3 tablespoons sugar

¼ cup water, warmed to 115°F

2 eggs

1 cup mashed or riced cooked potatoes

1½ teaspoons salt

1 teaspoon coarsely ground black pepper

1 cup (2 sticks) unsalted butter, melted and
    cooled

1¾ cups milk

6½ cups flour

GLAZE

1 egg, beaten

TOPPING

Kosher salt or coarse salt (optional)

1. Dissolve the yeast and 1 tablespoon of the sugar in the warm water, and set aside for 10 minutes to proof.

2. In the bowl of a stand mixer fitted with the paddle attachment, beat the eggs, potatoes, the remaining 2 tablespoons sugar, the salt, pepper, and butter to combine. Add the yeast mixture and incorporate. Add the milk and the flour alternately to the dough, continuing to beat until a soft dough forms.

3. *Preheat the oven to 175°F.* Coat a medium bowl with butter or vegetable oil spray. Place the dough in the greased bowl and swirl to coat. Cover the bowl with plastic wrap or a clean dish towel. Place the bowl on the back of the stove or in a warm place and allow to rise for 1 hour, or until doubled in size. Punch down the dough.

4. Coat the bottom and sides of two 9- by 5- by 3-inch loaf pans with vegetable oil spray or butter. Divide the dough in half with a spatula or a knife, and transfer to the prepared pans. Smooth the top of loaves with an offset spatula. Brush lightly with beaten egg, and sprinkle lightly with kosher or coarse salt, if desired. Cover the loaf pans loosely with plastic wrap or dish towels and allow to rise in a warm place for 1 hour, or until doubled in size. Remove the wraps.

5. Place the oven rack in the middle position. *Raise the oven temperature to 375°F.* Bake the bread for 40 minutes, or until the crust is a golden brown. Turn the breads out of the pans onto a wire rack. The breads are done when they make a hollow sound when tapped on their bottoms. Cool the breads completely before cutting. Store the breads, loosely wrapped in wax paper, at room temperature. Salt and Pepper Potato Bread freezes well.

Yield: 2 loaves; 10 to 12 slices each

SWEET TOUCH: Ricing the potatoes will result in a finer-textured bread.

• Grated Parmesan cheese can be sprinkled on top of the loaves before baking. Omit the salt on top if using cheese.

5 Easy as Pie

THE RECIPES

*T*here's nothing like an honest piece of pie. The crust consists of buttery flakes of dough or sweetened crumbs. The filling hides no surprises—just seasonal fruit, soft, lightly sweetened custard, or syrup-encrusted nuts. Meringue or whipped cream often alternate to enhance the appearance of pies we eat, whether at a four-star restaurant or the familiar neighborhood diner.

During the early 1950s, we learned of a movement to encourage eaters of pie to polish off their slices. It seemed that the edge of the crust where the bottom and top layers form a union were being discarded on plates all over New England. We found this hard to believe since our mother was the Queen of Piecrust, a title that eventually passed to Sheila. We would no more have given up that delectable buttery morsel of crust than give up pie eating forever. Thrifty Yankee pundits came up with the idea of serving slices of pie with the conjoined edge of the crust facing forward, the tines of the fork coyly balanced on this enticing area of pastry. We don't know if this ploy worked, but we believe any leftover crust means that the pie maker doesn't know how to make good piecrust.

An honest piece of pie means that the piecrust should be baked thoroughly and well. There should be no soggy bottom crust. The top crust should be golden brown, not charred or speckled. There should be a proper balance between crust and filling, and the topping should be appropriate to the pie.

There are those home bakers who use shortening or lard, or a combination of both, instead of butter in their piecrusts, but it is not the choice of an ingredient, but the quality of it, and the skill with which they use it that matters. Different pies call for different crusts. Cheese pies often call for crumb crusts. Some pies, such as the Buttery Maple Walnut Pie, can be made with a crust enriched with nuts.

That said, pie baking should be fun, and pies should be beautiful to look at and wonderful to eat. Sheila's recipe for Perfect Piecrust and its variations are important addenda to our recipes for pies.

We like looking back at the history of pie. It encourages us to occasionally have a slice for breakfast when we consider that hardy eighteenth- and nineteenth-century farmers and laborers started their day with a generous slice of apple, berry, or mincemeat pie. However, the slice of pie history that we cherish most is the memory of the pie man, who used to deliver commercially baked New England pies to our front door. We willingly paid a five-cent deposit for the tin pie plate. Some of us returned the pie plates for a refund, but others kept one or two for their own home baking. We admit that the occasional pies we bought at our front door were a novelty, but of any pies sold, they came the closest to what we could bake ourselves.

Accustomed to being served apple pie with a slice of sharp New England cheese, we came up with a recipe for Cheese Crumble Apple Pie that we bake with cheddar cheese in both the piecrust and the filling. We traveled to the southern part of the country to replicate Mama Ruth's burnished Georgia Pecan Pie and we tried our hand at baking a Chocolate Chess Pie. We did due diligence in researching once unfamiliar stalks of rhubarb and baking them into a rosy butter-crumbed Rhubarb Streusel Pie.

We sneak a bit of lemon juice or lemon zest into most of the fruit pies we bake, but there is nothing like an actual lemon pie. We revisited our memory of the Lemon Rio Pie we baked in the 1960s and 1970s and updated it for the twenty-first century. Richer and creamier, it is filled with a lovely lemon custard made with a cooked sugar syrup, is topped with whipped cream, and has ribbons of dark melted chocolate running through it.

Baking a pie should be a joyful respite from life's stresses, and not a harried session in the kitchen. We counsel you to allow enough time to read through the recipe at least twice, gather your ingredients and utensils before you start, and think of the pleasure your pie will bring to those who eat it.

NOTE: When a recipe requires a pie shell, we refer readers to the recipe for Sheila's Perfect Piecrust (page 154) that contains the basic pastry recipe as well as the methods for a single-crust pie, a double-crust pie, and a prebaked shell.

Quick Tips

- Rerolling piecrust may toughen it.
- Cut slits in the top crust to allow steam to escape.
- Brush the top of the pie with egg wash before baking for a shiny finish.

- Tent the pie with aluminum foil if it is browning too quickly.

Kahlúa Pie

This recipe is similar to one that came to us handwritten on an index card and called for rum, but we substituted Kahlúa, our favorite coffee liqueur, which brought back memories of the White Russians we sipped in the 1960s and 1970s. We decided to "translate" this recipe by using the boiled sugar syrup meringue technique to "cook" the egg whites. This chilled pie is delicious with a cup of hot black coffee.

CRUST

13 graham crackers, 2½ inches by 5 inches each
    (1 sleeve from a 3-sleeve box)
¼ cup (½ stick) unsalted butter, melted and cooled
½ cup confectioners' sugar

FILLING

1 cup heavy cream
4 eggs, separated
½ teaspoon salt
¾ cup Kahlúa
¼ cup water
1 envelope unflavored gelatin
½ cup granulated sugar

SUGAR SYRUP

¼ cup water
½ cup granulated sugar

TOPPING

½ cup heavy cream, whipped
Chocolate coffee beans (optional)

1. Set the oven rack in the middle position. Preheat the oven to 375°F. Coat a 9-inch ovenproof glass pie plate with vegetable oil spray.

2. To make the crust: Place the graham crackers in the bowl of a food processor fitted with a metal blade. Pulse to make crumbs the size of cornmeal; you should have about 1½ cups. Add the butter and confectioners' sugar and pulse to combine. Press the crumbs onto the bottom and sides of the pie plate. Bake the crust for 8 minutes. Transfer to a wire rack and cool for 10 minutes. Place in the refrigerator to chill.

3. To start the filling: Add the cream to the bowl of the stand mixer fitted with the whisk attachment and beat until thick. Transfer the cream to another container, cover, and store in the refrigerator until ready to use.

4. Set a medium metal bowl for the filling and a larger bowl for an ice water bath near your work surface. Have some ice cubes handy, but keep frozen until ready to use. Whisk the egg yolks together in a small bowl. Add the salt and Kahlúa and whisk to combine. Set aside.

5. Add the water to a heavy-bottomed 6-cup saucepan. Sprinkle the gelatin on top of the water and allow to stand for 1 minute. Whisk the gelatin and water together. Add the granulated sugar, and whisk the mixture again. Add the egg yolks, salt, and Kahlúa mixture to the gelatin-and-sugar mixture and whisk to combine. Cook the mixture over medium heat, stirring with a wooden spoon, for 4 to 5 minutes, or until the mixture thickens and coats the back of the spoon. Strain the custard mixture into the medium metal bowl. Set the bowl in the ice bath. Stir occasionally until the custard is cool. This will take about 10 minutes. Remove the whipped cream from the refrigerator, fold into the cooled custard, and place in the refrigerator.

6. Add the egg whites to the bowl of the stand mixer fitted with the whisk attachment and beat until soft peaks form. Set aside.

7. To make the sugar syrup: *Keep a large bowl*

filled with cold water and ice cubes at hand when making the sugar syrup for safety. This is not the same as the ice bath used for the custard (step 4). Add the water and sugar to a heavy-bottomed 6-cup saucepan and whisk to combine. Using a wooden spoon, stir the mixture over medium heat until it begins to boil. Reduce the heat slightly and continue to stir the mixture until it has boiled for 3 minutes. If sugar crystals form on the inside of the pan, wash them down with a wet pastry brush. Keep a glass

measuring cup filled with water near the stove so that you can dip the pastry brush in it after you wash down the sides of the pan. Do not scrape any sugar crust that forms on the sides of pan into the syrup. Transfer the syrup to a glass measuring cup. With the mixer turned *off,* pour the syrup down the inner side of the bowl into the whipped egg whites. *The bottom of the mixer bowl will be very hot.* Turn the mixer on, and whisk until the bottom of the mixer bowl is cold, 10 to 12 minutes. The beaten

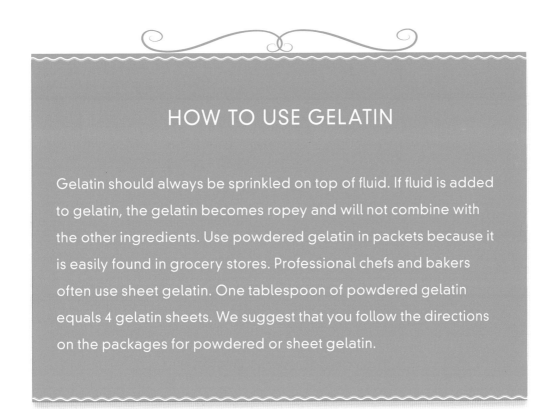

HOW TO USE GELATIN

Gelatin should always be sprinkled on top of fluid. If fluid is added to gelatin, the gelatin becomes ropey and will not combine with the other ingredients. Use powdered gelatin in packets because it is easily found in grocery stores. Professional chefs and bakers often use sheet gelatin. One tablespoon of powdered gelatin equals 4 gelatin sheets. We suggest that you follow the directions on the packages for powdered or sheet gelatin.

egg whites should form soft peaks and are now a meringue.

8. Remove the custard-cream mixture from the refrigerator. Fold the meringue into custard-cream mixture in three additions. Scoop the filling into the cooled pie shell. Transfer the pie to the refrigerator and chill for at least 6 hours, or overnight, before cutting and serving. Any leftover pie should be stored, loosely covered with plastic wrap, in the refrigerator.

Yield: one 9-inch pie; 8 slices

SWEET TIPS: Read through the recipe at least two times before making the pie, and be sure to have all of the ingredients laid out before you start the recipe.

• Be sure to sprinkle the gelatin over the water; do not add the water to the gelatin.

SWEET TOUCHES: When the pie is set, pipe a circle of whipped cream rosettes along the edge. Garnish the rosettes with chocolate coffee beans.

TENTING PIES AND PIECRUSTS WHILE BAKING AND STORING

When baking pies or piecrusts in the oven, they should be loosely tented with foil if the crust or filling is browning too quickly. One-crust filled pies and frosted cakes should be loosely tented with wax paper or foil when stored in the refrigerator. Tenting is simply loosely folding foil (or wax paper) in a tent shape. *Do not use wax paper tents in the oven.*

Black and White Cheese Pie

This recipe is very much like the one we made as sweet young things in the 1960s and 1970s. Although the original recipe had been lost, we found a similar one in our collection of living recipes. We decided to try this pie with a chocolate piecrust rather than a crumb crust, but it can be made with either. The melted bittersweet chocolate drizzled on a bed of sweetened sour cream makes this cheese pie something special.

FILLING

12 ounces cream cheese, at room
    temperature
2 eggs, beaten
1 teaspoon vanilla extract
½ cup sugar

CRUST

Unbaked single-crust chocolate piecrust
    (see page 156)

TOPPING

1 cup sour cream
3 tablespoons sugar
1 teaspoon vanilla extract
¼ cup American natural nonalkalized cocoa
    powder
2 tablespoons bittersweet chocolate, melted
    and slightly cooled (optional)

1. Set the oven rack in the middle position. Preheat the oven to 375°F.

2. To make the filling: Add the cream cheese, beaten eggs, and vanilla to the bowl of a food processor fitted with the metal blade and process until smooth. Add the sugar and continue processing until completely combined. The filling should be smooth, but any small lumps will melt when the pie is baked.

3. Pour the filling into the prepared pie shell. Bake the pie for 20 minutes and cover with tented aluminum foil if the crust is browning too quickly. Do not allow the foil to touch the filling.

4. While the pie is baking, make the topping: Add the sour cream, sugar, vanilla, and cocoa to the bowl of the food processor fitted with the metal blade and pulse until combined.

5. Remove the pie from the oven and place on a wire rack. *Increase the oven temperature to 425°F. Gently* spoon the sour cream topping onto the pie and return it to the oven for 5 minutes. Remove the pie from the oven and place on a wire rack to cool completely. Place the cooled pie in the refrigerator, uncovered, for at least 3 hours, or overnight. The pie will firm up in the refrigerator. Remove the pie from the refrigerator and drizzle the melted bittersweet chocolate over the top, if desired. Allow the chocolate drizzle to cool and set before serving. Any leftover pie should be loosely tented with foil and stored in the refrigerator.

Yield: one 9-inch pie; 10 to 12 slices

SWEET TOUCH: Rosettes of whipped cream can be piped around the edges.

Buttery Maple Walnut Pie

This pie started out as a handwritten recipe for a Buttery Pecan Pie, but it had a northern twist: a cup of dark maple syrup. Since we're Yankees, we fell in love with the idea of maple syrup, and decided to take it one step further by adding chopped toasted walnuts to the pie instead of pecans. We still have pleasant memories of those bygone days when we indulged in a forbidden slice of Mrs. Smith's Frozen Walnut Pie. The flavor of the maple syrup is not predominant in our pie, but it combines nicely with the walnuts and butter to become a pie rich in flavor and texture.

CRUST

Unbaked double-crust piecrust (see page 154)

FILLING

3 eggs

1 cup Grade A maple syrup

⅔ cup sugar

¼ teaspoon salt

⅓ cup (5⅓ tablespoons) unsalted butter, melted and cooled

1 teaspoon vanilla extract

1¾ cups walnuts, toasted and coarsely chopped

1. Set the oven rack in the middle position. Preheat the oven to 400°F to partially prebake the piecrust. To prevent spills in the oven, line a rimmed baking sheet with aluminum foil on which to place the unbaked *filled* pie.

2. To make the filling: Add the eggs to an 8-cup bowl and whisk. Add the maple syrup, sugar, and salt and beat to combine. Add the butter and vanilla and continue whisking to incorporate. Using a spatula, fold in the walnuts. Set the filling aside.

3. Cover the unbaked piecrust with a sheet of foil coated with vegetable oil spray. Place the foil with coated side on top of piecrust, and gently press into the crust. Prebake the crust for 10 minutes. Remove the partially baked piecrust from oven and transfer to a wire rack. Remove the foil and let cool for 2 minutes before filling. *Reduce the oven temperature to 350°F.*

4. Pour the filling into the partially baked pie shell. Using oven mitts, place the filled pie on the foil-lined baking sheet and return the pie to the oven. Bake for 60 minutes. Check the pie at 30 minutes to be sure that the crust is not browning too quickly. Place a foil tent over the pie for the rest of the baking if needed. The pie may be a bit wobbly in the center, but it will bubble when done.

5. Remove the pie from the oven, carefully lift the pie off the foil-covered baking sheet, and place on a wire rack to cool. When the pie is completely cool, place it in the refrigerator. Store any leftover pie, loosely covered with wax paper, in the refrigerator. Allow the pie to come to room temperature before serving.

Yield: one 9-inch pie; 8 to 10 slices

SWEET TIPS: Although we never had this pie filling run over while baking in the oven, placing it on a foil-covered rimmed baking sheet will prevent spills.

• Using broken or chopped walnuts rather than whole walnuts prevents the top of the pie from fusing into a solid sphere.

SWEET TOUCH: Before baking the pie, cut out decorative leaves from the remaining dough. Bake separately at 350°F for 10 minutes or until tops are golden.

Buttery Maple Walnut Pie

Cheese Crumble Apple Pie with Cheddar Cheese Crust

~~~~~~

We decided to make an apple pie with cheddar cheese in the crust and in the filling. Serving apple pie with a generous slab of cheese seems to be an old New England tradition since substantial pies such as apple, mincemeat, or pear were often part of the breakfasts enjoyed by farmers and laborers in the early days of our country. Savory farmhouse tarts mixing fruit, cheese, herbs, and even onions are also a part of the legacy from our English forebears.

CHEDDAR PIE CRUST
(for double-crust 9-inch pie)

2½ cups flour

2 tablespoons sugar

¼ teaspoon salt

1 cup (2 sticks) cold unsalted butter, cut into
    ½-inch dice

4 ounces sharp cheddar cheese, cut into
    ½-inch dice

¼ cup ice water

FILLING

5 large Golden Delicious or other baking apples,
    peeled, cored, and cut into thin chunks,
    10 to 12 thin chunks per apple

½ cup sugar

¼ teaspoon salt

½ teaspoon cinnamon

½ teaspoon ginger

2 tablespoons plus 1 teaspoon flour

4 ounces cheddar cheese, cut into ½-inch dice

1½ tablespoons cold unsalted butter,
    cut into small dice

EGG WASH

1 egg, beaten

1. Set the oven rack in the middle position. Preheat the oven to 425°F. Coat a 9-inch ovenproof glass pie plate with vegetable oil spray. To prevent spills in the oven, cover a 14 by 16-inch baking sheet, or a pizza pan, with aluminum foil, shiny side up. Coat the foil with vegetable oil spray.

2. To make the cheddar piecrust: Place the flour, sugar, and salt in the bowl of a food processor fitted with the metal blade and pulse three times to mix. Add the butter and cheddar cheese and pulse until crumbly. Add the water and pulse until the mixture comes together. Remove the dough from the bowl of the processor, divide in half, and shape each half into a disk. Unless your kitchen is very warm, you don't have to chill the dough before rolling it out.

3. To prepare the crust: Roll out the pastry dough. Fit half of the dough into the bottom of pie plate and trim off excess. Chill in the refrigerator. (For detailed instructions, see "To Make a Double-Crust Pie," steps 2 and 3, page 154.)

4. To make the filling: Add the apples to a large bowl and set aside. Put the sugar, salt, cinnamon, ginger, and the 2 tablespoons flour in a smaller bowl and whisk to combine. Add the dry ingredients to the apples and mix together until the apples are completely coated. Add the cheddar cheese to the apple mixture and stir to combine. Let the filling stand for 10 to 15 minutes to allow the flavors to meld.

5. Sprinkle the remaining 1 teaspoon flour over the bottom crust of the pie. Add the filling to the bottom crust. Scatter the diced butter over the top of the filling. Add the top crust. Seal the edges, cut off the excess piecrust with clean kitchen scissors, and trim the upper crust to fit the pie. Crimp the edges, using the tines of a fork, and cut decorative slits in the top of the piecrust. Brush the top of the crust and edges with beaten egg. (For detailed instructions, see "To Make a Double-Crust Pie," step 4, pages 154.)

6. Place the pie on the foil-lined baking sheet. Bake for 30 minutes at 425°F. Check the crust for browning. If the crust is browning too quickly, cover the pie loosely with foil. *Reduce the oven temperature to 350°F* and bake for another 10 minutes, or until the top crust is evenly brown. The bottom crust should be light brown when completely baked. A sharp knife inserted into an apple slice in the filling should go in easily. Cool the pie on a wire rack for at least 2 hours before serving. Store the pie, loosely covered with wax paper, in the refrigerator. Remove the pie from the refrigerator 10 minutes before serving, and warm in a 300°F oven for 5 to 7 minutes.

Yield: one 9-inch pie; 10 slices

Cobblestone Apple Tart

Cobblestone Apple Tart

This recipe came from a cookbook compiled by a boy named Harry as a gift to his mother for Christmas, 1941. He had handwritten her personal recipes. We were intrigued by the name of the pie, which featured wedges of apple laid out in uniform rows, much like cobblestones. We added the toasted almonds betwen the rows for "mortar," brushed the cobblestones with molasses before baking, and sprinkled the apples with sanding sugar. We baked the pie as a tart.

TART SHELL

Unbaked pastry for a single-crust pie
     (see page 154)

FILLING

2 tablespoons flour

½ cup firmly packed brown sugar

¼ teaspoon salt

½ teaspoon cinnamon

½ teaspoon nutmeg

⅛ teaspoon cloves

1 tablespoon grated lemon zest

2 large baking apples, peeled, cored, and cut
     into ¼-inch wedges (about 27 wedges)

1 tablespoon molasses

¼ cup almonds, toasted slivered

2 tablespoons coarse clear sanding sugar

1 tablespoon cold unsalted butter,
     cut into ⅛-inch dice

1. Coat a 9 by 9-inch square metal tart pan with a removable bottom with vegetable oil spray. Line the bottom with a sheet of parchment paper, cut to fit.

2. To make the tart shell: Roll out the pastry, lightly dusted with flour, between two sheets of wax paper or parchment paper to a 10½-inch square. Place the pastry into the prepared tart pan. Trim the edges with a knife to remove the excess crust. If the crust seems too thin around the edges, use extra pastry to reinforce the sides of the tart. Chill the tart shell in the refrigerator for 10 minutes. Remove from the refrigerator and place a sheet of nonstick aluminum foil on the inside of the tart shell. Set the oven rack in the middle position. Preheat the oven to 400°F. Bake the tart shell for 10 minutes. Remove from the oven and place on a wire rack. Carefully remove the foil and allow to cool for 10 minutes. Leave the oven on.

3. To make the filling: Add the flour, brown sugar, salt, cinnamon, nutmeg, cloves, and lemon zest to a large bowl and whisk to combine. Add the apples to the dry ingredients and mix well. Lay out apples in three uniform rows, resembling cobblestones, staggering the apples. Brush the apples with molasses, and sprinkle slivered almonds in spaces between the rows of apples. Sprinkle the top of the tart with coarse sanding sugar and the diced butter. Bake for 20 minutes. *Reduce the oven temperature to 375°F* and bake for an additional 25 minutes. The edges of the tart should be golden brown and the apples should be bubbling when the tart is fully baked.

4. Remove the tart from the oven and transfer to a wire rack until completely cool. Remove the tart from the pan and place on a serving platter or white cardboard square. Cut into squares and serve with whipped cream or vanilla ice cream. Store any leftover tart, covered with plastic wrap, in the refrigerator. Bring the tart to room temperature before serving.

Yield: one 9-inch square tart; 9 servings when cut into 3-inch squares

Chocolate Chess Pie

We liked the Lemon Chess Pie recipe (page 217) so much that we decided to experiment and make it as a Chocolate Chess Pie. We found that unlike the filling for the Lemon Chess Pie, this filling puffs up like a high hat because of the addition of the chocolate, but the surface retreats to a lovely fudgy density on standing as the filling condenses. This pie should be baked 5 minutes longer than the Lemon Chess Pie.

FILLING

1 tablespoon flour

2 cups sugar

1 tablespoon cornmeal

¼ teaspoon salt

4 eggs

¼ cup (½ stick) unsalted butter, melted and
    cooled

½ cup milk

2 teaspoons vanilla extract

½ cup (4 ounces) bittersweet chocolate,
    melted and slightly cooled

CRUST

Unbaked single-crust piecrust (see page 154)

1. Set the oven rack in the middle position. Preheat the oven to 375° F. Coat a 9-inch ovenproof glass pie plate with vegetable oil spray.

2. To make the filling: In a small bowl, combine the flour, sugar, cornmeal, and salt and set aside.

3. Using a whisk, beat the eggs in a large bowl. Add the butter and whisk it into the eggs. Add the milk and vanilla and whisk to combine. Whisk in the dry ingredients. Add a small amount of the pie filling to the melted chocolate and whisk to temper and combine. Add the tempered and slightly cooler chocolate mixture back to the rest of the filling and

whisk to combine. Pour the filling into the prepared pie shell.

4. Bake the pie for 25 minutes and cover with tented foil if the crust is browning too quickly. Do not allow the foil to touch the filling. Continue baking for another 25 minutes and check to see if the center is still loose. If loose (not wobbly), cover again with foil and bake for another 5 minutes, approximately 55 minutes in all.

5. Remove the pie from the oven and transfer to a wire rack to cool. The pie will be high but will settle when cool. Place the cooled pie in the refrigerator, uncovered, for at least 3 hours before cutting. Any leftover pie should be loosely wrapped with wax paper and stored in the refrigerator. If the surface of the pie forms small cracks, it can be covered with rosettes or swirls of whipped cream.

Yield: one 9-inch pie; 8 to 10 slices

SWEET TIP: *Melted chocolate should be warm when added to the filling. Chocolate that is completely cooled will not combine with filling and will congeal and form lumps.* Adding some of the pie filling to slightly warm chocolate lowers the temperature of the chocolate and prevents the eggs in the filling from "cooking."

Chocolate Chess Pie

Dang Good Pie

This handwritten recipe produced a simple piece of pie with an almost candylike filling. We found that the pie originated in the nineteenth-century South. Found in the files of many families whose home bakers diligently passed down recipes as part of their heritage, we decided to pay homage to its Southern origins by adding chopped toasted pecans. Please see the sidebars on page 147 on melting butter in the microwave and chopping pecans with sugar.

FILLING

3 tablespoons flour

¼ teaspoon salt

3 eggs

6 tablespoons (¾ stick) unsalted butter, melted and cooled

1 cup canned crushed pineapple, drained

1 cup sweetened shredded coconut

1½ cups sugar

½ cup pecans, toasted and coarsely chopped

CRUST

Unbaked single-crust piecrust (see page 154)

1. Set the oven rack in the middle position. Preheat the oven to 350°F.

2. To make the filling: Add the flour and salt to a small bowl and whisk to combine. Set aside.

3. Add the eggs to a large bowl and whisk. Add the butter to the eggs and whisk to combine. Add the flour and salt and continue whisking. Add the crushed pineapple and coconut and mix in. Add the sugar and chopped pecans.

4. Pour the filling into the piecrust. Bake the pie for 25 minutes, covering with tented aluminum foil if the crust is browning too quickly. Do not allow the foil to touch the filling. Continue baking for another 30 to 35 minutes. The pie is done when a metal tester inserted into the center comes out clean. The surface of the pie should be golden brown and firm.

5. Remove the pie from the oven and transfer to a wire rack to cool. Place the cooled pie in the refrigerator, uncovered, for at least 3 hours before cutting. Decorate with puffs of sweetened whipped cream around the edge of the pie before serving. Any leftover pie should be loosely wrapped with wax paper and stored in the refrigerator.

Yield: one 9-inch pie; 8 slices

SWEET TIP: Dang Good Pie will cut more easily if the coconut shreds are placed in a food processor fitted with the metal blade and pulsed a few times to shorten the shreds.

HOW TO MELT BUTTER IN A MICROWAVE OVEN

Cut the butter into ½-inch dice and put in a 2-cup glass bowl. To prevent the butter from spurting or "spitting" over the interior of the microwave oven, it is important to use a large enough bowl and cover it with plastic wrap. Microwave the butter in 25-second intervals two times. If not completely melted, microwave again in 10-second increments.

HOW TO CHOP NUTS IN A FOOD PROCESSOR

Chopping nuts in a food processor can be tricky because you can end up with a nut paste if you overprocess the nuts. When chopping nuts in the bowl of a food processor fitted with the metal blade, adding sugar along with the nuts to be chopped will prevent this from happening. The nuts and sugar should be pulsed only a few times until the desired texture and size of nuts is achieved.

Lemon Rio Pie

This is the pie we made for family and friends in the 1960s and 1970s. It is a chiffon pie, so the filling, while rich, is still light and fluffy. This sunny pie reminds us of things tropical and festive. We suggest that you make this pie the day before you plan to serve it because there are several steps to preparing the filling. Since we wanted to avoid using raw egg whites in the pie, we have added a recipe for a cooked sugar syrup to be added to the beaten egg whites to form a meringue.

FILLING

1 cup heavy cream

4 eggs, separated

¼ cup water

1 envelope unflavored gelatin

½ cup sugar

½ teaspoon salt

½ cup lemon juice

2 tablespoons grated lemon zest

⅓ cup chopped bittersweet chocolate, melted and slightly cooled

CRUST

Baked single-crust piecrust (see page 154)

SUGAR SYRUP

¼ cup water

½ cup sugar

1. To make the filling: Add the cream to the bowl of a stand mixer fitted with the whisk attachment and beat until thick. Turn off mixer. Remove the cream from the bowl of the mixer and place in another bowl or container. Cover and store in the refrigerator until ready to use.

2. Set up a medium metal bowl for the filling and a larger bowl for an ice water bath near the

work surface. Have ice cubes handy, but keep frozen until ready to use. Whisk the egg yolks together in a small bowl and set aside.

3. Add the water to a heavy-bottomed 6-cup saucepan. Sprinkle the gelatin on top of the water and allow to stand for 1 minute. Whisk the gelatin and water together. Add the sugar, and whisk the mixture again. Add the egg yolks, salt, and lemon juice to the gelatin-and-sugar mixture and whisk to combine. Cook the mixture over medium heat, stirring with a wooden spoon, for 4 to 5 minutes, or until the mixture thickens and coats the back of the spoon. Strain the mixture into the medium metal bowl, add the lemon zest, and stir to mix in. Set the custard in the metal bowl and set the bowl in the ice water bath. Stir occasionally until the custard is cool. This will take about 10 minutes. Remove the whipped cream from the the refrigerator and fold the cooled custard into the whipped cream. Return to the refrigerator until ready to combine with the egg white mixture.

4. Add the egg whites to the bowl of the stand mixer fitted with the whisk attachment and beat until soft peaks form. Set aside.

5. To make the sugar syrup: *Keep a large bowl filled with cold water and ice cubes at hand when making the sugar syrup for safety. This is not the same as the water bath used for the lemon custard (step 3).* Add the water and sugar to a heavy-bottomed 6-cup saucepan and whisk to combine. Using a wooden spoon, stir the mixture over medium heat until it begins to boil. Reduce the heat slightly and continue to stir the mixture until it has boiled for 3 minutes. If sugar crystals form on the inside of the pan, wash them down with a wet pastry brush. Keep a glass measuring cup filled with water near the stove so that you can dip the pastry brush after you wash down the sides of the pan. Do not scrape any sugar crust that forms on the sides of pan into the syrup. Transfer the syrup to the glass measuring cup. With the mixer turned off, pour the syrup down the inner side of the bowl into the whipped egg whites. *The bottom of the mixer bowl will be very hot.* Turn the mixer on, and beat until the bottom of the mixer bowl is cool, 10 to 12 minutes. The beaten egg whites should form soft peaks and are now a meringue.

6. Remove the lemon-custard-and-cream mixture from the refrigerator. Fold the meringue into the custard-and-cream mixture in three additions. Spoon half of the filling into the prepared pie shell. Drizzle half of the melted chocolate over the top of the filling. Add the remaining filling to the pie, piling it into peaks, and drizzle the remaining chocolate over the top of the pie. Chill the pie in the refrigerator for at least 6 hours, or overnight, before cutting and serving. Any leftover pie should be stored, loosely covered with plastic wrap, in the refrigerator. Lemon Rio Pie can be frozen. Remove the pie from the freezer 10 minutes before cutting and serving.

Yield: one 9-inch pie; 8 slices

SWEET TIPS: Read through the recipe for Lemon Rio Pie at least two times before making it, and be sure to have all of the ingredients laid out before you start the recipe.

• Be sure to sprinkle the gelatin over the water; do not add the water to the gelatin.

SWEET TOUCH: Pipe sweetened whipped cream around the edges of the pie to enhance the appeal of Lemon Rio Pie.

HOW TO USE AN ICE WATER BATH
TO COOL HOT MIXTURES

An ice water bath is a simple method for cooling hot mixtures before combining them with cooler mixtures. An ice water bath will prevent a hot mixture from "cooking" anything cooler to which it is added. It is easy to make an ice water bath in a home kitchen by using two bowls, one smaller than the other. The mixture to be cooled should be added to the smaller heatproof bowl, and then the bowl containing the hot mixture should be placed in the larger bowl, which has been filled with cold water and ice cubes. The hot mixture should be stirred every few minutes until it is cold and can then be added to another mixture. Ice water baths are particularly helpful when working with eggs.

Ice water baths can also be used for safety purposes when working with hot liquids or hot syrups.

Mama Ruth's Georgia Pecan Pie

This pecan pie is based on a recipe from Ruth Mozley O'Shields, a gracious lady, the daughter of a gentleman farmer from Atlanta. This is a very typical Southern recipe. The pecans are candied into the rich buttery filling. This pecan pie calls for a side of whipped cream or vanilla ice cream.

CRUST

Unbaked single-crust piecrust (see page 154)

FILLING

3 eggs

1 cup sugar

¼ teaspoon salt

1 cup dark corn syrup

4 tablespoons (½ stick) unsalted butter, melted

1 teaspoon vanilla extract

1¼ cups toasted pecans, coarsely chopped

1. Set the oven rack in the middle position. Preheat the oven to 400°F. To prevent spills in the oven, line a heavy rimmed baking sheet with aluminum foil on which to place the unbaked *filled* pie.

2. Place a 9-inch glass pie plate lined with unbaked piecrust on the foil-covered, rimmed baking sheet before placing it in oven. Place a sheet of nonstick aluminum foil facedown on the inside of pie shell. Partially bake the pie shell for 10 minutes. While the piecrust is in the oven, prepare the filling. Remove the partially baked piecrust from the oven and transfer to a wire rack. Remove the foil and let rest for 2 minutes before filling. Leave the oven on.

3. To make the filling: Add the eggs to a stand mixer fitted with the paddle attachment and beat until frothy. Add the sugar, salt, corn syrup, butter, and vanilla and beat to combine. Turn off the mixer, remove the bowl from the stand, and fold in the chopped pecans with a spatula. Pour the filling into the partially baked pie shell and place on foil-lined baking sheet. Place in oven, still set to 400°F. Bake for 10 minutes. *Reduce the oven temperature to 350°F,* and continue to bake for 30 minutes. Check the pie at 30 minutes to be sure that crust is not browning too quickly. Place a foil tent over pie if necessary. Continue to bake the pie for another 25 minutes; 65 minutes in all.

4. Remove the pie on the baking sheet carefully from the oven, and transfer to a wire rack to cool. The pie may be a bit wobbly in the center, but the top of the filling will be a burnished brown, and the filling will set when cool. When the pie is cool, place it in the refrigerator. Store any leftover pie, loosely covered with wax paper, in the refrigerator. Allow the pie to come to room temperature before serving.

Yield: one 9-inch pie; 8 to 10 slices

SWEET TIP: Using coarsely chopped pecans, rather than whole pecans, in the filling prevents the top of the pie from fusing into a solid sphere and makes it is easier to cut.

Rhubarb Streusel Pie

This Rhubarb Streusel Pie from the 1930s is sour and sweet at the same time. The pie's crunchy buttery streusel topping contrasts nicely with the syrupy filling. This recipe comes with a caution about placing the unbaked pie on a foil-covered rimmed baking sheet when placing it in the oven. The pie should also be tented with foil after 30 minutes to prevent the crust from browning too quickly. Choose only the tenderest stalks of rhubarb for this pie. We switched the almonds and the nutmeg we sometimes use in a streusel for the cinnamon and walnuts that can stand up to the robust flavor of the rhubarb. This pie will be very hot when it comes out of the oven.

FILLING

4 cups rhubarb, rinsed, trimmed, and cut
    into ½-inch pieces

1½ cups sugar

1 tablespoon flour

⅛ teaspoon salt

¼ cup lemon juice

3 tablespoons cornstarch

Grated zest of 1 lemon

STREUSEL TOPPING

¾ cup firmly packed brown sugar

2 tablespoons flour

¼ teaspoon salt

¼ teaspoon cinnamon

2 tablespoons cold unsalted butter, cut
    into small dice

¾ cup chopped walnuts

CRUST

Unbaked single-crust pie crust (see page 154)

1. To make the filling: Combine the rhubarb, sugar, flour, salt, and lemon juice in a large bowl. Set aside for 2½ hours. Pour the rhubarb mixture into a strainer, over a bowl. Collect the drained juice and pour into a saucepan. Reserve 3 tablespoons of juice in a small bowl. Add the cornstarch to the reserved juice in the small bowl and whisk to combine. Set aside. Cook the rest of rhubarb juice in the saucepan over medium heat until it starts to boil. Add the cornstarch mixture to the boiling rhubarb juice and whisk to combine. Continue cooking until the rhubarb juice starts to thicken. Add the lemon zest to the thickened juice, which is now a syrup. Pour the syrup into a heatproof bowl and set aside to cool. The bowl can be placed in the refrigerator to hasten cooling. When the syrup has cooled, add it to the reserved drained rhubarb.

2. To make the streusel: Add the brown sugar, flour, salt, and cinnamon to a bowl and whisk to combine. Wearing disposable gloves, or using your hands, add the diced butter to the dry ingredients and combine until the mixture has the texture of irregular crumbs. Add the walnuts and distribute. Chill the streusel for 20 minutes.

3. Set the oven rack in the middle position. Preheat the oven to 400°F. Line a heavy rimmed baking sheet or pizza pan with aluminum foil on which to set the filled pie.

4. Add the rhubarb mixture to the prepared pie shell, sprinkle the streusel on top of the pie, and gently pat down the streusel. Place the pie on the foil-lined baking sheet or pizza pan. Bake the pie for 30 minutes. At 30 minutes, check to see that the pie is not browning too quickly. If necessary, make a foil tent and place it over the pie. Bake for another 35 minutes, or until the filling bubbles. This pie

will be very hot when it comes out of the oven. Remove the pie from the baking sheet or pizza pan and place it on a wire rack to cool. When cool, transfer the pie to the refrigerator and chill until cold before cutting and serving. Any leftover pie should be covered with waxed paper, and stored in the refrigerator.

Yield: one 9-inch pie; 8 to 10 slices

SWEET TIP: The foil-covered baking sheet or pizza pan prevents any syrup that escapes from the pie in the oven from smoking.

SWEET TOUCHES: Any juice from the rhubarb filling in the baked pie forms a syrup, which can be spooned over slices of the pie.
- A scoop of vanilla ice cream goes nicely with this pie.

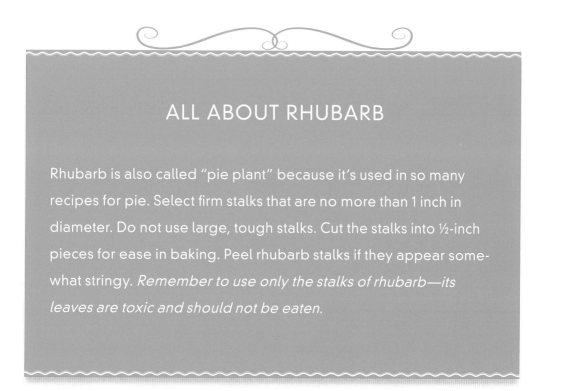

ALL ABOUT RHUBARB

Rhubarb is also called "pie plant" because it's used in so many recipes for pie. Select firm stalks that are no more than 1 inch in diameter. Do not use large, tough stalks. Cut the stalks into ½-inch pieces for ease in baking. Peel rhubarb stalks if they appear somewhat stringy. *Remember to use only the stalks of rhubarb—its leaves are toxic and should not be eaten.*

Sheila's Perfect Piecrust

Most of the home bakers we've chatted with have raised questions about making piecrust. We've used this easy-to-make piecrust for years, and have found that it is similar to many of the recipes we've discovered in our manuscript cookbooks. The sweet version is similar to that of Bertha Bohlman, an heirloom baker and cook. Several professional bakers have adopted our piecrust recipe with wonderful results.

TO MAKE A DOUBLE PIECRUST

2½ cups flour

3 tablespoons sugar

¼ teaspoon salt

1 cup (2 sticks) cold unsalted butter, cut into
    16 slices

¼ cup ice water

1 egg, beaten (optional glaze for double-
    crust pie)

1. Put the flour, sugar, and salt in the bowl of a food processor fitted with a metal blade and pulse three times to mix. Add the sliced butter and pulse until crumbly. Add the ice water and pulse until the mixture just comes together.

2. Remove the dough from the bowl of the processor, divide in half, and shape each half into a disk. Unless your kitchen is very warm, you don't have to chill the dough before rolling it out.

Yield: dough for one 9-inch
double-crust piecrust

TO MAKE A DOUBLE-CRUST PIE

1. Coat a 9-inch ovenproof glass pie plate with vegetable oil spray.

2. Roll out each disk of dough between two sheets of floured wax paper or parchment paper until 2 inches wider than the diameter across the top of the pie plate.

3. Fold one rolled dough disk in half and then in quarters. Place the folded dough into the bottom quarter of the pie plate. Carefully unfold the dough and let it relax into the pie plate. Trim the excess dough from the rim. Transfer to the refrigerator and chill the bottom crust while preparing the filling.

4. Brush the edges of the bottom crust with the beaten egg. Fill the pie and flip the second crust over the top of the pie. Trim the excess dough around the rim of pie, leaving just enough to make a crimped edge. Press the edges of the crust together gently with your fingers to seal. Crimp the edge with the tines of a fork or a pie crimper. Cut six 1-inch decorative slits in the center of the top crust to allow steam to escape. Brush the top crust and edges with the beaten egg. Bake as directed in the recipe.

TO MAKE A SINGLE-CRUST PIE

1. Coat a 9-inch ovenproof glass pie plate with vegetable oil spray.

2. Roll out one disk of dough between two sheets of floured wax paper or parchment paper until 2 inches wider than the diameter across the top of the pie plate.

3. Fold the rolled dough disk in half and then in quarters. Place the folded dough into the bottom quarter of the pie plate. Carefully unfold the dough and let it relax into the pie plate. Trim the excess dough around the rim, leaving enough to form a decorative edge. Flute the edge, or shape as desired.

4. Transfer to the refrigerator and chill the crust while preparing the filling. Fill and bake the pie as directed in the recipe.

TO PREBAKE A PIE SHELL

1. Place the oven rack in the middle position. Preheat the oven to 400°F.

2. Prick the pie shell pastry with a fork. Cut a piece of aluminum foil slightly larger than the pie shell and coat it with vegetable oil spray. Place the foil, greased side down, in the pie shell, fitting it loosely into the bottom and sides. Fill the foil with uncooked rice or beans to prevent the crust from bubbling up during baking. Bake for 20 minutes. Alternatively, a piece of nonstick foil, which doesn't require rice or beans, may be loosely pressed into the bottom of the crust.

3. Remove the foil, or rice or bean filling carefully. Prick any existing bubbles in the dough. Return the shell to the oven and continue baking, checking every 5 minutes for browning. If the edge of the crust appears to be browning too quickly, cover loosely with foil. Remove the pie shell from the oven when it is golden brown. Cool on a wire rack before adding the pie filling, unless otherwise directed.

4. The rice or beans can be cooled, sealed in a plastic bag, and reused several times to prebake pie shells. *They should not be eaten.*

Chocolate Piecrust

This is the Chocolate Piecrust we have been making for the past forty years. It is simple to make and enhances pies made with chocolate, mocha, lemon, orange, or vanilla fillings. It is especially good for sweet cheese pies.

1 teaspoon vanilla extract

¼ cup ice water, less 1 teaspoon

2 cups flour

½ cup American natural nonalkalized cocoa powder

3 tablespoons sugar

¼ teaspoon salt

1 cup (2 sticks) cold unsalted butter, cut into 16 slices

1. Add the vanilla to a ¼-cup measuring cup, then add enough ice water to fill the cup, and set aside. Place the dry ingredients in the bowl of a food processor fitted with the metal blade and pulse three times to mix. Add the butter and pulse until crumbly. Add the vanilla and ice water and pulse until the mixture comes together.

2. Remove the dough from the bowl of the processor, divide in half, and shape each half into a disk. Unless your kitchen is very warm, you don't have to chill the dough before rolling it out.

Yield: one double-crust 9-inch pie;
two single-crust 9-inch pies;
or two 8- or 9-inch tarts

SPRINKLE CHOCOLATE PIECRUST WITH COCOA RATHER THAN FLOUR

When working with Chocolate Piecrust, sprinkle cocoa powder, not flour, on wax paper before rolling it out. This prevents "white" flour from staining the chocolate piecrust.

6
We Gather Together

THE RECIPES

W e always look forward to gatherings of family and friends, as long as we can bring the desserts. There's nothing like that journey on a snowy day, arriving laden with tins of cookies, boxes of pies, and our ultimate contribution, the Chocolate *Bûche de Noël.*

We relish the stories from the older generations and the conviviality of those who are younger. We laugh at the duplication of recipes. How many similar pumpkin breads or brownies can a person eat? We moderate between home bakers, as they compete for votes as to which is the best.

We watch with pride as daughters or daughters-in-law assume responsibility for providing the familiar cake or pie that once was the province of a mother, grandmother, or aunt.

We commemorate Thanksgiving with raisin-and-nut-studded spicy June's Pumpkin Cookies and Cranberry Raisin Pie. We honor the Jewish holidays of Rosh Hashanah and Passover with something sweet, Grandma Goldberg's Honey Cake, and a Passover Sponge Cake, a light raspberry jam–filled cake pretending to be a Victoria sponge with its cloak of confectioners' sugar. Easter with good friends means Hot Cross Buns, fresh from the oven.

For the times when we're feeling like something exotic or we're welcoming someone from far away, we serve a syrup-drenched Armenian *Basbousa*, an Italian Cream Cake, or a diamond-shaped piece of Grandma Rometo's Torte.

Sometimes, gatherings are smaller, informal, and more intimate, with plates of Peanut Butter "Hermits," Central Squares, and the ever-popular Brown Sugar Brownies. These offerings are accompanied by pots of tea or strong black coffee, amended with irregular cubes of Demerara sugar and generous pitchers of cream and milk.

Gatherings are when we spend time with each other and enjoy the recipes that come from that sacred territory known as the home kitchen. If it's only the immediate family or just two of us, a square of Old-Fashioned Gingerbread and a glass of milk seem right. Although most of the gatherings we attend seem to be at midday or in the evening, we treasure our impromptu middle-of-the-night coming together, when the books we've read are discussed, solutions are offered for problems that seem unsolvable, and that unexplained need for something sweet is satisfied and shared in good company.

Quick Tips

- Sift confectioners' sugar after measuring, to remove lumps.
- Pipe whipped cram on tops of pies or cakes with uneven tops or sift tops with confectioners' sugar. No one will know your secret.
- Use footed cake and pie stands of varied heights so that baked accompaniments are all visible.
- When serving large groups, serve tea or coffee at one table and a buffet of sweets at another.

Brown Sugar Brownies
(Back by Popular Demand)

This recipe for Brown Sugar Brownies from Heirloom Baking *is the recipe most requested by home bakers at our demonstrations and events. Bittersweet chocolate and brown sugar makes these moist brownies perfect with a glass of milk or a cup of tea. Save the cut edges to mix with ice cream or for snacking.*

1 cup cake flour

½ teaspoon salt

1 cup American natural nonalkalized cocoa powder, sifted

1½ cups (3 sticks) unsalted butter, cut into ¼-inch slices, at room temperature

12 ounces bittersweet chocolate, chopped

2 cups granulated sugar

1 cup firmly packed brown sugar

6 eggs

2 teaspoons vanilla extract

1. Set the oven rack in the middle position. Preheat the oven to 350°F. Cover the bottom and sides of a 9 by 13 by 2-inch metal pan with aluminum foil, shiny side up. Coat the foil with butter or vegetable oil spray.

2. Add the cake flour, salt, and cocoa to a bowl and whisk to combine. Set aside.

3. Melt the butter and bittersweet chocolate in a large metal bowl set over a saucepan of slightly simmering water, stirring occasionally, until smooth. Carefully remove the bowl from the pan using pot holders.

4. Pour the melted chocolate and butter into the bowl of a stand mixer fitted with the paddle attachment. Add the granulated sugar and brown sugar and beat. Add the eggs one at a time, and beat to combine. Add the vanilla and beat to combine. Add the dry ingredients to the egg-sugar mixture in three additions, beating well after each addition.

5. Pour the batter into the prepared pan. Bake the brownies for about 40 minutes, or until the top seems firm and a metal tester inserted into the middle comes out fairly clean. There may be a few cracks on top. Do not overbake. Cool the brownies in the pan on a wire rack to room temperature. For easier cutting, place the pan in the refrigerator for 3 hours or overnight to chill. Remove the uncut brownies from the pan, discard the foil, and place on a cutting surface. (If you prefer, trim the edges using a wide-bladed knife and reserve the scraps.) Cut into 1-inch squares, wiping the knife clean as needed. Store the brownies in layers between sheets of wax paper in a covered tin. These brownies freeze well.

Yield: forty to fifty 1-inch brownies

NOTE: A version of the Brown Sugar Brownies recipe was originally published in *Heirloom Baking with the Brass Sisters*, published by Black Dog & Leventhal Publishers.

Chocolate *Bûche de Noël*

Chocolate *Bûche de Noël*

We've always loved making a Bûche de Noël, *that rolled cake made in the shape of a Yule log, hiding a filling of rich chocolate ganache. We consider any* bûche *we bake an opportunity for us to try out our idea of what edible holiday decorations are all about. We cover our* bûche *with a frosting of rich bittersweet chocolate, and we dust it with toasted finely chopped pistachios. We mold some tiny chocolate stars for the top, and we're off to a friend's house to celebrate the season.*

CHOCOLATE GANACHE FILLING

6 ounces heavy cream

8 ounces bittersweet chocolate, coarsely chopped

1 teaspoon vanilla extract

⅛ teaspoon salt

JELLY ROLL

⅔ cup flour

⅓ cup American natural nonalkalized cocoa powder, sifted

1 teaspoon baking powder

¼ teaspoon salt

3 eggs, separated

1½ cups granulated sugar

4 tablespoons water

1 teaspoon vanilla extract

½ cup granulated sugar, for dusting the dish towel

CHOCOLATE FROSTING

½ cup (1 stick) unsalted butter, at room temperature

2 cups confectioners' sugar, sifted

⅛ teaspoon salt

½ teaspoon vanilla extract

3 ounces bittersweet chocolate, melted and cooled to room temperature

1 tablespoon water, plus additional if needed

GARNISH

½ cup pistachio nuts, finely ground in a food processor

Chocolate stars or other decorations

1. To make the chocolate ganache filling: Add the cream to a heavy-bottomed saucepan and scald over low to medium heat, mixing with a wooden spoon until small bubbles form around the edges of the pan. Remove the pan from the heat and add the chocolate. Allow to sit for 5 minutes, or until the chocolate melts into the cream mixture. Add the vanilla and salt and continue to slowly stir with a wooden spoon until completely combined. Set aside to cool until spreadable.

2. Set the oven rack in the middle position. Preheat the oven to 375°F. Coat the bottom and sides of an 11 by 17 by 1-inch rimmed metal jelly roll pan with vegetable oil spray. Line the pan with parchment paper, and coat with vegetable oil spray. If too much spray accumulates, remove the excess with a small piece of paper towel.

3. To make the jelly roll: Add the flour, cocoa, baking powder, and salt to a small bowl and whisk to combine. Set aside.

4. Add the egg whites to the bowl of a stand mixer fitted with the whisk attachment and beat until firm peaks form. If you have only one mixer bowl, transfer the beaten egg whites to another bowl and set aside.

5. Add the egg yolks, 1 cup of the granulated sugar, and the water to the bowl of the stand mixer fitted with the paddle attachment and beat until pale yellow. Add the vanilla and beat in. Add the dry ingredients to the egg-sugar mixture in two additions and continue to beat until combined. Turn off the mixer, remove the bowl from the stand, and fold the egg whites into the batter in three additions. Pour the batter into the prepared pan and level with an offset spatula. Bake for 17 to 18 minutes or until the jelly roll springs back to the touch. Do not overbake or the jelly roll may crack.

6. Wet a dish towel with water, wring it out, and dust generously with the remaining ½ cup granulated sugar. Turn the jelly roll onto the prepared dish towel, and carefully peel the parchment paper from the jelly roll. Using the dish towel, quickly roll up the jelly roll from one wide end, and let rest and cool for 10 minutes.

7. Unroll the jelly roll, and spread the cooled ganache over the entire surface with an offset spatula. Reroll the jelly roll and roll onto a sheet of wax paper longer than the jelly roll itself.

8. Place the jelly roll on a wire rack and allow to cool. Transfer the jelly roll to a serving platter by picking it up from the wax paper sheet with a large metal cake lifter. Store the jelly roll in the refrigerator until ready to decorate.

9. To make the chocolate frosting: Add the butter, confectioners' sugar, and salt to the bowl of a stand mixer fitted with the whisk attachment and beat together. Add the vanilla and continue to beat. Add the cooled chocolate to the mixture and beat until the mixture is light and fluffy. Add the water, one tablespoon at a time, and mix until the frosting is the desired consistency. Remove the jelly roll from the refrigerator when ready to decorate. Place sheets of wax paper on either side of the *bûche*. Cover the entire *bûche* with frosting, except for the ends. Run the tines of a fork vertically down the sides and top of the *bûche* to form a bark-like texture. Trim both ends of *bûche* at the same angle. Dust the *bûche* with the finely ground pistachios. Place chocolate stars randomly over the top of the *bûche*. Place the *bûche* in the refrigerator until ready to serve. The *bûche* is fragile and should be eaten the day it is baked. *Any leftover* bûche *should be kept refrigerated if being used again, especially for trifle.*

Yield: 1 bûche; 10 slicess

SWEET TIP: Plastic molds for stars are available in craft stores. Follow the directions that come with the mold to make the stars.

Cranberry Raisin Pie
(Mock Cherry Pie)

We received this recipe from Kristina Bracciale, whose family came from England in the early 1800s, and substituted the more plentiful cranberries found in Massachusetts for the more expensive summer cherries. They combined the cranberries with raisins to enhance the flavor of the pie. They probably would have had to "stone" or remove the seeds from the raisins before using them.

CRUST

1 double-crust piecrust (see page 154)

FILLING

2 cups plus 2 tablespoons water, at room
    temperature

1½ cups sugar

½ teaspoon salt

3 cups raw cranberries, rinsed, drained,
    and cut in half

2 cups raisins, jumbo if possible

2 tablespoons grated lemon zest

4 tablespoons lemon juice

1 teaspoon vanilla extract

3 tablespoons minus 1 teaspoon cornstarch

EGG WASH

1 large egg

1 tablespoon water

1. Set the oven rack in the middle position. Preheat the oven to 450°F. Cover a 14 by 16-inch baking sheet with aluminum foil, shiny side up. Coat the foil with vegetable oil spray.

2. Prepare the double crust according to the detailed instructions, steps 1 through 3, on page 154. Chill in the refrigerator.

3. To make the filling: Add 2 cups of the water, sugar, salt, cranberries, raisins, lemon zest, lemon juice, and vanilla to a heavy-bottomed saucepan and whisk to combine. Stirring with a wooden spoon, bring the mixture to a boil over medium heat. Reduce to a simmer and cook, stirring, for 5 minutes. Remove from the heat. In a small bowl, combine the cornstarch and remaining 2 tablespoons water and slowly add to the cranberry mixture. When the mixture has thickened, transfer the filling to a bowl and cool to room temperature.

4. Pour the cooled cranberry filling into the bottom crust. Whisk the egg and water together. Apply egg wash to the edge of the bottom crust. After rolling out the top crust, and decorating it with circle cut-outs or other motifs, place it on the filled pie, and press together the top and bottom edges of the crusts to seal. Using clean kitchen scissors, trim the excess crust from the edges so it fits the pie plate. Make a decorative edge with the tines of a fork, or with your fingers. Brush egg wash over the top and edges of the pie.

5. Place the pie in the oven on the prepared baking sheet and bake for 10 minutes. *Reduce the oven temperature to 350°F*, and bake for another 30 to 35 minutes, or until the top crust is golden brown and the filling bubbles in the slits or cut-outs in the top of the pie. Check the pie halfway through the baking to be sure the crust is not browning too quickly. Place a foil tent over the pie for the rest of baking time if necessary. Transfer the pie to a wire rack to cool. The slices of pie will cut more evenly if the pie is completely cool. Store the pie, covered with wax paper, at room temperature.

Yield: one 9-inch pie; 8 to 10 slices

Grandma Goldberg's Honey Cake

This recipe from the 1930s comes from Hilary Finkel Buxton, a friend from our days at WGBH, the public television station in Boston, and her sister, Sandy. Their grandma Celia Goldberg admitted to 101 before she died. She was beloved by her family, and they treasured the sometimes cryptic notes she bequeathed to them for her Honey Cake, Mandlebread, and Noodle Pudding. Grandma called her sister, Yetta, who lived to be 102, every day when they both lived in the Bronx.

2 teaspoons instant coffee or instant espresso

1 cup hot water

3 cups flour

½ teaspoon salt

1 teaspoon cinnamon

1 teaspoon ginger

3 eggs, separated

1 cup sugar

1 teaspoon baking soda

3 tablespoons warm water

½ cup oil

1 cup honey

½ cup thinly sliced almonds, toasted

1. Set the oven rack in the middle position. Preheat the oven to 350°F. Coat two 9 by 5 by 3-inch loaf pans with vegetable oil spray. Line the bottom and ends of the pans with a single strip of wax paper and coat with vegetable oil spray. Dust the pans with flour and tap to remove the excess.

2. Add the instant coffee to the hot water and allow to cool, or place in the refrigerator to hasten the cooling.

3. Add the flour, salt, cinnamon, and ginger to a large bowl and whisk to combine. Set aside.

4. Add the egg whites to the bowl of a stand mixer fitted with the whisk attachment and whip the whites until they form firm peaks. Set aside. If you don't have a second mixer bowl, transfer the egg whites to another bowl and set aside. The honey cakes come together quickly so the beaten egg whites will not have time to deflate.

5. Add the sugar and egg yolks to the bowl of the stand mixer fitted with the paddle attachment and beat to combine. Turn off the mixer and, using a rubber spatula, scrape down the mixture from the sides and bottom of the bowl. Turn the mixer on and continue to beat and combine with the rest of the mixture.

6. Add the baking soda to the warm water and stir to combine. Set aside. Whisk together the oil, honey, and cooled coffee in a small bowl. Add the baking soda mixture, and continue to whisk until combined.

7. Add the sifted dry ingredients to the mixture alternately with the liquid ingredients. Remove the bowl from the stand and fold in the beaten egg whites in three additions. Pour the batter into the prepared pans. *The batter will be very loose.* Sprinkle the almonds on top of the loaves and bake for 30 minutes. Tent each cake with aluminum foil and bake for an additional 25 to 30 minutes, or until a metal tester inserted into the center of each cake comes out clean. Transfer the cakes to a wire rack and cool for at least 20 minutes. Go around the edges of each cake with a butter knife and turn out onto a second wire rack. Invert the cakes onto the first rack and continue to cool. Grandma Goldberg's Honey Cake should be wrapped in wax paper and stored at room temperature.

Yield: 2 loaves; 9 slices per loaf

Grandma Goldberg's Honey Cake

Joe Wells's Dingbat Cookies

We found this handwritten recipe for little iced tea cakes in a manuscript cookbook from Patterson, New Jersey. We assume that Joe is a gentleman and not a lady. Whoever he was, he was quite a baker. His recipes for raisin and chocolate filling were also found in the same collection. Dingbat refers to a typographical symbol, but it is sometimes used as a derogatory name. Would Edith have baked these cookies for Archie Bunker?

COOKIES

2½ cups flour

¼ teaspoon salt

1 teaspoon baking soda

2 teaspoons cinnamon

2 teaspoons allspice

½ teaspoon cloves

1 cup (2 sticks) unsalted butter, at room temperature

½ cup granulated sugar

3 eggs

1 cup buttermilk

1 cup raisins

1 cup pecans, toasted and coarsely chopped

1 cup sweetened shredded coconut

VANILLA ICING

2 cups confectioners' sugar

Pinch of salt

2 teaspoons vanilla extract

2 tablespoons plus 2 teaspoons water

1. Set the oven rack in the middle position. Preheat the oven to 375°F. Line a 14 by 16-inch baking sheet with a silicone liner or aluminum foil, shiny side up. Coat the foil with vegetable oil spray.

2. Add the flour, salt, baking soda, cinnamon, allspice, and cloves to a large bowl and whisk to combine. Set aside.

3. In the bowl of a stand mixer fitted with the paddle attachment, cream the butter and granulated sugar until light and fluffy. Add the eggs and continue to beat until well combined. Add the dry ingredients and the buttermilk alternately to the creamed mixture in three additions, beating well after each addition. Add the raisins, pecans, and coconut and run the mixer slowly a few times until they are distributed into the cookie dough. The raisins, pecans, and coconut can also be folded in by hand. Drop the dough by tablespoons onto the prepared baking sheet, 3 across and no more than 12 to a baking sheet. These cookies spread when baked. Bake for 15 minutes. The tea cakes will puff up and brown around the edges. Place the baking sheet with the tea cakes on a wire rack. Remove the tea cakes with a metal spatula and place on a second wire rack. *Cool for 3 minutes before icing.*

4. To make the vanilla icing: Sift the confectioners' sugar and salt into a small bowl and whisk to combine. Add the vanilla and 1 tablespoon of the water and continue to whisk until the icing comes together. Add more water, by the teaspoon, if necessary to achieve the desired consistency. Slip a sheet of wax paper under the wire rack. Using a teaspoon or fork, drizzle the icing on top of the Dingbats. After the icing has set, store the tea cakes, between sheets of wax paper, in a covered tin at room temperature.

Yield: about 5 dozen cookies

SWEET TIP: Dingbats should be warm when iced so that the icing will melt into them.

• Use an offset spatula to spread the icing.

Grandma Rometo's Torte

This is based on an old Slovak recipe we received from our friend Leslie Gaydos. Her grandmother Mary Agnes Sader Rometo was given the recipe by her neighbor Mrs. Burin, who spoke little English and measured ingredients by the handful. We adapted the original filling and made it more as a frosting. Grandma Rometo, who was born in Czechoslovakia and lived in Tarentum, Pennsylvania, loved to bake for her family, and they treasure her recipes.

TORTE

1 cup flour

⅛ teaspoon salt

2 teaspoons baking powder

I cup graham cracker crumbs

1 cup walnuts, toasted and finely chopped

8 eggs, separated

1 cup granulated sugar

1 teaspoon vanilla extract

5 tablespoons cold black coffee

FILLING

4 cups confectioners' sugar, sifted

⅛ teaspoon salt

1 cup (2 sticks) unsalted butter, at room temperature

1 teaspoon vanilla extract

2 tablespoons water plus more water, if necessary

1 cup walnuts, toasted and finely chopped

TOPPING

2 tablespoons confectioners' sugar

1. Set the oven rack in the middle position. Preheat the oven to 375°F. Coat the bottom and sides of an 11 by 17 by 1-inch rimmed jelly roll pan with vegetable oil spray. Line the pan with parchment paper, and coat the parchment paper with vegeta-ble oil spray. If too much spray accumulates in the corners, remove the excess with a small piece of paper towel.

2. To make the torte: Add the flour, salt, baking powder, graham cracker crumbs, and walnuts to a bowl and whisk together. Set aside.

3. Add the egg whites to the bowl of a stand mixer fitted with the whisk attachment and beat until firm peaks form. If you only have one mixer bowl, transfer the beaten egg whites to another bowl and set aside.

4. Add the egg yolks and granulated sugar to the bowl of the stand mixer fitted with the paddle attachment and beat until pale yellow. Add the dry ingredients to the creamed mixture in two additions and continue to beat until combined. Add the vanilla and coffee and beat in. Turn off the mixer, remove the bowl, and fold the egg whites into the batter in three additions. Pour the batter into the prepared pan, and level with an offset spatula. Bake for 20 minutes, or until the torte springs back to the touch. Do not overbake.

5. Remove the pan from the oven, and place it on a wire rack. When cool, cover the pan with a cutting board and flip it over. Carefully remove the parchment paper and flip over again, right side up.

6. To make the filling: In the bowl of the stand mixer fitted with the paddle attachment, beat together the sifted confectioners' sugar, salt, and butter to combine. Add vanilla. Add the water and beat to combine. If necessary, add more water a teaspoon at a time, and continue beating until the filling comes together. Add the walnuts and combine.

7. Place the torte on a cutting board. Carefully slice the torte in half horizontally with a thin, sharp knife. Place the top on another flat surface.

Frost the bottom of the torte with the entire filling. Replace the top of torte on the filling. Cut the torte into diamond shapes and sift confectioners' sugar over the top.

8. Keep the torte slices refrigerated until 10 minutes before serving. Save any leftover diamonds, loosely covered with wax paper, in the refrigerator.

Yield: about 4 dozen diamonds

SWEET TIP: This torte dries out easily, so keep it covered and refrigerated.

SWEET TOUCH: Grandma Rometo's Torte is elegant, and is definitely a cloth-napkin-and-best-china recipe.

Hot Cross Buns

Hot Cross Buns are a traditional Easter bread. We've added golden raisins, candied or dried apricots, and candied ginger to the buns. These buns are also good baked with currants. This is a great dough, and the Hot Cross Buns are easy to make. They come out of the oven shiny, plump, and golden brown.

YEAST SPONGE

One 1¼-ounce package active dry yeast

1 tablespoon granulated sugar

1 cup milk, warmed to 115°F

DOUGH

1 cup golden raisins

¾ cup dried or candied apricots, cut into ¼-inch pieces

¼ cup candied ginger, cut into ¼-inch pieces

½ cup candied citron (optional)

3 cups flour

3 tablespoons granulated sugar

⅛ teaspoon salt

¼ teaspoon nutmeg

¼ teaspoon allspice

4 tablespoons (½ stick) unsalted butter, at room temperature

2 eggs

1 teaspoon vanilla extract

1 egg, beaten, for egg wash

FROSTING

⅔ cup confectioners' sugar

Pinch of salt

2 tablespoons milk

¼ teaspoon vanilla extract

2 tablespoons unsalted butter, at room temperature

1. To make the yeast sponge: Dissolve the yeast and sugar in the warmed milk. Set in a warm place for 10 minutes to proof.

2. To make the dough: Add the raisins, apricots, candied ginger, and candied citron (if using) to a small bowl and set aside. Add the flour to a larger bowl and remove 1 tablespoon and sprinkle over the fruit in the small bowl. Mix the flour through the fruit to coat, and set aside. To the flour in the larger bowl, add the granulated sugar, salt, nutmeg, and allspice and whisk to combine. Set aside.

3. In the bowl of a stand mixer fitted with the paddle attachment, combine the butter, eggs, vanilla, and proofed yeast mixture. Slowly add the dry ingredients and beat until thoroughly mixed. Add the floured fruit and mix to distribute. Change to the dough hook and knead for 5 minutes, or until the dough comes together in a small ball.

4. Preheat the oven to 175°F. Coat a medium bowl with butter or vegetable oil spray. Place the dough in the greased bowl and, using a spatula, turn the dough so that the whole mixture has a thin coat of butter or vegetable oil spray. Cover the bowl with plastic wrap or a clean dish towel. Place the bowl on the back of the stove or in a warm place and allow to rise for 1 hour, or until doubled in size.

5. Line a 14 by 16-inch baking sheet with a silicone liner or aluminum foil, shiny side up. Coat the foil with vegetable oil spray. Set aside.

6. Remove the raised dough from the bowl and turn it out onto a sheet of wax paper or a breadboard dusted with flour. Punch down the dough. Divide the dough into two pieces and form into two rolls, 12 inches long. Divide each roll into six sections and form each section into a round bun by

Hot Cross Buns

rotating the dough on the work surface with the palm of your hand.

7. Place the buns on the prepared pan and let rise in a warm place until doubled in size, 45 to 60 minutes. When ready to bake, set the oven rack in the middle position. *Raise the temperature to 400°F.* Brush the tops of buns with the beaten egg and bake for 15 minutes until shiny and golden. Transfer the buns to a wire rack to cool.

8. To make the frosting: Sift the confectioners' sugar and salt into a bowl and whisk to combine. Add the milk and vanilla and whisk in. Add the butter and continue whisking until the butter is fully incorporated into the frosting. Add more sifted confectioners' sugar or milk to the frosting to achieve the desired consistency; the frosting should be fairly thick.

9. When the buns are completely cool, pipe wide ribbons of frosting in the shape of a cross on top of each bun using a disposable frosting bag and a #10 piping tube with a ¼-inch opening. Let the frosting set before serving. Any leftover buns can

be stored, loosely covered with wax paper, at room temperature.

Yield: 1 dozen large buns

SWEET TIPS: Most of the Hot Cross Buns we've tried have contained candied citron. Because it is not frequently found on pantry shelves, we have made the citron optional.
• The frosting can also be applied with a large spoon, or by filling a plastic bag with frosting, snipping a corner, and piping a cross on the bun.
• Leave space between the wax paper and tops of the frosted buns when storing so that the frosting will not smear.

SWEET TOUCH: Traditionally, if not frosting Hot Cross Buns, a cross is cut about ¼ inch deep in the dough before brushing with the beaten egg and baking.

Italian Cream Cake

This handwritten recipe came from the manuscript cookbook of the lady from North Carolina whose recipes for Milk Chocolate Pound Cake and Red Velvet Cake we found to be wonderful. Growing up in Massachusetts, we were used to cream cakes laden with rum-flavored whipped cream that we found in Boston's Italian North End. We were pleased to find that this recipe produced a cake with the delicate taste of coconut. We frosted it with a Whipped Cream Cheese Frosting from our friend Mandy Timney Finizio.

CAKE

1 cup chopped sweetened shredded coconut

2 cups flour

1 teaspoon salt

1 teaspoon baking soda

5 eggs, separated

1 cup (2 sticks) unsalted butter, at room temperature

2 cups sugar

1 teaspoon vanilla extract

1 cup buttermilk

WHIPPED CREAM CHEESE FROSTING

2 cups heavy cream

8 ounces cream cheese, at room temperature

½ cup sugar

Pinch of salt

1½ teaspoons vanilla extract

1 cup chopped sweetened shredded coconut (optional)

1. Set the oven rack in the middle position. Preheat the oven to 350°F. Coat the bottoms and sides of three round 7-inch cake pans or two 9-inch cake pans with vegetable oil spray. Line the pans with parchment paper, and coat with vegetable oil spray. Dust the pans with flour and tap the pans to remove the excess flour.

2. To make the cake: Place the coconut in the bowl of a food processor and pulse three times to chop finely. Do not overpulse the coconut. Set aside. *If you plan to apply coconut to the sides of the cake, process the additional cup of coconut (see Frosting) at this time.*

3. To make the cake: Add the flour, salt, baking soda, and chopped coconut to a large bowl and whisk to combine. Set aside.

4. Add the egg whites to the bowl of a stand mixer fitted with the whisk attachment and whisk until peaks form. The peaks should be firm, but still a little soft. If you don't have an second bowl for your stand mixer, transfer the whipped egg whites to another bowl, and set aside. The egg whites won't deflate while you put the cake together.

5. Add the butter and sugar to the bowl of the stand mixer fitted with the paddle attachment and cream to combine. Add the egg yolks and vanilla and continue beating until they are incorporated. Add the dry ingredients to the creamed mixture alternately with the buttermilk in three additions, beating well after each addition. Gently fold the beaten egg whites into the batter in three additions, until no trace of the egg whites can be seen in the batter.

6. Transfer the batter to the prepared pans and bake for 45 minutes, or until a metal tester inserted into the centers of the cakes comes out clean. Place the cakes on a wire rack and allow to cool in the pans for 15 minutes. Run a butter knife gently

around the edges if necessary to loosen and invert the cakes onto a second rack. Remove parchment liners. Let cool completely.

7. To make the frosting: Add the cream to the bowl of the stand mixer fitted with the whisk attachment and beat until thick. If you don't have a second mixer bowl, remove the cream from the bowl of the mixer and place in another bowl or container. Cover and store in the refrigerator until ready to use.

8. Add the cream cheese, sugar, salt, and vanilla to the bowl of the stand mixer fitted with the whisk attachment and beat until fluffy. Add the reserved chilled whipped cream to the cream cheese mixture and beat a few times until well combined; the frosting will be fluffy. Refrigerate the frosting until ready to use.

9. When ready to frost the cakes, remove them from the refrigerator. Carefully slice a thin layer off the top of each cake to level, if necessary. Place the bottom layer of cake on a cake round, lined with four small pieces of wax paper. Spread the frosting over the top of this cake layer with an offset spatula. Frost only the tops of the bottom and middle layers. Add the third layer and frost the top and the sides of the entire cake. Immediately cover the sides of the cake with the shredded coconut, if using. Allow the frosted cake to set for 30 minutes to 1 hour in the refrigerator before slicing. Remove the cake from the refrigerator 10 minutes before serving. Store any leftover cake, covered with wax paper, in the refrigerator. Use toothpicks to keep the wax paper from sticking to the frosting.

Yield: one 7-inch 3-layer cake or one 9-inch 2-layer cake; 8 slices; about 3 cups Whipped Cream Cheese Frosting

SWEET TIP: Chopping the coconut in the food processor releases the coconut flavor and makes cutting the cake easier than if the shreds were longer.

Joyce's Basbousa Cake
(Armenian Farina Cake)

This is a simple recipe that can be mixed by hand. The Basbousa diamonds have the consistency of candy, and the flavors of the honey and lemon are concentrated. Serving the Basbousa with softly whipped cream makes a pleasant contrast to the chewy texture of the farina and walnuts.

SYRUP

6 tablespoons sugar

6 tablespoons honey

6 tablespoons water

Juice of ½ large lemon

CAKE

1 cup farina

1 cup sour cream

1 cup sugar

1 teaspoon baking powder

3 tablespoons unsalted butter, melted

¼ cup walnuts, toasted and finely
    chopped

1. Set the oven rack in the middle position. Preheat the oven to 350°F. Cover the bottom and sides of a 9 by 9 by 2-inch metal pan with aluminum foil, shiny side up. Coat the aluminum foil with vegetable oil spray.

2. To make the syrup: Add the sugar, honey, water, and lemon juice to a saucepan, mix with a wooden spoon, and place over medium heat. Bring mixture to a boil, reduce the heat, and continue to simmer, stirring, for 5 minutes. The mixture will thicken slightly and form a syrup. *Carefully* pour the syrup into a heatproof container and allow to cool.

3. To make the cake: Add the farina, sour cream, sugar, and baking powder to a mixing bowl and whisk to combine. Spoon the batter into the prepared pan, and pour the butter evenly over the top of the cake. Sprinkle the top of the cake with the walnuts. Bake for 45 minutes, or until the top is golden brown. Remove the Basbousa from the oven and cut it into squares or diamonds while still hot. Pour the cooled syrup over the squares or

FARINA

Farina is a milled grain meal, usually made with wheat. It is sold under the brand name Cream of Wheat. It is often used to make Middle Eastern pastries or sweets.

diamonds and return to the oven for 5 minutes. Let cool slightly and remove from the pan with the foil attached. Carefully lift the squares or diamonds off the foil with a metal spatula and place on a serving plate. Serve slightly warm, or at room temperature, with whipped cream. Store any leftover Basbousa, between sheets of wax paper, in a covered tin. The Basbousa should be eaten within 2 days.

Yield: 18 to 20 diamonds; 1 cup of syrup

SWEET TIP: We used two glass liquid measuring cups to measure the honey and water for the syrup, using one cup to measure and one cup to receive the measured honey and water.

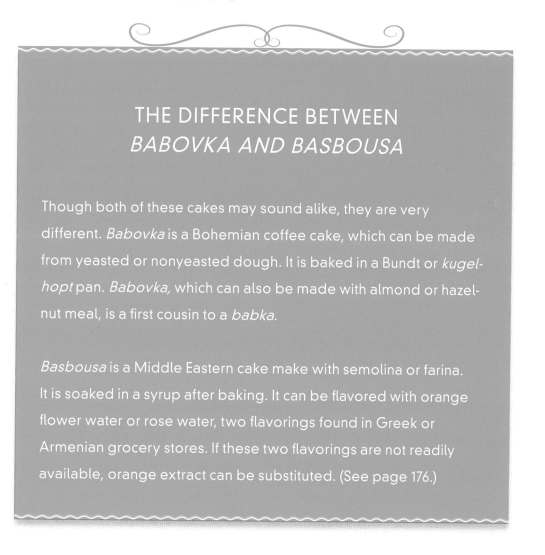

THE DIFFERENCE BETWEEN
BABOVKA AND BASBOUSA

Though both of these cakes may sound alike, they are very different. *Babovka* is a Bohemian coffee cake, which can be made from yeasted or nonyeasted dough. It is baked in a Bundt or *kugelhopt* pan. *Babovka,* which can also be made with almond or hazelnut meal, is a first cousin to a *babka.*

Basbousa is a Middle Eastern cake make with semolina or farina. It is soaked in a syrup after baking. It can be flavored with orange flower water or rose water, two flavorings found in Greek or Armenian grocery stores. If these two flavorings are not readily available, orange extract can be substituted. (See page 176.)

June's Pumpkin Cookies

These delightfully cakelike cookies from the 1950s, with their hint of spice, are not overly sweet. These moist morsels benefit from the addition of toasted walnuts and golden raisins. They remind us of pumpkin pie without the crust. Adding an orange or vanilla glaze, or dusting them with confectioners' sugar, adds additional sweetness.

COOKIES

1 cup walnuts, toasted and coarsely chopped
½ cup golden raisins
2½ cups flour
½ teaspoon salt
1 teaspoon baking powder
1 teaspoon baking soda
1 teaspoon cinnamon
1 teaspoon nutmeg
¼ teaspoon cloves
½ cup (1 stick) unsalted butter, at room temperature
1½ cups granulated sugar
1 egg
1 cup cooked or canned pure pumpkin puree (see sidebar page 37)
1 teaspoon vanilla extract

GLAZE

1 cup confectioners' sugar, sifted
1 teaspoon grated orange zest
Pinch of salt
2 to 3 tablespoons orange juice

1. Set the oven rack in the middle position. Preheat the oven to 350°F. Line a 14 by 16-inch baking sheet with a silicone liner or aluminum foil, shiny side up. Coat the foil with vegetable oil spray.

2. To make the cookies: Add the walnuts and golden raisins to a small bowl and set aside.

3. Add the flour, salt, baking powder, baking soda, cinnamon, nutmeg, and cloves to a separate bowl and whisk to combine. Set aside.

4. Add the butter and granulated sugar to the bowl of a stand mixer fitted with the paddle attachment and cream to combine. Add the egg to the creamed mixture and continue to beat. Add the pumpkin puree and vanilla and beat to incorporate.

5. Add the dry ingredients to the creamed mixture in three additions, mixing well until combined. Remove the bowl from the stand and fold in the walnuts and raisins. Drop the dough by heaping teaspoons onto the prepared sheet, 12 cookies to a baking sheet. Bake for 15 minutes, or until lightly browned around the edges. The bottoms of the cookies will be golden brown. Slide the foil or the silicone liner with the baked cookies onto a wire rack to cool for at least 5 minutes. Remove the cooled cookies with a metal spatula and transfer to a second wire rack.

6. To make the glaze: Whisk together the confectioners' sugar, orange zest, and salt in a small bowl. Add the orange juice, 1 tablespoon at a time, and whisk until the desired consistency is achieved. Slip a sheet of wax paper under the wire rack to catch drips. Using a teaspoon or fork, drizzle the glaze over the tops of the cookies. After the glaze has set, store the cookies, between sheets of wax paper, in a covered tin.

Yield: 5 dozen cookies

SWEET TOUCHES: A vanilla glaze can be substituted for the orange glaze by omitting the orange juice and grated orange zest and adding a teaspoon of vanilla extract. Water can be substituted for the orange juice.

• Wait until the Pumpkin Cookies are completely cool before dusting with confectioners' sugar.

Lemon Almond Biscotti

This is a delectable variation of our friend Lisa Ann Schraffa's Nana Rose's Anise Biscotti. Since we had a recipe for Mrs. Marasi's Anise Biscotti in Heirloom Baking, *we thought it would be fun to bake Nana Rose's recipe, substituting butter for the olive oil and lemon oil for the anise oil. For some crunch, we added toasted almonds. Nana Rose, one of twenty children, grew up on a farm in Arlington, Massachusetts, and baked wonderful biscotti.*

BISCOTTI

2½ cups flour

½ teaspoon salt

1 teaspoon baking powder

½ teaspoon cloves

½ cup (1 stick) unsalted butter, at room
     temperature

1 cup granulated sugar

3 eggs

1 teaspoon lemon oil, or 1½ teaspoons
     lemon extract

1½ cups whole almonds, toasted

LEMON GLAZE (optional)

2 cups confectioners' sugar

¼ teaspoon salt

¼ cup lemon juice

1. Set the oven rack in the middle position. Preheat the oven to 350°F. Line two 14 by 16-inch baking sheets with a silicone liner or aluminum foil, shiny side up. Coat the foil with vegetable oil spray.

2. Add the flour, salt, baking powder, and cloves to a bowl and whisk to combine. Set aside.

3. In the bowl of a stand mixer fitted with the paddle attachment, cream the butter and granulated sugar. Add the eggs and continue beating until combined. Add the lemon oil or extract and mix in. Add the dry ingredients in three additions and beat until combined; a soft dough will come together. Fold in the almonds.

4. Transfer the dough to a plastic container or bowl, cover with plastic wrap, and allow to chill in the freezer for 30 to 45 minutes. Remove the dough from the freezer when firm, and divide into two portions. Place each portion on one of the prepared baking sheets.

5. Wearing disposable gloves, shape the portions into loaves measuring 12 inches long by 2½ inches wide and ¾ inch high. Alternatively, dip your fingers in a little cold water and form the loaves. Bake the first baking sheet for 25 to 30 minutes, until the loaves are golden brown and a metal tester inserted into each loaf comes out dry. Transfer the baking sheet to a wire rack and cool for 15 to 20 minutes.

6. Transfer one loaf at a time from the baking sheet to a cutting board. Using a serrated knife, cut the loaf into diagonal slices ½ inch thick. Repeat with the remaining loaf. Divide the biscotti slices, cut side down, between two baking sheets and return one pan to the oven for 10 minutes. Remove from the oven, turn the biscotti over (the second cut side will be up), and return to the oven for another 10 minutes. Slide the foil or the silicone liner with the baked cookies onto a wire rack to cool. Remove the cooled cookies with a metal spatula and transfer to a second wire rack. Repeat this with the remaining pan of biscotti.

7. To make the glaze (if using): Sift the confectioners' sugar and salt into a small bowl and whisk

to combine. Whisk the lemon juice, a little at a time, into the confectioners' sugar mixture, adding the rest as needed. The glaze will come together. Drizzle the lemon glaze on the tops of the cooled biscotti. Allow the glaze to set. Store the biscotti in a covered tin. The biscotti should keep crisp for a week.

Yield: 4 dozen biscotti

SWEET TOUCH: Instead of glazing the biscotti, sprinkle clear coarse sanding sugar on top of the biscotti loaves before baking.

Central Squares
(Lemon Cream Cheese Squares)

We've named these squares in honor of Central Square in Cambridge, Massachusetts, where Marilynn first lived at the YWCA. It seems that everyone has a recipe for Lemon Squares, but this one combines three wonderful elements: A toasted almond crust, cream cheese sweetened with confectioners' sugar, and a tangy lemon curd. What makes these squares unusual is that the crust is the only part of the recipe that needs to be baked. We found this one handwritten on the back of an American Automobile Association membership card. We wonder if the home baker who was responsible for this recipe took it with her on her automobile trips. Central Squares are wonderful to take to gatherings with family and friends, and they are just the thing to grace a tea table. The lemon curd should be made ahead.

CRUST

1 cup flour

2 tablespoons granulated sugar

⅛ teaspoon salt

½ cup (1 stick) cold unsalted butter, cut into
¼-inch dice

½ teaspoon vanilla extract

½ cup slivered almonds, toasted and
chopped

FILLING

8 ounces cream cheese, at room-temperature

¾ cup confectioners' sugar, sifted

1½ cups Lemon Curd (see recipe, page 185)

1. Set the oven rack in the middle position. Preheat the oven to 375°F. Cover the bottom and sides of an 8-inch square metal pan with aluminum foil, shiny side up. Coat the foil with butter or vegetable oil spray.

Central Square

2. To make the crust: Add the flour, granulated sugar, and salt to a 4-cup mixing bowl and whisk to combine. Work the butter into the dry ingredients with your fingers (wear disposable gloves, if desired) until the butter is incorporated and the mixture has the texture of coarse cornmeal. Add the vanilla and slivered almonds and gently work them into the dough. When all of the ingredients are combined, press the dough into the bottom of the prepared pan. Bake for 20 minutes; the crust will be lightly brown. Transfer the pan to a wire rack to cool completely.

3. To make the filling: Add the cream cheese and confectioners' sugar to bowl of a stand mixer fitted with the paddle attachment and beat until combined.

Central Squares

4. Place the cream cheese filling on the cooled crust and spread with an offset spatula. Spread the lemon curd over the cream cheese layer using an offset spatula, bringing the curd out to the corners and sides of the pan. Refrigerate the squares for at least 4 hours before serving. Remove the squares from the pan by lifting them by the ends of the foil. Place on a cutting board, remove the foil, and cut into 2-inch squares with a wide-bladed serrated knife. Garnish the squares with rosettes of whipped cream. Any leftover Central Squares can be stored, between sheets of wax paper, in the refrigerator.

Yield: 16 squares

SWEET TIP: Be sure that the pan of Central Squares has set completely before cutting them.
- This recipe can be doubled and baked in a 9 by 13 by 2-inch metal pan.

Lemon Curd

This is the lemon curd recipe we've been making for more than forty-five years. It's wonderful on top of cheesecakes, combined with whipped cream for fillings and frostings, and served with scones and muffins. This is what we make when we serve an English tea. Lemon curd can be stored in the refrigerator for 3 weeks.

1 whole egg

4 egg yolks

¾ cup sugar

Pinch of salt

1 teaspoon grated lemon zest

1 cup lemon juice

¼ cup (½ stick) unsalted butter, cut into large dice, at room temperature

Whisk the whole egg and egg yolks in a 6-cup heavy-bottomed saucepan. Add the sugar, salt, and lemon zest and whisk to combine. Whisk in the lemon juice. Add the butter and whisk over medium heat until the butter has melted. Switch to a wooden spoon and continue to cook, stirring, until the curd thickens, about 5 minutes. If you prefer a smooth curd, strain it to remove the lemon zest. Cover with a piece of plastic wrap, pressed directly on the surface to prevent skin from forming. Let the curd cool completely. Keep refrigerated; *do not let lemon curd stand out of the refrigerator for long periods of time.*

Yield: about 1½ cups lemon curd

SWEET TIP: Use a wooden-handled metal whisk if possible because a metal handle can become hot.

Old-Fashioned Soft Gingerbread

This recipe was written on the blank half of a greeting card made by The Paramount Card Company. The card cost 15 cents, so this is probably from the 1940s. Easy to make, this soft gingerbread is very delicate, almost a ginger cake. We made it in a stand mixer, but it can be made with a whisk and a bowl. The sanding sugar gives a nice crunch to the crust.

½ cup small raisins

1½ cups flour

1 teaspoon baking soda

½ teaspoon salt

¾ teaspoon ginger

½ teaspoon cinnamon

⅛ teaspoon cloves

½ cup granulated sugar

½ cup (1 stick) unsalted butter, at room temperature

½ cup molasses

2 eggs

½ cup buttermilk

¼ cup ginger jam or orange marmalade

3 tablespoons coarse sanding sugar

1. Set the oven rack in the middle position. Preheat the oven to 350°F. Cover the bottom and sides of a 9 by 13 by 2-inch metal pan with aluminum foil, shiny side up. Coat the foil with butter or vegetable oil spray.

2. Put the raisins in a small bowl. Add the flour to a large bowl. Remove 1 tablespoon of the flour, and add it to the raisins. Stir the raisins and flour together until the raisins are coated with the flour. Add the baking soda, salt, ginger, cinnamon, and cloves to the larger bowl containing the remaining flour and whisk to combine. Set aside.

3. In the bowl of a stand mixer fitted with the paddle attachment, cream the granulated sugar and butter. Add the molasses and beat to combine. Add the eggs, and continue to mix until incorporated. Add the sifted dry ingredients alternately with the buttermilk and continue to beat. Add the ginger jam or orange marmalade and mix in. Fold in the raisins and spoon the batter into the prepared pan. Sprinkle coarse sanding sugar evenly over the top of the cake.

4. Bake for 35 minutes or until a metal tester inserted into the center comes out clean. Transfer the pan to a wire rack, and allow to cool for 30 minutes. When cool, remove the gingerbread from the pan. Remove the foil and cut the gingerbread into squares. Serve with sweetened, lightly whipped cream. Store any leftover gingerbread, covered with paper towels and wrapped in wax paper, at room temperature.

SWEET TIP: Apricot jam can be substituted for the ginger jam or orange marmalade.

Yield: one 9 by 13 by 2-inch cake; twelve 3-inch squares;

Passover Sponge Cake

This came to us written in the Palmer Method, on a lined recipe card. Most Passover sponge cakes we've baked are made with cake meal, which is made from pulverized baked matzo, and they are leavened with egg whites. This sponge cake also uses egg whites for leavening, but uses potato starch instead of the cake meal. Since potato starch is available year round, this sponge cake can be enjoyed anytime, and since this cake uses no flour, it is gluten-free.

CAKE

7 eggs

⅛ teaspoon salt

¼ cup water

1¼ cups granulated sugar

Grated zest of 1 large lemon

1 tablespoon lemon juice

1 cup minus 1 tablespoon potato starch

TOPPING

2 tablespoons confectioners' sugar
   (kosher for Passover, optional)

1. Set the oven rack in the middle position. Preheat the oven to 350°F. Cut a parchment paper or wax paper liner to fit the bottom of an 8-inch tube pan. Insert the liner.

2. Separate 5 eggs, adding the whites to the bowl of a stand mixer fitted with the whisk attachment. Place the yolks in a separate bowl and set aside. Add the salt to the whites and whisk until stiff peaks form. If you don't have a second mixer bowl, transfer the beaten whites to a separate bowl and set aside.

3. Add the remaining 5 yolks, 2 whole eggs, and the water to the bowl of the stand mixer fitted with the paddle attachment and beat on high speed for 5 minutes. Add the granulated sugar, lemon zest, and lemon juice and beat again on high speed for 5 minutes. Remove the bowl from the mixer and, using a sieve, gradually sift the potato starch into the batter, gently folding it in. Fold in the beaten egg whites in thirds until well distributed.

4. Pour the batter into the prepared tube pan. Do *not* bang the pan to remove air bubbles; the bubbles are necessary for the cake to rise. Bake the cake for 50 minutes, or until a metal tester inserted into the center comes out clean. Cool the cake in the pan on a wire rack for 20 minutes. Run a butter knife gently around the edges and tube of the pan and invert the cake onto a second rack. Remove the parchment paper liner. Turn the cake right side up and allow to cool completely. Sift the top of the cake with confectioners' sugar. Store the cake, loosely covered with wax paper, at room temperature.

Yield: one 8-inch tube cake; 12 slices

SWEET TIP: The cake may be sliced into three layers with a serrated knife, layered with raspberry jam, topped with confectioners' sugar, and served with whipped cream as a Victoria sponge.

• A tablespoon of vanilla can be substituted for the lemon zest and lemon juice.

• Passover Sponge Cake can be split in half horizontally, filled with lemon curd, put together, and dusted with confectioners' sugar.

• Always refrigerate cake when filled with lemon curd.

Peanut Butter "Hermits"

This treat came from a simple handwritten recipe we found in a copy of Lebanon Valley Cookery. *We think the recipe is from the 1920s or 1930s. It has only four ingredients, and it contains no eggs or butter. These are more cookies than hermits. The peanut butter flavor is subtle, but evident. The cookies will crisp up after they cool. They taste even better the next day because the peanut butter flavor really comes through, and the cookies have a nice snap to them. We used red-skinned peanuts to garnish them, but regular salted peanuts are fine.*

COOKIES

¾ cup graham cracker or chocolate graham
    cracker crumbs
¼ teaspoon salt
1 cup sweetened condensed milk
⅓ cup smooth or chunky peanut butter

TOPPING

36 salted red-skinned peanuts, toasted

1. Set the oven rack in the middle position. Preheat the oven to 350°F. Line a 14 by 16-inch baking sheet with a silicone liner or aluminum foil, shiny side up. Coat the foil with vegetable oil spray.

2. To make the cookies: Add the graham cracker crumbs and salt to a mixing bowl and whisk to combine. Add the sweetened condensed milk and whisk into the crumbs and salt. Add the peanut butter and whisk to combine. The batter will be loose.

3. Using a disposable plastic piping bag with a small opening cut off, pipe the cookies, 2 inches apart, on the prepared baking sheet. Do not place more than 12 cookies on a sheet. The piped cookies should be 1¾ inches in diameter before baking. Place 1 peanut in the center of each cookie. Bake

for 13 minutes, or until lightly brown around the edges. Transfer the baking sheet to a wire rack and let cool for 5 minutes. Remove the cooled cookies with a metal spatula and transfer to another rack. The cookies will firm up as they cool. Store the cookies, between sheets of wax paper, in a covered tin.

*Yield: 3 dozen crisp,
round, waferlike cookies*

SWEET TIPS: We used one package of 9 double graham crackers to make our graham cracker crumbs, saving any extra crumbs for piecrusts.
• Coat measuring cups used for condensed milk and peanut butter with vegetable oil spray for ease in removing the contents.
• A small food storage plastic bag with one end snipped off can be substituted for a disposable piping bag.

7 Teatimes and Coffee Hours

THE RECIPES

*T*here has always been a need to connect socially with others. Whether it's bridge with the girls, a tea to honor an old friend, or attending a coffee klatch to meet a political candidate, tea and coffee have always brought people together.

We learn from history that both tea and coffee were once exotic and expensive, and were often kept under lock and key. They were first enjoyed publicly more than two hundred years ago in the atmosphere of the tea shop and the coffeehouse, both of which institutions still exist today.

Although taking tea or drinking coffee can be informal, it is reassuring to know that these occasions can also be elegant. When served with sweet accompaniments and fine china, teatime becomes formal. Coffee, served with frothy warmed milk or crested with whipped cream, when served in a dimly lit atmosphere similar to that of an old world coffeehouse, becomes an experience.

Tea and coffee can be taken by one, shared by two, or served to several. It's not just the tea or coffee we find ourselves drinking, it is the ritual of partaking and sharing them with others.

We find ourselves lingering over a tea tray, multitiered and full of choices.

We like our accompaniments for tea to be sweet and diminutive—a thin slice of Pumpkin Tea Cake with Toasted Walnut Brown Sugar Topping, a morsel of Lemon Drizzle Cake. Bars and cookies should be served in miniature, an Evelyn's Strawberry Blondie, small enough to consume in two bites or a tiny Big Mama's Lemon-Lime Tassie, so delicate and delicious that it becomes a memorable mouthful. Plates should be large enough to support a portable sampling of teatime offerings, but small enough to manage if there is not ample seating.

Because we like to think of coffee as a robust drink, its accompaniments can be served in larger portions. Coffee drinkers like to sit when they sip, and so generous slices of Irish Sweet Bread with Bourbon Glaze or Ukrainian Prune and Walnut Cake can be enjoyed for themselves and not as finger food. Tutti Frutti Biscotti, Almond Jam Clothespin Cookies, and *Alfajores* filled with guava jam can mingle on the coffee drinker's plate of sweets, not in competition, but in refreshing harmony.

We salute the diversity of the sweet accompaniments we serve when we meet for tea or coffee, but we also celebrate the comfort and friendship we experience by lifting our cups together.

Quick Tips

- Warm the pot before brewing tea, and allow tea to steep for the correct amount of time.
- A plate of thinly sliced lemon and a pitcher of milk are good teatime accompaniments.
- When taking tea, cakes, cookies, and bars should be served in finger-size pieces.
- Serving a variety of teas and coffees, together with both granulated and cube sugars, enhances the experience of teatimes and coffee hours.

Big Mama's Lemon-Lime Tassies

We received this very old Southern recipe in an e-mail from Amy Geer. Big Mama was Ethel Johnson Geer from Ashburn, Georgia, and she was married to Amy's grandfather Judge William I. Geer. The couple resided in Colquitt, Georgia. Most recipes for Lemon Tassies use a dough made with cream cheese, but we decided to use Sheila's Perfect Piecrust. These dear little "tarts" are made in tiny muffin pans and are a delicious mouthful.

LEMON-LIME CURD

1 whole egg

4 egg yolks

¾ cup sugar

Pinch of salt

1 teaspoon grated lemon zest

1 teaspoon grated lime zest

¼ cup lemon juice

¼ cup lime juice

¼ cup (½ stick) cold unsalted butter, cut into
  large dice

PASTRY

1¼ cups flour

1½ tablespoons sugar

⅛ teaspoon salt

½ cup (1 stick) cold unsalted butter,
  cut into ½-inch dice

2 tablespoons ice water

1. To make the curd: Whisk the whole egg and egg yolks in a 6-cup heavy-bottomed saucepan. Add the sugar, salt, lemon zest, and lime zest and whisk to combine. Whisk in the lemon and lime juices. Add the butter and whisk over medium heat until the butter has melted. Switch to a wooden spoon and continue to cook, stirring, until the curd thickens, about 5 minutes. If you prefer a smooth curd, strain it to remove the lemon and lime zests. Press plastic wrap directly on the surface of the curd to prevent a skin from forming. Let the curd cool completely, and keep refrigerated.

2. To make the pastry: Put the flour, sugar, and salt in the bowl of a food processor fitted with the metal blade and pulse three times to mix. Add the butter and pulse until crumbly. Add the ice water and pulse until the mixture comes together.

3. Remove the dough from the bowl of the processor and shape it into a disk. Unless your kitchen is very warm, you don't have to chill the dough before rolling it out.

4. Set the oven rack in the middle position. Preheat the oven to 400°F. Have ready two ungreased 12-cup or one 24-cup miniature muffin pan(s).

5. Roll out the dough to a thickness of ⅛ inch between two sheets of lightly floured wax paper. Using either a 2½-inch round or scalloped cookie cutter dipped in flour, cut out rounds of the dough. Place the rounds in the muffin pans, and gently press down and around the dough with your finger to fit the tassies into the muffin cups. Chill for 30 minutes in the refrigerator. Bake the tassie shells for 10 to 12 minutes. Remove the pan from the oven, and transfer to a wire rack to cool completely.

6. Remove the cooled tassie shells from the pan(s) and place on a platter. Fill with the lemon-lime curd. Place the filled tassies in the refrigerator until ready to serve. Just before serving, pipe a tiny swirl of whipped cream on top of each tassie. *Do not leave tassies out at room temperature for long periods of time.* Store any leftover tassies in the refrigerator.

Yield: 2 dozen tiny tassies; about 1½ cups lemon-lime curd

Almond Jam Clothespin Cookies

We love these cookies! Marilynn says they bring back childhood memories of those inexpensive Danish cookies that came in a tin and were so good with a cup of tea on a cold winter afternoon. She still remembers those sparkling little gems with their chewy jam centers, in their crisp white paper cups, sitting on a plate in our kitchen in Winthrop. The cookies can be rolled either in chopped almonds or sweetened shredded coconut after forming into balls. These cookies are called Clothespin Cookies because home bakers often used a clothespin to make the indentation for the jam in the balls of dough.

2½ cups flour

½ teaspoon salt

1 cup (2 sticks) unsalted butter, at room
    temperature

¾ cup sugar

2 egg yolks

1 teaspoon vanilla extract

2 egg whites, beaten

1 cup almonds, toasted and coarsely chopped,
    or 1 cup sweetened shredded coconut

½ cup seedless raspberry jam

1. Set the oven rack in the middle position. Preheat the oven to 350°F. Line a 14- by 16-inch baking sheet with a silicone liner or aluminum foil, shiny side up. Coat the foil with vegetable oil spray.

2. Add the flour and salt to a bowl and whisk to combine. Set aside.

3. Add the butter and sugar to the bowl of a stand mixer fitted with the paddle attachment and cream until combined. Add the egg yolks to the creamed mixture one at a time, and beat until combined. Add the vanilla and beat in. Add the dry ingredients to the creamed mixture gradually until well blended. Turn off the mixer, remove the dough

from the bowl, wrap the dough in plastic wrap, and chill in the refrigerator for 2 hours, or until firm enough to handle.

4. Remove the dough from the refrigerator and, using floured hands or wearing disposable gloves, form 1-inch balls. Dip the balls in the beaten egg whites and roll in the chopped almonds or coconut. Continue until all the dough is rolled into balls. Make an indentation in the balls with your thumb, and fill the indentations with ¼ teaspoon of jam. *Do not fill the indentations with too much jam.* Place the clothespin cookies on the prepared baking sheet, spaced at least 1½ inches apart, or 12 cookies per sheet, to allow for spreading. Bake for 25 minutes; the cookies will be a light brown. Slide the foil or the silicone liner with the baked cookies onto a wire rack to cool. Remove the cooled cookies with a metal spatula and transfer to a second wire rack. Store the cookies, between sheets of wax paper, in a covered tin.

Yield: 3½ dozen cookies

SWEET TIP: A disposable piping bag or a plastic bag with a corner snipped can be used to add jam to the cookies.

SWEET TOUCH: We used raspberry jam, but strawberry or apricot jam will do.

Big Mama's Lemon Lime Tassies and Almond
Jam Clothespin Cookies

Evelyn's Strawberry Blondies

Evelyn's Strawberry Blondies

We received a master recipe for Evelyn Cardozo's Blondies from her daughters, Maria and Carol. We found her recipe lends itself to wonderful adaptations such as this one for Strawberry Blondies. Maria and Carol grew up in Cambridge, Massachusetts, and joyfully recall family gatherings in the garden with their parents. Maria and Carol gifted us with their mother's mixing bowl, and we continue to use it lovingly.

2 ¾ cups flour

2 ½ teaspoons baking powder

½ teaspoon salt

1 cup (2 sticks) unsalted butter, at room temperature

2 ½ cups sugar

3 eggs

1 teaspoon lemon extract

5 ½ ounces (half of an 11-ounce bag) white chocolate chips

¾ cup strawberry jam

1. Set the oven rack in the middle position. Pre- heat the oven to 350°F. Cover the bottom and sides of an 11 by 17 by 1-inch metal jelly roll pan with aluminum foil, shiny side up. Run the foil over the edges of the pan. Coat the foil with butter or vegetable oil spray

2. Add the flour, baking powder, and salt to a mixing bowl and whisk to combine. Add the butter and sugar to the bowl of a stand mixer fitted with the paddle attachment and cream until combined. Add the eggs one at a time, beating well after each addition. Add the lemon extract and beat in. Add the dry ingredients in three additions, beating until incorporated. Remove the bowl from the stand and fold the white chocolate chips into the batter.

3. Turn the batter into the prepared pan and distribute evenly, smoothing the top with an offset spatula. Add the strawberry jam by spoonfuls evenly spaced over the top of the batter. Using a spoon, swirl the jam through the batter. Smooth the top again with an offset spatula, dipping the spatula in warm water if necessary. Bake the blondies for 40 minutes, or until the top seems firm and a metal tester inserted into the center comes out clean. The blondies will firm up when cooled.

4. Transfer the pan to a wire rack and allow to cool. Flip the bars from the pan in one piece and place on a cutting board or on a rimless metal cookie sheet. Remove the foil and flip onto another cutting board. Cut into 2-inch squares with a wide-bladed knife. Store the bars, between sheets of wax paper, in a covered tin. The blondies can be successfully frozen, brought to room temperature, and served at a later date.

Yield: about forty 2-inch squares

SWEET TIP: Coat the offset spatula and wide-bladed knife with vegetable oil spray before using.

Edna's Feather Gingerbread

This recipe from the 1930s is a special quick bread. The texture is dense, spicy, and satisfying. The flavor intensifies on standing. This recipe makes two loaves, one to serve and one to give away.

GINGERBREAD

3 cups cake flour

2 teaspoons baking soda

⅛ teaspoon salt

¼ teaspoon finely ground black pepper

½ teaspoon ginger

½ teaspoon cinnamon

½ teaspoon cloves

½ cup (1 stick) unsalted butter, at room temperature

1 cup granulated sugar

1 cup molasses

2 eggs

1 teaspoon vanilla extract

1 cup boiling water

VANILLA GLAZE

1 cup confectioners' sugar

Pinch of salt

¼ teaspoon vanilla extract

2 tablespoons water, plus more if needed

1. Set the oven rack in the middle position. Preheat the oven to 350°F. Coat two 9 by 5 by 3-inch loaf pans with vegetable oil spray. Cover the bottom and ends of each pan with a single strip of wax paper. Coat the wax paper liners with vegetable oil spray. Dust the pans with flour and tap the pans to remove the excess flour.

2. To make the gingerbread: Add the flour, baking soda, salt, pepper, ginger, cinnamon, and cloves to a bowl and whisk to combine. Set aside.

3. In the bowl of a stand mixer fitted with the paddle attachment, cream the butter and granulated sugar. Add the molasses and combine. Add the eggs and vanilla and beat until the mixture is smooth.

4. Add the dry ingredients to the creamed mixture in three additions, and continue to beat until all the ingredients are combined. Add the boiling water and continue beating until incorporated. Pour the batter into the prepared pans and place in the oven. Bake for 45 to 50 minutes, or until a metal tester inserted into the center of each loaf comes out clean. Remove the gingerbread from the oven and transfer to a wire rack to cool. After 20 minutes, invert the loaves onto the rack, remove from the pans, and remove the wax paper strips.

5. To make the vanilla glaze: Sift the confectioners' sugar and salt into a small bowl. Add the vanilla and water and whisk to combine. Add additional water to the glaze if needed, one teaspoon at a time, to achieve the desired consistency.

6. When the gingerbread is completely cool, brush each loaf with the vanilla glaze.

7. When the glaze has set, store the gingerbreads, loosely covered with wax paper, at room temperature or in the refrigerator. Insert six toothpicks evenly spaced on top of the gingerbreads to prevent the wax paper from sticking to the glaze.

Yield: 2 loaves; 10 to 12 slices per loaf

SWEET TOUCHES: For Raisin Gingerbread, add 1 tablespoon of the flour to 1 cup raisins and fold into the batter.

• For Double Ginger Gingerbread, add 2 tablespoons finely chopped candied ginger.

Irish Sweet Bread with Bourbon Glaze

We found this recipe that had been handwritten by Marilynn on a narrow scrap of paper forty years ago. It's not an Irish Soda Bread, but more of a tea or sweet bread, something like the Bram Brack that Irish bakers make on Halloween. It's studded with candied cherries, candied pineapple, ginger, and rich meaty walnuts. This is a substantial sweet bread with an assertive bourbon glaze.

BREAD

½ cup candied cherries, cut into ¼-inch dice

1 cup candied pineapple, cut into ¼-inch dice

¼ cup candied ginger, cut into ¼-inch dice

1 cup walnuts, toasted and coarsely chopped

3 cups flour

1½ teaspoons salt

¾ teaspoon baking soda

½ teaspoon ground ginger

1 teaspoon mace

1 cup (2 sticks) unsalted butter, at room temperature

½ cup granulated sugar

2 eggs

¼ cup molasses

1 teaspoon vanilla extract

1½ cups buttermilk

GLAZE

¾ cup confectioners' sugar

Pinch of salt

2 tablespoons bourbon

1. Set the oven rack in the middle position. Preheat the oven to 350°F. Coat a 9-inch metal springform pan with vegetable oil spray. Line the bottom of the pan with parchment paper or wax paper cut to fit.

2. To make the bread: Put the chopped candied cherries in a small bowl and set aside. Add the remaining chopped candied fruit and walnuts to another small bowl and set aside. Put the flour in a large bowl. Remove 1 tablespoon of the flour and add to the candied cherries. Mix to coat the cherries with the flour. Transfer the cherries to a wire strainer over the bowl containing the flour. Strain the excess flour from the cherries back into the larger bowl of flour. Set the floured cherries aside. Add the salt, baking soda, ground ginger, and mace to the flour and whisk to combine. Set aside.

3. Add the butter and granulated sugar to the bowl of a stand mixer fitted with the paddle attachment and cream until combined. Add the eggs one at time, beating well after each addition. Add the molasses and combine. Add the vanilla to the buttermilk in a glass measuring cup and mix to combine.

4. Add the dry ingredients and the buttermilk mixture alternately in three additions to the creamed mixture, beating after each addition. Turn off the mixer and remove the bowl and fold in the floured cherries. Fold in the remaining fruits and nuts. Transfer the batter to the prepared pan, cut three slashes on top of the dough, and place in the oven. Bake for 65 minutes, or until a metal tester inserted into the center comes out clean. Transfer the bread to a wire rack and cool for 20 minutes. Gently go around the edges of the pan with a butter knife to loosen the bread. Remove the sides from the pan, and carefully slide the bread from the bottom of the pan. Remove the parchment or wax paper from the bottom of the bread. Allow the bread to cool completely on the wire rack.

5. To make the glaze: Sift the confectioners' sugar and salt through a strainer into a small bowl.

Add the bourbon, 1 tablespoon at a time, until the desired consistency is achieved. Add more bourbon, 1 teaspoon at a time, if the glaze is too thick. Slip a sheet of wax paper under the wire rack to catch drips. Brush any crumbs from the sides and top of the bread with a pastry brush. Using a teaspoon or fork, drizzle the glaze over the top of the bread. Store the bread, loosely covered with wax paper, at room temperature.

Yield: one 9-inch cake; 14 to 16 slices

SWEET TIP: Since the flavor of the bourbon in the glaze is strong, lemon juice can be substituted in the glaze if desired.

• Fruits and nuts are sometimes lightly coated with flour to prevent them from falling to the bottom of a cake or bread as it bakes. Since the candied pineapple and ginger are heavily coated with sugar, coating them with flour isn't necessary because the flour wouldn't adhere to them.

Lemon Drizzle Tea Cake

We first tasted a Lemon Drizzle Cake when we met with our editor, Valerie Lewis, at the office of Miller's Publications in Kent, England. One of the staff baked a lemon cake with a lovely lemon glaze for us to have with our tea. This handwritten recipe from the 1960s came from Arline Ryan, whose recipe files we acquired a few years ago. We turned what was a recipe for a Lemon Tea Bread into a Lemon Tea Cake topped with a light lemon and sugar drizzle. One thing you must remember: Once the cake has been in the oven for 45 minutes, begin to make the topping.

TEA CAKE

1½ cups flour

1 teaspoon baking powder

1 teaspoon salt

⅛ teaspoon cloves

½ cup (1 stick) unsalted butter, melted

1 cup sugar

2 eggs, beaten

Grated zest of 1 large lemon (about 2 tablespoons zest)

½ cup milk

½ cup walnuts, toasted and coarsely chopped

LEMON DRIZZLE TOPPING

Juice of 1 large lemon

⅓ cup sugar

1. Set the oven rack in the middle position. Preheat the oven to 350°F. Coat a 9 by 5 by 3-inch loaf pan with vegetable oil spray. Cover the bottom and ends of the pan with a single strip of wax paper. Coat the wax paper liner with vegetable oil spray. Dust the pan with flour and tap the pan to remove the excess flour.

2. To make the tea cake: Sift the flour, baking powder, salt, and cloves into a bowl and whisk to combine. Set aside.

3. Add the butter and sugar to the bowl of a stand mixer fitted with the paddle attachment and beat to combine. With the mixer running, add the eggs one at a time, beating well after each addition. Add the lemon zest and beat in.

4. Add the sifted dry ingredients and milk alternately to the creamed mixture until all of the ingredients have been added, beating well after each addition. Add the walnuts and beat in just until evenly distributed. Pour the batter into the prepared pan and tap gently to remove any air bubbles.

5. Bake the cake for 55 minutes, or until a metal tester inserted into the center comes out clean.

6. Once the cake has been in the oven for 45 minutes, begin to make the topping: *Keep a large bowl filled with cold water and ice cubes at hand when making the sugar syrup for safety.* Add the lemon juice and sugar to a heavy-bottomed metal saucepan and stir with a wooden spoon to combine. Continue to cook, stirring, over medium heat until the topping begins to boil. Boil for 1 minute, stirring continuously, or until slightly thickened. Set the topping aside; it will continue to thicken as it stands.

7. After removing the tea cake from the oven, transfer it to a wire rack. Poke holes in the cake with a cake tester and, while still hot, spoon the topping over the hot cake. Continue until all of the topping has been used, spreading with an offset spatula until it is evenly distributed over the top of the tea cake.

8. Allow the cake to cool for 15 minutes on a wire rack. Use a smooth butter knife to loosen the

cake from the edges of the pan. The cake will pull away from sides. When completely cool, remove the cake by lifting it by the ends of the wax paper lining. Place the cake back on the wire rack and peel off the wax paper. Cut the cooled cake with a wide-bladed serrated knife. Store any leftover tea cake, wrapped in wax paper, at room temperature. Lemon Drizzle Tea Cake can be frozen and re-heated for a few minutes in a 300°F oven before serving.

Yield: 1 loaf; 12 slices

SWEET TIP: There will be a very small amount of the Lemon Drizzle Topping, but it will be enough to add another layer of tartness to the tea cake.

SWEET TOUCH: Since serving whipped cream never subtracts from the pleasure of something baked, we recommend its addition, but we also believe that a bit of lemon gelato on the side of this Lemon Drizzle Tea Cake wouldn't be in excess.

• Lemon Drizzle Cake can be decorated with half slices of lemon dipped in clear coarse sanding sugar.

Lemon Drizzle Tea Cake

Maria's Alfajores
(South American Jam-Filled Cookies)

A cross between linzer torte cookies and shortbread, this recipe for Alfajores *came to us from Maria Orlich O'Brien, the sister-in-law of our friend George Geuras. Maria came to this country from Costa Rica, where she owned a bakery. These cookies are fun to bake and have a good texture. They're flaky and crisp, and and are lightly brown when baked. We used guava jam or* dulce de leche *when we baked them, but use any jam you prefer.*

COOKIES

1½ cups flour

2 cups cornstarch

½ teaspoon salt

½ teaspoon baking powder

1 cup (2 sticks) unsalted butter, at room
    temperature

1 cup granulated sugar

2 eggs

2 tablespoons rum or rum extract

1 teaspoon vanilla extract

FILLING

One 8-ounce can *dulce de leche* or 1 cup
    guava jam

TOPPING AND GARNISH

Sweetened shredded coconut, toasted

¼ cup confectioners' sugar (optional)

1. Set the oven rack in the middle position. Preheat the oven to 300°F. Line a 14 by 16-inch baking sheet with a silicone liner or aluminum foil, shiny side up. Coat the foil with vegetable oil spray.

2. To make the cookies: Add the flour, cornstarch, salt, and baking powder to a bowl and whisk to combine. Set aside.

3. Add the butter and granulated sugar to the bowl of a stand mixer fitted with the paddle attachment and cream until combined. Add the eggs one at a time, and continue beating. Add the rum and vanilla and beat until combined. Add the dry ingredients to the creamed mixture in two additions and beat until thoroughly incorporated and the dough has come together.

4. Turn off the mixer. Using a spatula, remove the dough from the bowl and transfer to a plastic food storage bag. Pat or roll out the dough flat in the bag to hasten the chilling. Place the bag in the freezer for 1 hour to chill.

5. Remove the chilled dough from the plastic bag. Place the dough on a sheet of wax paper and divide it into four equal portions. Lightly dust each portion with flour and form into four individual balls.

6. Place the first ball of dough on a lightly floured sheet of wax paper. Place the rest of the dough in the plastic bag and return it to the refrigerator until ready to use.

7. Sprinkle the dough with a small amount of flour. Cover with another sheet of wax paper and roll out into a circle or a rectangle ¼ inch thick. Remove the top sheet of wax paper. Using a 2-inch round cookie cutter, dipped in flour each time, cut out the cookies. Dust the dough with a small amount of additional flour if necessary. Place no more than 12 cookies on a baking sheet. Using a pastry brush, remove any excess flour from the cookies. Bake the cookies for 20 minutes, or until *lightly* browned. Slide the foil or the silicone liner with the baked cookies onto a wire rack to cool. Remove the cooled cookies with a metal spatula and transfer to a *second* wire rack.

8. Place the cooled cookies from the second

rack on a sheet of wax paper on the first wire rack. Spread the bottoms of half of the cookies with the *dulce de leche* or guava jam. Place the bottom of another cookie on top of the filling and press gently to make a cookie sandwich, allowing some of the filling to squeeze out from the sides. Roll the edges of the filled cookies in the coconut. Dust the top of the cookie sandwiches with confectioners' sugar, if desired. The cookies can be stored, in a covered metal container, for up to 2 days.

Yield: 30 cookie sandwiches

SWEET TOUCH: Raspberry or apricot jam can be substituted for the *dulce de leche* or guava jam.
• *Alfajores* are good simply dusted with sifted confectioners' sugar on the tops.

Mary Frances's Brown Sugar Tea Cake

This tea cake came from the recipe file of Gertrude Smith, the mother of our good friend Ronn Smith. It is a delightful little tea cake, unpretentious and simple to make. We enjoy it with a cup of strong Irish breakfast tea. This is a good recipe to make with supervised young bakers because it teaches them how to prepare pans, measure ingredients, and put together a recipe.

TEA CAKES

2½ cups flour

3½ teaspoons baking powder

1 teaspoon salt

1 teaspoon nutmeg

⅔ cup (10⅔ tablespoons) unsalted butter,
    at room temperature

1⅔ cups firmly packed brown sugar

3 eggs

2 teaspoons vanilla extract

1¼ cups milk

TOPPING

Confectioners' sugar (optional)

1. To make the tea cakes: Set the oven rack in the middle position. Preheat the oven to 350°F. Coat two 9 by 5 by 3-inch loaf pans with vegetable oil spray. Cover the bottom and ends of each pan with a single strip of wax paper. Coat the wax paper liners with vegetable oil spray. Dust the pans with flour and tap the pans to remove the excess flour.

2. Add the flour, baking powder, salt, and nutmeg to a bowl and whisk together. Set aside.

3. Cream together the butter and brown sugar in the bowl of a stand mixer fitted with the paddle attachment. With the mixer running, add the eggs one at a time.

4. Add the vanilla to the milk in a glass measuring cup and set aside. Add the dry ingredients and the milk-and-vanilla mixture alternately to the creamed mixture until all of the ingredients have been incorporated. Pour the batter into the prepared pans and tap gently to remove any air bubbles. Bake the tea cakes for 40 to 45 minutes, or until the cakes pulls away from the sides of the pans and a metal cake tester inserted into the center of each cake comes out clean.

5. Transfer the pans to a wire rack and cool for 15 minutes. Run a smooth butter knife around the edges. Turn out the cakes onto a second wire rack, remove the wax paper, and allow to cool completely. The tea cakes can be sprinkled with sifted confectioners' sugar before serving, if desired. Cut the cooled cakes with a wide-bladed serrated knife. Store any leftover tea cakes, loosely covered with wax paper, in the refrigerator. Bring the tea cakes to room temperature before serving. Mary Frances's Brown Sugar Tea Cake can be frozen, defrosted, and reheated for a few minutes in a 300°F oven before serving.

Yield: 2 tea cakes; 12 slices per cake

SWEET TOUCH: Serve with whipped cream or vanilla ice cream.

Pumpkin Tea Cake with Toasted Walnut Brown Sugar Topping

This recipe from the 1920s makes a delicious tea cake with a fine crumb. Cake flour was introduced as early as 1895. This recipe originally called for sifting the flour twice before and after measuring. We whisk instead of sift because modern cake flour is lighter and more delicate.

TEA CAKES

2½ cups cake flour

4 teaspoons baking powder

1 teaspoon salt

¼ teaspoon cloves

¾ teaspoon ground ginger

1 teaspoon cinnamon

⅔ cup (10⅔ tablespoons) unsalted butter, at room temperature

1½ cups granulated sugar

2 large eggs

1 cup canned pure pumpkin puree (see sidebar, page 37)

1 teaspoon vanilla extract

¾ cup milk

TOPPING

¼ cup plus 2 tablespoons firmly packed brown sugar

¼ cup plus 2 tablespoons toasted walnuts, coarsely chopped

1. To make the tea cakes: Set the oven rack in the middle position. Preheat the oven to 350°F. Coat two 9 by 5 by 3-inch loaf pans with vegetable oil spray. Cover the bottom and ends of each pan with a single strip of wax paper. Coat the wax paper liners with vegetable oil spray. Dust the pans with flour and tap the pans to remove the excess flour.

2. Add the cake flour to a bowl. Add the baking powder, salt, cloves, ground ginger, and cinnamon to flour and whisk together until well blended. Set aside.

3. Cream the butter and granulated sugar in the bowl of a stand mixer fitted with the paddle attachment. With the mixer running, add the the eggs one at a time, and beat after each addition. Add the pumpkin puree and beat to incorporate.

4. Add the vanilla to the milk in a glass measuring cup. Add the dry ingredients and the milk-and-vanilla mixture alternately to the creamed mixture until all of the ingredients have been added. Pour the batter into the prepared pans and tap gently to remove any air bubbles.

5. To make the topping: Pulse the brown sugar and nuts in the bowl of a food processor fitted with the metal blade to make a finely ground mixture. Scatter the mixture over the tops of the cakes and press down gently on the topping with the palm of your hand. Bake the cakes for 45 minutes, or until the cakes pull away from sides of pans and a metal tester inserted into each cake comes out clean.

6. Transfer the pans to a wire rack and let cool for 15 minutes. Run a smooth butter knife around the edges. Turn out the cakes on one side onto the rack, carefully remove the wax paper, turn right side up, and allow to cool completely. The topping is fragile and might crack if the cakes are turned on their tops. Cut the cooled cakes with wide-bladed serrated knife. Store any leftover cake, loosely covered with wax paper, in the refrigerator. Let the cake come to room temperature before serving. The cakes can be frozen and reheated for a few minutes in a 300°F oven before serving.

Yield: 2 tea cakes; 12 slices per cake

Soft Molasses Cookies

We found several recipes for soft molasses cookies in our collection of manuscript cookbooks. Credit for this recipe goes to Julia Greevsky, and P. Finelli, a home baker from the 1930s. These are chewy, spicy cookies, great with a glass of cold milk or a cup of Earl Grey tea. We used mace, but you can substitute nutmeg or ginger.

1 tablespoon instant coffee or instant espresso

¼ cup cold water

2¼ cups flour

1 teaspoon baking soda

½ teaspoon salt

¾ teaspoon cinnamon

½ teaspoon mace

¼ teaspoon cloves

½ cup vegetable oil

¼ cup molasses

¾ cup sugar

1 egg

1¼ cups raisins

¾ cup walnuts, toasted and coarsely chopped

1. Set the oven rack in the middle position. Preheat the oven to 350°F. Line a 14 by 16-inch baking sheet with a silicone liner or aluminum foil, shiny side up. Coat the foil with vegetable oil spray.

2. Add the instant coffee or instant espresso to the cold water and whisk to dissolve. Set aside.

3. Add the flour, baking soda, salt, cinnamon, mace, and cloves to a bowl and whisk to combine. Set aside.

4. Add the oil, molasses, sugar, and dissolved coffee to the bowl of a stand mixer fitted with the paddle attachment and combine thoroughly. Add the egg and continue to blend. Add the dry ingredients to the wet ingredients in two additions, and combine. Unplug the mixer, remove the bowl from the stand, and fold in the raisins and walnuts.

5. Drop the cookie dough by heaping teaspoonful onto the prepared sheet, about 2 inches apart or 12 cookies per sheet. Bake for 10 minutes. The cookies will still be a bit soft. Remove the baking sheet from the oven and slide the foil or the silicone liner with the baked cookies onto a wire rack to cool. Remove the cooled cookies with a metal spatula and transfer to second wire rack. Store the cooled cookies, between sheets of wax paper, in covered tin. Do not crowd the cookies.

Yield: about 4 dozen cookies

SWEET TIP: We used golden raisins or sultanas in our Soft Molasses Cookies, but you can use any raisins you want.

Tutti Frutti Biscotti

This recipe for Tutti Frutti Biscotti is an adaptation or alias of one of our other biscotti recipes. Tutti Frutti Biscotti are a little bit like the biscotti found in the glass-fronted cases of the pastry shops of Boston's Italian North End. We suggest that you make this confection with candied cherries, candied pineapple, and golden raisins, either dried or plumped. To achieve the desired texture, do not chop the candied fruit and walnuts too finely. These crisp biscotti should be dipped in coffee or tea for the real North End experience.

1 cup candied fruit, coarsely chopped

½ cup large golden raisins, dried or plumped

1 cup walnuts, toasted and coarsely chopped

2½ cups flour

1 teaspoon baking powder

½ teaspoon salt

1 teaspoon cinnamon

½ teaspoon nutmeg

½ teaspoon ground ginger

¼ teaspoon cloves

1 cup sugar

¾ cup light or mild olive oil

3 eggs

1 tablespoon rum or one teaspoon rum extract

1. Set the oven rack in the middle position. Preheat the oven to 350°F. Line a 14 by 16-inch baking sheet with a silicone liner or aluminum foil, shiny side up. Coat the foil with vegetable oil spray.

2. Add the candied fruit, raisins, and walnuts to a small bowl and set aside. Add the flour to a larger bowl, remove 2 tablespoons, and mix with the candied fruit, raisins, and walnuts in the small bowl. Add the baking powder, salt, cinnamon, nutmeg, ground ginger, and cloves to the remaining flour in the larger bowl and whisk to combine.

3. Add the sugar and oil to the bowl of a stand mixer fitted with the paddle attachment and beat to combine. Add the eggs and rum or rum extract and continue beating until thoroughly mixed. Add the dry ingredients in three additions to the creamed mixture until all of the dry ingredients are incorporated and the dough has come together. Add the floured candied fruit, raisins, and walnuts and continue beating slowly to combine; the dough will be soft. Place the dough in a covered freezer-proof container or in a sealed plastic bag, and place in the freezer for at least 1 hour, or until the dough has firmed up.

4. Remove the dough from the freezer and, using a spatula, divide the dough in half on a silicone-lined baking sheet. Shape the dough into 2 loaves, measuring 12½ inches long by 3 inches wide and about ½ inch high. Dip your hands in water, or wear disposable gloves, when forming the loaves.

5. Place the baking sheet in the oven and bake the biscotti loaves for 30 minutes, or until the loaves are golden brown and a metal tester inserted into loaves comes out clean. The loaves will spread. Transfer the baking sheet to a wire rack and allow to cool for 10 minutes. Transfer one loaf at a time from the baking sheet to a cutting board. Using a long serrated knife, cut each loaf into diagonal slices about ½ inch thick. Trim any fruit or raisins sticking out of the slices. Place the slices, cut side down, on the same baking sheet and return to the oven for 10 minutes. Remove the baking sheet from the oven, turn the biscotti over (the second side will be up), and return to the oven for another 10 minutes. Slide the foil or the silicone liner with the baked cookies onto a wire rack to cool. Remove

the cooled cookies with a metal spatula and transfer to a second wire rack. Repeat for the second biscotti loaf if there was not enough room for slices from both loaves on one pan. Store the biscotti between sheets of wax paper, in a covered tin.

SWEET TIP: Candied pineapple, candied lemon peel, candied orange peel, and candied ginger can also be used in this recipe.

• The ends of the biscotti may be leaned, cut side up, between two other slices for even baking.

Yield: about 3 dozen biscotti

PLUMPING RAISINS

There are several ways to plump raisins. Raisins can be plumped by heating or soaking them in warm orange juice. Alternatively, to plump raisins quickly, place the raisins in a bowl, cover with boiling water, and set aside.

PLUMPING RAISINS IN WINE, RUM, OR BRANDY

Place the raisins in a bowl, cover with wine, rum, or brandy, place plastic wrap over the bowl, and set aside at room temperature for at least 6 hours, stirring every hour. The raisins can also be soaked overnight in wine, rum, or brandy in the refrigerator.

Ukrainian Prune and Walnut Cake
(Prune and Walnut Bars)

The handwritten recipe for this confection refers to it as a "cake," but the cake when cut into 2-inch pieces, suddenly becomes a lovely old world bar, rich with dried fruit and walnuts. A drizzle of vanilla glaze or a light dusting of confectioners' sugar takes this sweet to a new level.

CAKE

1¼ cups pitted moist prunes, cut into ½-inch pieces (about 35 prunes)

1 cup walnuts, toasted and finely chopped

2¼ cups flour

1¼ teaspoons vanilla extract

¾ cup buttermilk or sour milk (see page 212)

1 teaspoon salt

2¼ teaspoons baking powder

¾ teaspoon baking soda

½ teaspoon cinnamon

½ teaspoon nutmeg

¼ teaspoon cloves

1 cup (2 sticks) unsalted butter, at room temperature

1½ cups granulated sugar

3 medium eggs

VANILLA GLAZE

1 cup confectioners' sugar

Pinch of salt

1 tablespoon vanilla extract

1 tablespoon water, plus more if needed

OPTIONAL TOPPING

Confectioners' sugar

1. Set the oven rack in the middle position. Preheat the oven to 350°F. Cover the bottom and sides of a 9 by 13 by 2-inch metal pan with aluminum foil, shiny side up. Coat the foil with vegetable oil spray.

2. To make the cake: Put the prunes and walnuts in a bowl. Measure the flour into a large bowl. Remove ¼ cup of the flour and add it to the bowl containing the prunes and walnuts. Stir to coat the prunes and walnuts with the flour and set aside. Add the vanilla to the buttermilk or sour milk in a glass measuring cup and set aside.

3. Add the salt, baking powder, baking soda, cinnamon, nutmeg, and cloves to the large bowl containing the flour and whisk to combine. Set aside.

4. Add the butter and granulated sugar to the bowl of a stand mixer fitted with the paddle attachment and cream until combined. Add the eggs and continue to beat until combined. Add the flour mixture and buttermilk alternately to the creamed mixture and beat until incorporated. Fold the prunes and walnuts into the batter with a spatula. Scrape the batter into the prepared pan. Bake the cake for 50 minutes, or until a metal cake tester inserted into the center comes out clean. Transfer the cake to a wire rack and let cool for 2 hours. Remove the cake from the pan with the foil attached. Invert the cake and peel off the foil carefully. Invert the cake back onto the rack.

5. To make the vanilla glaze: Sift the confectioners' sugar and salt into a small bowl. Add the vanilla and water and whisk to combine. Add additional water to the glaze, by teaspoons, to achieve the desired consistency. Drizzle the top of cake with the glaze. Alternatively, confectioners' sugar can be sifted over the top. Cut the cake into 2-inch bars. Store the bars, loosely wrapped in wax paper, at room temperature, or in a covered tin.

Yield: 2 dozen 2-inch bars

SWEET TIPS: Lightly coat a clean pair of scissors, which have been dedicated for use only with food, with vegetable oil spray, and use them to cut the prunes.

• If your prunes are not moist, cut them in half, pour an equal amount of boiling water over them, and let them sit for 10 minutes to rehydrate. Stir after 5 minutes. Drain the prunes before using.

HOW TO SOUR MILK

Make a quick buttermilk substitute by placing 1 tablespoon lemon juice or apple cider vinegar into a glass measuring cup. Add milk to the 1-cup line. Let stand at room temperature for 5 minutes before using.

8 Summertime Treats

THE RECIPES

*S*ummertime will always mean sunshine and saltwater to us because we grew up just a few minutes walk from Winthrop Beach. Most of our early summer childhood was spent walking on sand and pebbles and eating homemade tuna fish sandwiches from a cooler, while wearing chenille-trimmed cotton capes over our bathing suits.

To us, summer was a state of mind. When we remember summer it is with thoughts of sand between our toes, the briny smell of the ocean, the sound of seagulls overhead, the sticky, chewy taste of cotton candy, and the slap, slap, slap of a beach ball tossed from one of us to the other.

To everything there is a season, and to us, the treats our mother baked in the summer months were special to that stretch of time from June to the beginning of September. Many of the treats were portable, so we could enjoy glistening sugar cookies or vanilla wafers while sitting on the seawall or on our front porch. Sometimes we'd bring the radio up to the window on the front porch and listen through the screen to *Stop the Music* or *Baby Snooks*.

The more elaborate desserts, those that required a fork and plate, whether plastic and paper or regular metal and china, seemed to taste even better than some of the desserts we ate at other times of the year. What we were learning was that foods prepared and eaten in their season could be spectacular, like a rustic peach pie or plum squares. Green tomatoes were not just for pickling. They could be turned into a delectable, gingery chocolate cake.

We experienced rhubarb only at the tables of friends when we were sweet young things in the 1960s and 1970s. It seemed foreign to us, but when we learned to tame the sturdy stalks and turn them into unforgettable pies, cakes, and conserves, we felt that we had truly expanded our baking repertoire.

In later years, our memories of blueberries and cherries came to fruition in our Summertime Blueberry Kugel and Marilynn's Fresh Cherry Tart. Apples, which we always seemed to rediscover during the later days of summer and early days of autumn, show their worth in a golden crisp with a buttery vanilla wafer and brown sugar topping.

August brought rough seas and the uncertainty of tropical weather with its possibility of hurricanes. We revisit the taste and form of the peanut butter and jelly sandwiches we ate on those humid rainy days of late summer, in our large family kitchen. We bake and eat Rolled Peanut Butter Cookies, but we sandwich them, not with grape jelly, but with chocolate ganache.

Finally, like the color of summer sunshine, the sharply sweet citrus taste of a simple Lemon Chess Pie captures the elusive joy of summertime.

Quick Tips

- Take pies from the refrigerator and let warm to room temperature before serving.
- Do not leave pies containing custard, such as the Lemon Chess Pie, at room temperature for long periods of time or in hot weather. Store leftover custard pie in the refrigerator.
- Use crumb crusts for pies that are served frozen because slices are easier to cut.
- Use firm, not ripe or soft, seasonal fruit when baking with peaches and plums.

Lemon Chess Pie

This is a simple economical nineteenth-century recipe for a delicious lemon pie. Lemon Chess Pie originated in the Southern United States. It is adapted from an English recipe, which referred to it as a "cheese pie" because the filling formed a lemon curd. You will need just a bowl and whisk to make this recipe. You could even use a spoon. This is a very delicate pie, and because you're baking it at a fairly high temperature, 375°F, you may have to tent it with foil to prevent the crust from browning too quickly.

FILLING

1 tablespoon flour

1 tablespoon cornmeal

¼ teaspoon salt

4 eggs

2 cups sugar

¼ cup (½ stick) unsalted butter, melted,

2 teaspoons grated lemon zest

¼ cup milk

1 teaspoon vanilla extract

¼ cup lemon juice

Sprinkle of nutmeg (optional)

CRUST

1 unbaked 9-inch pie shell in an ovenproof
glass pie plate, (see page 154)

1. Set the oven rack in the middle position. Preheat the oven to 375°F.

2. To make the filling: In a small bowl, combine the flour, cornmeal, and salt and set aside.

3. Using a whisk, beat the eggs in a bowl. Add the sugar and butter and whisk into the eggs. Add the dry ingredients and combine. Add the lemon zest, milk, and vanilla to the mixture. Add the lemon juice and whisk quickly to combine. Pour the filling into the prepared pie shell. Sprinkle with nutmeg, if desired.

4. Bake the pie for 20 minutes and cover with tented aluminum foil or a ring made of foil if the crust is browning too quickly. Do not allow the foil to touch the filling. Continue baking for another 25 minutes, then check to see if the center is still loose. If it is loose (not wobbly), cover again with foil and bake for another 5 minutes; 50 minutes in all.

5. Remove the pie from the oven and transfer to a wire rack to cool. When cool, place the pie in the refrigerator, uncovered, for at least 3 hours before cutting. The filling will form a custardlike curd. Decorate with puffs of sweetened whipped cream around the edge of pie just before serving. Any leftover pie should be stored, loosely wrapped with wax paper, in the refrigerator.

Yield: one 9-inch pie; 8 to 10 slices

Marilynn's Fresh Cherry Tart

Marilynn's Fresh Cherry Tart

When we were faced with the challenge of baking a cherry tart made with fresh, pitted cherries, we decided to try a variation of the blueberry pie recipe we found handwritten in a copy of Laboratory Recipes *owned by Rachel W. Banks. We've tasted cherry pie before, and it turned out to be a gluey slice loaded with bright artificially pink, canned cherries. This cherry tart has the perfect balance of sweet and sour because of the addition of lemon zest and lemon juice. The touch of cinnamon gives it some complexity, and the flaky crust is just firm enough to support the wealth of fresh cherries within.*

GLAZE

2 tablespoons (⅛ cup) seedless raspberry
    jam

CRUST

Prebaked and cooled 9-inch tart shell
    (see page 154)

FILLING

4 cups pitted fresh cherries
½ cup plus 2½ tablespoons water
2½ tablespoons cornstarch
½ cup sugar
2 teaspoons grated lemon zest
1 teaspoon lemon juice
½ teaspoon cinnamon
⅛ teaspoon salt

Sweetened whipped cream, for serving
    (optional)

Marilynn's Fresh Cherry Tart

1. To make the glaze: Add the raspberry jam to a small glass bowl and cover with plastic wrap. Heat the jam in the microwave oven for 25 to 30 seconds on low, or cook the raspberry jam in a heavy-bottomed metal saucepan over low heat until bubbles form around the edges. Brush the bottom and sides of the cooled pie shell with the glaze and let cool.

2. To make the filling: Place a cup of the cherries and ½ cup of the water in a heavy-bottomed metal saucepan and bring to a boil over medium heat. Boil gently for 3 to 4 minutes, then remove from the heat. Add the cornstarch to the remaining 2½ tablespoons water and whisk to dissolve. Add the cornstarch mixture, sugar, lemon zest, lemon

juice, cinnamon, and salt to the cooked cherries. Bring to a boil over medium heat and cook, stirring, for about 1 minute, or until the cherries have the consistency of jam.

3. Transfer the cooked cherry mixture to a 6-cup bowl. Fold in the remaining 3 cups cherries. *If using a metal bowl, the bowl will be hot.* Add the filling to the tart shell and let cool for at least 2 hours. After the tart has cooled, and just before serving, pipe whipped cream around the edge of the tart. This tart is best served the day it is made, but it will still be delicious the next day if loosely wrapped in wax paper or placed in a covered container and refrigerated.

Yield: one 9-inch tart; 8 to 10 slices

SWEET TIPS: *Be sure to count the pits as you prepare the cherries.*

SWEET TOUCHES: After the tart shell is filled with the cherry filling, you can carefully flip any cherries so that the unbroken skin sides of the cherries are on top, *but be careful, the filling will be hot.*
• Whipped cream, slightly sweetened with confectioners' sugar, can be piped around the edge of the tart, if desired.

Crisp Vanilla Butter Wafers

These are similar to the Dark Chocolate Butter Cookies in the chocolate chapter, but we like to think of them as more wafers than cookies. This is a great treat to make your own by embellishing with slivered almonds or a sprinkle of fine clear sanding sugar. These were the cookies we loved to eat with a glass of ginger ale after a day at Winthrop Beach.

1¾ cups flour

¼ cup cornmeal

½ cup granulated sugar

½ cup confectioners' sugar, sifted

½ teaspoon salt

¼ teaspoon baking soda

1 cup (2 sticks) cold unsalted butter, cut into
     16 slices

1½ teaspoons vanilla extract

Clear *fine* sanding sugar (optional)

1. Put the flour, cornmeal, sugars, salt, and baking powder in the bowl of a food processor fitted with the metal blade attachment and pulse until well mixed. Add the butter and pulse until crumbly. Add the vanilla and continue to pulse until the dough comes together.

2. Remove the dough from the bowl of the food processor and place on a sheet of wax paper or plastic wrap. Form into a disk and chill in the refrigerator for at least 2 hours, or overnight.

3. Set the oven rack in the middle position. Preheat the oven to 350°F. Line a 14 by 16-inch baking sheet with silicone liner or aluminum foil, shiny side up. Coat the foil with vegetable oil spray. Prepare two baking sheets, if desired.

4. Divide the chilled dough into four portions. Working with one section at a time, and keeping the remaining dough chilled, roll out the dough ¼ inch thick between two pieces of lightly floured wax paper. Cut out cookies with a 2½-inch round cookie cutter. Place them 2 inches apart on the prepared baking sheet(s), no more than 12 cookies per sheet. If you are using the sanding sugar, sprinkle it on the tops of the unbaked cookies now. Bake the cookies for 14 minutes. Slide the foil or the silicone liner with the baked cookies onto a wire rack to cool. Remove the cooled cookies with a metal spatula and transfer to a second wire rack to cool until firm. Store the cookies, between sheets of wax paper, in a covered tin.

Yield: 20 to 25 cookies

SWEET TIP: Dip the cookie cutter lightly in flour before cutting out the cookies.

Summertime Blueberry Kugel

This is the recipe we made for our audition tape for the Food Network. We truly believe it led to our throw-down with Bobby Flay, which we won by baking our mother's recipe for Pineapple Upside-Down Cake.

This is a "dessert" mac and cheese, but it's good any time for breakfast, lunch, or Sunday supper with a glass of cold milk.

BLUEBERRY JAM

4 cups fresh blueberries

½ cup plus 2 ½ tablespoons water

2 ½ tablespoons cornstarch

½ cup granulated sugar

2 teaspoons grated lemon zest

1 teaspoon lemon juice

1 teaspoon vanilla extract

½ teaspoon cinnamon

⅛ teaspoon salt

MAC AND CHEESE

12 ounces uncooked small elbow macaroni (approximately 3 ½ cups dry), or 7 ½ cups cooked macaroni

¼ teaspoon salt

½ cup granulated sugar

¼ teaspoon cinnamon

2 teaspoons grated lemon zest

1 cup ricotta cheese, at room temperature

1 cup cream cheese, at room temperature

1 cup sour cream

1 teaspoon vanilla extract

4 eggs, beaten

¼ cup (½ stick) unsalted butter, melted and cooled

TOPPING

3 tablespoons unsalted butter, melted

1 ½ cups walnuts, toasted and coarsely chopped

¾ cup firmly packed brown sugar

Sweetened whipped cream, for serving

1. Set the oven rack in the middle position. Preheat the oven to 350°F. Coat a 9 by 13-inch oven-proof glass baking dish with vegetable oil spray. Cover a rimmed baking sheet with aluminum foil.

2. To make the blueberry jam: Put 1 cup of the blueberries and ½ cup of the water in a metal saucepan and bring to a boil over medium heat. Boil gently for 3 to 4 minutes, then remove from the heat. Add the cornstarch to the remaining 2 ½ tablespoons water and whisk to dissolve. Add the cornstarch mixture, granulated sugar, lemon zest, lemon juice, vanilla, cinnamon, and salt to the cooked blueberries. Bring to a boil over low heat and cook, stirring, for about 1 minute, or until the blueberries have the consistency of jam. Set aside to cool. Transfer the cooked blueberry mixture to a 6-cup bowl. Fold in the remaining 3 cups blueberries. Set aside.

3. To make the mac and cheese: Cook the macaroni according to the package directions, for 10 to 12 minutes. Drain thoroughly, rinse with cold water, and drain again. Transfer the cooked macaroni to a bowl and set aside.

4. Add the salt, granulated sugar, cinnamon, and lemon zest to a small bowl and whisk to combine. Set aside.

5. Add the ricotta cheese, cream cheese, sour cream, and vanilla to a large bowl and whisk thoroughly to combine. Add the eggs and butter to the

cheese mixture and whisk in. Add the sugar, salt, cinnamon, and lemon zest in the small bowl to the mixture and whisk to combine. Add the cooked macaroni and fold into the mixture with a spatula.

6. Place half the macaroni mixture in the prepared baking dish. Spoon the blueberry jam over the macaroni and smooth it with a spatula. Add the other half of the macaroni to the dish and smooth it over the blueberry jam layer.

7. To make the topping: Spoon the butter over the top of the kugel. Add the walnuts and brown sugar to a small bowl and whisk to combine. Sprinkle the walnuts and brown sugar over the top of the kugel and press down gently so that the topping adheres to the top layer of the macaroni. The entire top should be covered.

8. Place the baking dish on the foil-covered heavy rimmed baking sheet to prevent the kugel from spilling over in the oven as it bakes. Bake for 55 minutes, or until the topping and sides are bubbling. Remove the kugel from the oven and place the baking dish on a wire rack to cool. When still slightly warm, or when cool, serve with sweetened whipped cream. Leftover kugel should be stored, covered with plastic wrap or wax paper, in the refrigerator.

Yield: one 9- by 13-inch kugel; 16 servings

SWEET TIP: Let leftover kugel come to room temperature before serving, but do not allow it to stay out of the refrigerator for too long because it is made with eggs.

SWEET TOUCH: The blueberry jam turns into a delicious syrup and can be spooned over the kugel when serving.

Green Tomato Chocolate Cake

The handwritten recipe for Green Tomato Chocolate Cake we found was credited to Marie. Her recipe called for beer and a mixture of cocoa and bitter chocolate. We tried it, and we found that it was a very nice cake, but we craved a deeper chocolate flavor so we omitted the cocoa and increased the melted bitter chocolate. We decided to rewrite the whole recipe, adding buttermilk instead of beer, and enriching the cake with more butter and eggs. Our version is very different from the original, and the baked nuggets of pureed tomatoes combine to make a delicate crumb. Although we added ample ginger, the spice is evident only as a minor note.

CAKES

3 cups flour

2 teaspoons baking soda

½ teaspoon salt

2 teaspoons ground ginger

1 teaspoon vanilla extract

1 cup buttermilk

1 cup (2 sticks) unsalted butter, at room temperature

2 cups granulated sugar

3 eggs

5 ounces bitter chocolate, melted and slightly cooled

1 cup pureed green tomatoes (see sidebar page 225)

GINGER GLAZE

1 cup confectioners' sugar

Pinch of salt

½ teaspoon vanilla extract

2 tablespoons cold water, plus more if needed

2 tablespoons ginger jam

1. Set the oven rack in the middle position. Preheat the oven to 350°F. Coat the bottoms and sides of two 9-inch round cake pans with vegetable oil spray. Line the bottoms of the pans with parchment paper. Coat the parchment paper with vegetable oil spray. Dust the bottoms and sides of the pans with flour and tap the pans to remove the excess flour.

2. To make the cake: Add the flour, baking soda, salt, and ground ginger to a bowl and whisk to combine. Set aside. Add the vanilla to the buttermilk in a glass measuring cup and set aside.

3. Add the butter and granulated sugar to the bowl of a stand mixer fitted with the paddle attachment and cream until combined. Add the eggs one at a time and beat to combine. Add the cooled chocolate, followed by the pureed tomatoes, and combine.

4. Add the dry ingredients and buttermilk alternately to the creamed mixture in three additions and beat until thoroughly mixed. Pour the batter into the prepared pans and bake the cakes for 35 minutes, or until a metal tester inserted into the centers comes out clean. Transfer the cakes to a wire rack to cool. The cakes will pull away from the edges as they cool. After 20 minutes, go around the edges of the pans with a butter knife, if necessary, and invert the cakes onto another wire rack.

5. To make the ginger glaze: Sift the confectioners' sugar and salt into a small bowl. Add the vanilla and cold water gradually, whisking until the glaze is the desired consistency, and adding more water, one teaspoon at a time, if necessary. Add the ginger jam and whisk to combine. Slip a sheet of wax paper under the wire rack with the cakes to catch drips. When the cakes are cool, using a teaspoon or fork, drizzle the glaze over the tops of the cakes. Allow the glaze to set for 1 hour. Place

the cakes in the refrigerator to chill before cutting. Allow the cakes to come to room temperature just before serving. Any leftover cake should be stored, loosely covered with wax paper, in the refrigerator.

Yield: two 9-inch round cakes;
8 to 10 slices per cake

HOW TO PREPARE GREEN TOMATO PUREE

This Green Tomato Chocolate Cake calls for unripe green tomatoes from the garden, not *heirloom* green tomatoes. The tomatoes used in this recipe are the ones that are available in late August or early September. They are the last of the crop and haven't had a chance to turn red. Cut the tomatoes into quarters, remove the tough cores and seeds, and place them in a food processor fitted with the metal blade. Pulse the tomato quarters two or three times until they turn into a puree. Do not overprocess or they will liquefy; however, it is not unusual for some liquid to form. Spoon the puree into a 1-cup measure. Turn the cup upside down, holding your hand over the top so that some of the excess liquid flows away, but the puree remains in the cup measure. Use the remaining puree in the recipe.

Merry's Upside-Down Plum Squares

We loved the name of the home baker whose recipe we found hand-printed on an index card from the 1950s. We liked, as well, the prospect of baking a recipe using summer's bounty of plums. The original recipe called for Italian plums, those small, sweet, intensely flavorful fruits available in late August through September. We decided to try it with plums that had a longer seasonal availability, such as red- or yellow-fleshed plums. The combination of jammy baked plums combined with the crunch of a graham cracker streusel captures the robust warmth of a summer orchard, but hints of autumn's more moderate temperatures. We suggest using plums that are fairly firm.

STREUSEL

⅓ cup firmly packed brown sugar

½ teaspoon cinnamon

¼ cup graham cracker crumbs

3 tablespoons cold unsalted butter, cut into
   ¼-inch dice

SQUARES

5 to 6 large firm plums, pitted and cut into
   12 slices each (5 or 6 cups of cut plums)

1½ cups flour

¾ teaspoon salt

1½ teaspoons baking powder

1½ teaspoons cinnamon

1 teaspoon nutmeg

¾ cup (1½ sticks) unsalted butter, at room
   temperature

1½ cups granulated sugar

3 eggs

Grated zest of 1 large lemon

2 teaspoons lemon juice

1. Set the oven rack in the middle position. Preheat the oven to 400°F. Line the bottom of a 9 by 13 by 2-inch metal pan with aluminum foil, shiny side up. Coat the foil with vegetable oil spray.

2. To make the streusel: Add the brown sugar, cinnamon, and graham cracker crumbs to a bowl and whisk to combine. Set aside. Reserve the diced butter in the refrigerator until ready to use.

3. To make the squares: Place the plum wedges on the bottom of the prepared pan. Add the flour, salt, baking powder, cinnamon, and nutmeg to a bowl and whisk together. Set aside.

4. In the bowl of a stand mixer fitted with the paddle attachment, beat the butter until fluffy. Add the granulated sugar and cream until smooth. Add the eggs and continue to beat until combined. Add the lemon zest and lemon juice and beat in. Add the dry ingredients in thirds and beat to incorporate.

Merry's Upside-Down Plum Squares

Merry's Upside-Down Plum Squares

5. Spoon the batter over the plums in the pan and spread with an offset spatula until all the plums are covered. Sprinkle the reserved streusel over the batter. Sprinkle the cold diced butter evenly over the streusel and place the pan in the oven. Bake for 40 minutes, or until a metal tester inserted into the cake part of the squares comes out dry. The tester will be moist if inserted directly into the plums, but the squares will pull away slightly from the sides of the pan when done.

6. Transfer the pan to a wire rack to cool for 1 hour. After an hour, place the cake in the refrigerator until completely cool. Remove the cooled cake from the refrigerator and run a butter knife around the edges to loosen the cake. Flip the pan onto a cutting board. Carefully remove the foil from the cake. The bottom of the cake will become the top.

Using a sharp knife, cut the cake into squares. The plum squares are best served the same day they are baked. The plums on the bottom of the squares will turn into jam. Any leftover squares should be stored, covered with wax paper, in the refrigerator. Bring leftover squares to room temperature before serving.

Yield: about 2 dozen 2-inch squares

SWEET TIP: Remove any coarse strands from the center of the pitted plums before using.

SWEET TOUCH: An embellishment of whipped cream or a scoop of vanilla ice cream enhances the plum square experience.

Rhubarb Royalle
(Rhubarb Upside-Down Cake)

We found this recipe for a Rhubarb Upside-Down Cake in a manuscript cookbook from the 1930s, owned by Ann E. Herzog, who received it from Grandmother Meinhold. This glistening jewel like cake served with whipped cream is wonderful for dessert, but the rhubarb confection is also suitable for those who like the sweeter side of breakfast. This is almost like an upside-down rhubarb cobbler.

RHUBARB LAYER

2 tablespoons unsalted butter, melted and cooled
2½ cups rhubarb, washed, trimmed, and cut into
    ½-inch pieces
1 tablespoon flour
1 teaspoon cinnamon
1 tablespoon grated orange zest
⅔ cup honey

CAKE

1 cup flour
½ teaspoon salt
2 teaspoons baking powder
¼ cup (½ stick) cold unsalted butter, cut into
    ¼-inch dice
3 eggs, beaten
1 tablespoon orange juice
2 tablespoons honey

TOPPING

2 tablespoons orange juice
1 tablespoon honey

1. Set the oven rack in the middle position. Preheat the oven to 350°F.

2. To make the rhubarb layer: Swirl the melted butter in a 9 by 2-inch round metal pan until the bottom and sides are completely coated. Arrange the rhubarb on the bottom of the pan. Combine the flour, cinnamon, and orange zest in a small bowl, then sprinkle over the rhubarb. Pour the honey over the rhubarb mixture.

3. To make the cake: Whisk the flour, salt, and baking powder together in a bowl. Add the butter to the dry ingredients and work it in with your hands until the mixture resembles coarse crumbs. Add the eggs, orange juice, and honey to the flour-and-butter mixture and stir until combined. Do not overwork. Spread the mixture evenly on top of the rhubarb layer in the prepared pan. Bake for 25 minutes.

4. To make the topping: Mix the orange juice and honey together in a small bowl. Remove the cake from the oven and pour the topping over the cake. Return the cake to the oven and bake for 15 minutes more, or until a metal tester inserted into the cake comes out clean. Transfer the pan to a wire rack and allow the cake to cool for 3 minutes. Go around the rim of the cake with a butter knife and invert the cake (*the cake will still be very hot*) onto a platter larger than the cake pan. If bits of fruit remain in the pan, retrieve them and place back on top of the cake. Serve the cake warm or at room temperature with whipped cream or vanilla ice cream, or topped with sifted confectioners' sugar. Rhubarb Royalle is best served the day it is made, but any leftover cake can be stored, wrapped loosely in wax paper, in the refrigerator.

Yield: one 9-inch cake; 12 servings

SWEET TOUCH: Crumbled leftover Rhubarb Royalle is very nice sprinkled over vanilla ice cream or orange sherbet.

Nanall Alleman's Sand Cookies

This recipe, originally called Sand Tarts, came from Leslie Baker, an artist who lives and paints on Martha's Vineyard. It was her grandmother Nanall Gertrude Brubaker Alleman's recipe. We like to think of these more as cookies than tarts because they have no filling. Nanall's recipe has been passed down to her great-granddaughter, Emma. They are similar to a cookie we used to eat on Winthrop Beach with fresh fruit punch. In the sunshine, the sugar on the tops of the cookies glistened like grains of sand.

COOKIES

2 ¼ cups flour
1 ¼ cups granulated sugar
¼ teaspoon salt
1 cup (2 sticks) cold unsalted butter, cut into
    ½-inch dice
1 egg, lightly beaten
1 teaspoon vanilla extract

"SAND" TOPPING

1 egg white, beaten
Coarse clear sanding sugar, or ¼ cup
    granulated sugar mixed with 2 teaspoons
    cinnamon
60 pecan halves, toasted

1. Set the oven rack in the middle position. Preheat the oven to 350°F. Line a 14- by 16-inch baking sheet with a silicone liner or aluminum foil, shiny side up. Coat the foil with vegetable oil spray.

2. To make the cookies: Add the flour, granulated sugar, and salt to the bowl of a food processor fitted with the metal blade and pulse three times to mix. Add the butter, egg, and vanilla and continue to pulse until the dough comes together.

3. Remove the dough from the bowl of the food processor and place on a floured sheet of wax paper. Divide the dough into four equal portions. Wrap each portion in plastic wrap and chill in the refrigerator for at least 2 hours, or overnight, before rolling out.

4. Remove one portion of the chilled dough from the refrigerator. Place the dough on a sheet of floured wax paper. Dust the top of the dough with flour and cover with a second sheet of wax paper. Roll out the dough to a thickness of ⅛ inch. Cut circles from the dough with a 2½-inch round scalloped cookie cutter, dipped in flour. Lift the cookies onto the prepared baking sheet. Brush the cookies with the beaten egg white and sprinkle with the coarse sanding sugar or granulated-sugar-and-cinnamon mixture. Place a toasted pecan half in the center of each cookie. Bake the cookies for 15 minutes. The cookies will be a little soft when they come out of the oven, but they will firm up a bit after cooling on a wire rack. Slide the foil or the silicone liner with the baked cookies onto a wire rack to cool. Remove the cooled cookies with a metal spatula and transfer to a second wire rack. Repeat with remaining cookies. Store the cookies, between sheets of wax paper, in a covered tin. They will be fragile, so handle them with care.

Yield: about 5 dozen cookies

SWEET TOUCHES: We chose to use coarse *gold* sanding sugar, but you can use the original cinnamon-and-sugar topping. They both glisten.
• Slivered almonds can be a substitute for pecan halves.

Nanall Alleman's Sand Cookies

Rustic Ginger Peach Pie

Rustic Ginger Peach Pie
(Peach Galette)

The joy in making this Rustic Ginger Peach Pie is in its delicious imperfections. There are no worries about irregular slices of peaches or cracks in the pastry. We like the combination of ginger with peaches, so we've added a bit to the piecrust and some ginger jam to the filling. The trick to a successful pie is to use peaches that are firm, and not overly juicy.

SWEET PIECRUST

1¼ cups flour

2 tablespoons granulated sugar

⅛ teaspoon salt

⅛ teaspoon ground ginger (optional)

½ cup (1 stick) unsalted cold butter, cut into 8 slices

2 tablespoons ice water

FILLING

3½ to 4 cups firm, but not hard, peaches, peeled, pitted, and sliced

3 tablespoons flour

¼ teaspoon salt

2 tablespoons ginger jam (optional)

2 tablespoons cold unsalted butter, cut into ½-inch dice

1 egg, beaten

2 tablespoons clear coarse sanding sugar

1. To make the sweet piecrust: Put the flour, granulated sugar, salt, and ground ginger, if using, in the bowl of a food processor fitted with a metal blade and pulse three times to mix. Add the butter and pulse until crumbly. Add the ice water and pulse until the mixture comes together.

2. Remove the dough from the bowl of the processor and shape it into a disk. Unless your kitchen is very warm, you don't have to chill the dough before rolling it out.

3. Set the oven rack in the middle position. Preheat the oven to 400°F. Place a sheet of parchment paper on top of a 14- by 16-inch rimmed baking sheet or a 13-inch metal pizza pan.

4. To make the filling: Add the peaches to a large bowl and set aside. Put 2 tablespoons of the flour, the salt, and ginger jam, if using, in a small bowl and whisk to combine. Add to the peaches and stir with a spatula until the peaches are completely coated. Set aside and let the filling stand for 10 to 15 minutes to allow the flavors to meld.

5. Roll out the piecrust into a 12- to 14-inch circle. Sprinkle the remaining 1 tablespoon flour over the crust. Place the crust in the refrigerator for 15 minutes to chill. Remove from the refrigerator and place on the prepared pan. Place the filling on top of the crust, leaving a 2½-inch margin around the edge the filling. Scatter the diced butter over the top of the filling. Brush the edges of the piecrust with the beaten egg. Bring up the dough over the fruit, pleating the edges all around; the filling will not be completely covered. Brush the dough with the remaining beaten egg, and sprinkle with the coarse clear sanding sugar.

6. Bake the pie for 25 to 30 minutes, or until the crust is golden brown and the peaches are soft and a little bubbly. Check the pie at 15 minutes. If the crust is browning too quickly, carefully tent with foil. When the pie is done, transfer to a wire rack to cool for about 15 minutes before serving. Any leftover pie should be stored, wrapped in wax paper, in the refrigerator. Let leftover pie come to room temperature before serving or reheat in a 300°F oven for 10 minutes.

Yield: 1 rustic pie (galette); 8 slices

HOW TO PEEL PEACHES

Peeling peaches was one of the first tasks Marilynn accomplished when she started her baking adventure.

Choose peaches that are not overly soft or ripe. They should be somewhat *firm* if their skins are to be peeled. Peaches can be peeled by hand with a vegetable peeler, but it is quicker and more efficient to dip the peaches in boiling water for a minute, and then in cold water. The skins can then be easily removed.

Rolled Peanut Butter Cookies

These cookies are a very different peanut butter cookie because the dough is rolled, and the cookies are cut with a cookie cutter. Most peanut butter cookies are drop cookies, flattened with the tines of a fork. These are crisp, thin, and rich. This recipe is a true "living recipe" because it came from a crumbling scrap of yellowed notebook paper from the 1930s. These cookies are also good filled with ganache, a delicious combination of cream and dark chocolate. See below.

COOKIES

2½ cups flour

½ teaspoon salt

1 teaspoon baking powder

1 cup (2 sticks) unsalted butter, at room temperature

1 cup granulated sugar

¾ cup firmly packed brown sugar

1 cup creamy peanut butter

2 eggs

1 teaspoon vanilla extract

Coarse clear sanding sugar (optional)

1. Set the oven rack in the middle position. Preheat the oven to 350°F. Line a 14- by 16-inch baking sheet with a silicone liner or aluminum foil, shiny side up. Coat the foil with vegetable oil spray. Prepare two baking sheets, if desired.

2. To make the cookies: Add the flour, salt, and baking powder to a bowl and whisk together. Set aside.

3. Cream the butter and the sugars in the bowl of a stand mixer fitted with the paddle attachment until fluffy. Add the peanut butter and continue to cream. Add the eggs and vanilla to the mixture and beat in. Add the dry ingredients gradually until well blended.

4. Scoop the cookie dough onto a sheet of wax paper or parchment paper and form it into disk. Cover and chill in refrigerator for at least 2 hours, or overnight. Place the dough in the freezer to chill more quickly.

5. Divide the chilled disk of dough into four equal portions. Place one portion of the dough between two pieces of wax or parchment paper. Return the rest of the dough to the refrigerator. Roll out the first portion of dough, dusted lightly with flour, to a thickness of ¼ inch. Cut out cookies with a 2½-inch round cookie cutter, dipped in flour. Remove the cookies from the paper with a 2-inch metal spatula dipped in flour, shaking off the excess flour. Place the cookies 2 inches apart on the prepared baking sheet(s), no more than 12 cookies per sheet. If the dough becomes too soft to reroll, place in freezer for 5 to 10 minutes to firm up. Continue to roll out the remainder of the dough

6. Bake the cookies for 13 to 14 minutes, or until they are a golden brown. Do not overbake. Slide the foil or the silicone liner with the baked cookies onto a wire rack to cool. Remove the cooled cookies with a metal spatula and transfer to a second wire rack to continue cooling. Store the cookies, between sheets of wax paper, in a covered tin.

Yield: 4 dozen or 2 dozen filled cookies

CHOCOLATE GANACHE

½ cup heavy cream

6 ounces bittersweet or semisweet chocolate, chopped

Pinch of salt

½ teaspoon vanilla extract

To make the ganache: Heat the cream in a heavy saucepan over medium heat until bubbles form around the edges. Remove from the heat, add the chocolate, and let sit for 5 minutes. Stir with a wooden spoon to combine. Stir in the salt and vanilla. Cool the ganache until thickened, and use as a filling between two cookies. Filled cookies should be stored, between sheets of wax paper, in a covered tin, and refrigerated because ganache tends to soften at room temperature.

SWEET TIP: Check during baking that the cookies do not turn dark brown.

SWEET TOUCHES: The cookies can be sprinkled with coarse sanding sugar before baking.

• Two cookies can be filled with chocolate ganache to make a cookie sandwich.

• Another type of cookie sandwich—a PB&J Cookie Sandwich—can be made by putting two cookies together and filling them with raspberry, strawberry, or apricot jam.

Washington Apple Crisp

We found this recipe hand-printed on a large index card. It seemed like a good recipe for a crisp, but we decided to add ginger, lemon zest, and vanilla wafer crumbs to the topping. We also added the cold diced butter at the very end, rather than mixing it into the topping. This is a wonderful dessert for those late August or early September evenings when twilight lingers, and supper or dessert on the porch seems like a good idea.

TOPPING

½ cup flour

1 cup finely crushed vanilla wafer crumbs

½ cup firmly packed brown sugar

½ teaspoon ground ginger

Grated zest of 1 large lemon

¼ cup (½ stick) cold unsalted butter, cut into ¼-inch dice

CRISP

8 Granny Smith apples, peeled, cored, and cut into ½-inch wedges

¼ cup granulated sugar

¼ cup firmly packed brown sugar

1 tablespoon flour

½ teaspoon cinnamon

1 teaspoon ginger

¼ teaspoon cloves

¼ teaspoon salt

2 teaspoons lemon juice

1. Set the oven rack in the middle position. Preheat the oven to 375°F. Liberally coat the bottom and sides of a 9 by 9 by 2-inch metal pan with butter.

2. To make the topping: Place the flour, vanilla wafer crumbs, brown sugar, ginger, and lemon zest in a bowl and whisk to combine. Set aside. Place the diced butter in the refrigerator until ready to bake the crisp.

3. To make the crisp: Add the apples to a large bowl and set aside. Add the sugars, flour, cinnamon, ginger, cloves, and salt to another bowl and whisk to combine. Add the dry ingredients and the lemon juice to the apples and mix with a large spoon until the apples are completely coated with the flour and spices.

4. Transfer the apple mixture to the prepared pan and press down gently to fit in. Sprinkle the topping over the apples. Scatter the cold diced butter over the topping. Bake the crisp for 45 minutes, or until the apples are tender and the topping is brown. Remove the crisp from the oven and place on a wire rack to cool. The crisp can be served slightly warm or at room temperature. Any leftover crisp should be stored, in the pan, covered with plastic wrap, in the refrigerator.

Yield: one 9-by-9-inch crisp; 6 servings

SWEET TIP: An alternative method for making the topping for the apple crisp is to add the cold diced butter to the topping, working it in with your fingers (wearing disposable gloves, if desired). The topping should be coarsely crumbled and placed in the refrigerator until you are ready to bake the crisp.

SWEET TOUCH: Any cookie crumbs can be added to the topping; homemade ones are the best.
• Vanilla ice cream or lightly sweetened whipped cream elevates this dessert to a new level.

9 *Make Mine Chocolate*

THE RECIPES

The title of this chapter says it all. We love to eat chocolate, and we love to bake with it.

Because the flavor of chocolate, like wine, tea, or coffee, is nuanced in flavor, chocolate can have notes of fruit, nuts, citrus, or spice. Chocolate, however, is complex, not only in flavor, but also in composition.

As we become more sophisticated, we request chocolate with different percentages of chocolate liquor and sugar. We no longer talk about dark chocolate or milk chocolate. Some of us want our chocolate dark and sweet, while there are those who choose a more intense chocolate experience. It's all in the percentages. The higher the percentages, the more robust and bitter the chocolate. For many of our recipes, we often choose unsweetened or bitter chocolate that is also known as baking chocolate. It contains no sugar, and has a very high percentage of chocolate liquor.

While we admit to increasing the amount of chocolate we eat, and adventurously nibbling different chocolates from Africa, South America, or Iceland, we also find ourselves baking with chocolate more often. Although more exotic chocolate is now available, we have not chosen the more costly exotic brands with which to bake our recipes. Our palates may have become more educated, but because we wanted to achieve a uniform result in testing the recipes, we used more readily available brands.

We pay homage to the history of chocolate with a nod to Baker's Chocolate where it all began in Massachusetts centuries ago. Although we've chosen to use dark chocolate and white chocolate chips in the recipe for Polka Dot Chocolate Bars on page 105, we have yet to include a variation on the iconic Toll House Cookie recipe, which was created in the Bay State. You don't mess with success.

We've varied the recipes we've chosen to bake for this chapter by selecting some that are simple, and some that demand a bit more dedication. The Chocolate Tea Cake and Shirley Broner's Fudge Squares, Palma Snarskis's Cranberry, White Chocolate, and Walnut Bars are easy treats to replicate, and while Jack's Chocolate Walnut Caramel Tart takes more time to prepare, it will be sublime.

We've offered recipes for cakes, pound, tea, buttermilk, and marble; for tarts, caramel and wal-nut, and mocha truffle; for bars and squares, Julia's Coconut and Fran's Sour Cream Espresso; and a Chocolate Guinness Bread Pudding that would thrill even an honorary Irishman, and we've done it just to show off the delights of chocolate.

Quick Tips

- Do not substitute semisweet chocolate when bitter or baking chocolate is called for.
- We have chosen to use natural or American cocoa powder, which is nonalkalized. European, or Dutched, cocoa powder, which is alkalized, can react differently in a recipe.
- White chocolate is not really chocolate. It is made from sweetened cocoa butter and contains milk solids.
- Store chocolate in a cool, dark, dry place. Do not refrigerate chocolate.

Chocolate Guinness Bread Pudding

We've always been fascinated by the robust flavor of Guinness stout. It evokes images of manly smoky pubs with dark wood paneling and plaintive Irish music. After finding that Guinness pairs well with chocolate and spices when baked into substantial cakes, we decided to make a very Irish bread pudding, and served it with whipped cream fortified with more stout to make it almost celestial.

BREAD LAYERS

Fourteen to sixteen ½-inch slices brioche or firm white bread, trimmed of crusts and cut in half

8 to 10 tablespoons (1 stick plus 2 tablespoons) unsalted butter, melted and cooled

CUSTARD

1 cup milk

1 cup heavy cream

1 cup Guinness stout

1 teaspoon vanilla extract

1 cup firmly packed brown sugar

¼ teaspoon salt

½ cup American natural nonalkalized cocoa powder

½ teaspoon cinnamon

½ teaspoon nutmeg

¼ teaspoon cloves

6 eggs, beaten

1 cup dark chocolate chips

TOPPING

¾ cup firmly packed brown sugar

3 tablespoons unsalted butter, melted and cooled

GUINNESS STOUT WHIPPED CREAM

1 cup heavy cream, whipped

¼ cup Guinness stout

1. Coat a 9 by 13-inch ovenproof glass baking dish with vegetable oil spray and set aside.

2. To prepare the bread layers: *Lightly* brush melted butter on both sides of each brioche slice.

3. To make the custard: Combine the milk, cream, Guinness, vanilla, brown sugar, salt, cocoa, cinnamon, nutmeg, and cloves in a bowl and whisk to combine. Add the beaten eggs to the custard mixture and combine.

4. Pour a small amount of the custard in the bottom of the prepared baking dish. Tilt and swirl the dish until the bottom is covered. Layer the brioche on top of the custard, filling in the spaces with extra brioche. Sprinkle ⅓ cup of the chocolate chips over the brioche. Pour one-third of the remaining custard over the brioche. Add another layer of brioche on top of the custard in the same manner. Sprinkle with another ⅓ cup of the chocolate chips and pour another third of the custard on top of the brioche. Add the remaining brioche on top of the custard. Sprinkle with the last of the chocolate chips, and pour the remaining custard mixture on top of the brioche.

5. Using a knife, cut 10 slits through the layered brioche and custard. Cover the top of the bread pudding with plastic wrap, and press down firmly with your palm until the custard rises to the top. Let stand for 10 minutes, then push down gently again on top of bread pudding. Place the pudding in the refrigerator for at least 4 hours, or overnight, if possible, and push down one more time to distribute the custard.

6. Set the oven rack in the middle position. Preheat the oven to 350°F. Remove the bread pudding from the refrigerator and wait 15 minutes before sprinkling with the brown sugar. Pour the melted butter over the top, cover with aluminum foil, and

place in the oven. *The baking dish can be placed on a foil-lined rimmed baking sheet, if desired, to prevent spills in the oven.* Bake for 60 minutes. Remove the top foil after 20 minutes. The bread pudding is done when it begins to pull away from the sides of the dish, and a metal tester inserted into the center comes out clean.

7. Remove the bread pudding, on the baking sheet, from the oven and place on top of the stove. Carefully remove the dish of bread pudding from the baking sheet, and place on a wire rack to cool. *The dish will be very hot.* Allow to rest for 5 minutes, cut into portions, and serve with the Guinness Stout Whipped Cream. Any leftover bread pudding should be covered with wax paper and stored in the refrigerator.

8. To make the Guinness Stout Whipped Cream: Add the cream to the bowl of a stand mixer fitted with the whisk attachment and beat until the cream is thick. Turn off the mixer. Remove the cream from the bowl of the mixer, fold in the Guinness stout, and transfer to another bowl or container. Cover and store in the refrigerator until ready to use.

Yield: one 9- by 13-inch bread pudding; 12 servings

SWEET TIP: We suggest that you *lightly* brush the brioche slices with the melted butter. They need just a touch of the melted butter.

Chocolate Tea Cake

This recipe comes from Gertrude Smith, a home baker who was known not only for her excellence in producing delicious cookies, tea cakes, and pies, but also for the beautiful presentation of her contributions to potluck suppers at the Bethlehem Lutheran Church in Lynchburg, Virginia. Her son, Ronn, treasures the dish she used for her gelatin desserts. This Chocolate Tea Cake, with its delicate crumb, is a prime example of a "Gertrude Smith Special."

TEA CAKES

2½ cups flour

2 teaspoons baking soda

½ teaspoon salt

1 cup (2 sticks) unsalted butter, at room
     temperature

1 cup granulated sugar

½ cup firmly packed brown sugar

5 eggs

3 ounces unsweetened chocolate, melted
     and cooled

2 teaspoons vanilla extract

1 cup buttermilk

½ cup chocolate chips

CHOCOLATE GLAZE

1 cup confectioners' sugar

1 teaspoon instant espresso powder

Pinch of salt

3 to 4 tablespoons warm water

1 tablespoon unsalted butter, melted and
     cooled to warm

¼ cup chocolate chips, melted and cooled to
     warm

½ teaspoon vanilla extract

1. Set the oven rack in the middle position. Preheat the oven to 350°F. Coat two 9 by 5 by 3-inch loaf pans with vegetable oil spray. Line the bottom and ends of the pan with a single strip of wax paper and coat with vegetable oil spray. Dust the pans with flour and tap the pans to remove the excess flour.

2. To make the tea cakes: Add the flour, baking soda, and salt to a bowl and whisk to combine. Set aside.

3. In the bowl of a stand mixer fitted with the paddle attachment, cream the butter, and sugars. With the mixer running, add the eggs one at a time, and mix well. Add the cooled unsweetened chocolate and beat into batter until completely combined.

4. Add the vanilla to the buttermilk in a glass measuring cup. Add the dry ingredients alternately with the buttermilk and vanilla to the creamed mixture in three additions, ending with the dry ingredients. Fold in the chocolate chips. Pour the batter into the prepared pans, level the tops with an offset spatula, and gently tap the pans. Place the pans in the oven and bake for 55 minutes, or until a metal tester inserted into the center of each loaf comes out clean.

5. Transfer the pans to a wire rack and cool the loaves for at least 15 minutes before turning out. Gently lift the cakes out of the pans onto a wire rack using the ends of the wax paper linings. *Be careful; the cakes will still be warm.* Remove the wax paper from the cakes and let cool completely. When the cakes are completely cool, pour the chocolate glaze over the top or sift confectioners' sugar over them.

6. To make the chocolate glaze: Sift the confectioners' sugar, espresso powder, and salt into a

small bowl. Add 2 tablespoons of the warm water and whisk to combine. Add the butter, melted chocolate, and vanilla and whisk until the glaze is glossy. If a looser glaze is desired, add more water, a teaspoon at a time, until you achieve the desired consistency. Slip a sheet of wax paper under the wire rack with the cakes to catch drips. Using a teaspoon or fork, drizzle the glaze over the tops of the cooled cakes, letting the glaze drip down the sides. Allow the glaze to set before cutting with a wide-bladed serrated knife. If glazed, gently wrap any leftover cake in wax paper and store in the re-frigerator. Remove the cakes from the refrigerator 10 minutes before serving. If dusted with confec-tioners' sugar, the cakes can be stored, wrapped in wax paper, at room temperature.

Yield: 2 loaves; 12 slices each

SWEET TOUCHES: Chocolate Tea Cake is delicious warmed in the microwave for 10 seconds.
• A small scoop of vanilla or chocolate ice cream goes well with this cake.

Dark Chocolate Butter Cookies

This is an elegant cookie because of its complexity of flavor and texture. The simple pairing of confectioners' and granulated sugars combined with the cocoa and bitter chocolate works well. The touch of cornmeal gives this not-too-sweet cookie an appealing crunch. This recipe was chosen for the Food & Wine *magazine's staff holiday guide a few years ago.*

1½ cups flour

¼ cup cornmeal

½ cup granulated sugar

½ cup confectioners' sugar, sifted

¼ cup natural American natural nonalkalized cocoa powder

½ teaspoon salt

¼ teaspoon baking soda

1 cup (2 sticks) cold unsalted butter, cut into 16 slices

1 ounce bitter or baking chocolate, melted and cooled

1 teaspoon vanilla extract

1. Put the flour, cornmeal, sugars, cocoa, salt, and baking soda into the bowl of a food processor fitted with the metal blade and pulse until well mixed. Add the butter and pulse until crumbly. Add the melted chocolate and pulse to mix. Add the vanilla and continue to pulse until the dough comes together.

2. Remove the dough from the bowl of the food processor and place on sheet of wax paper or plastic wrap and form into a disk. Chill in the refrigerator for at least 2 hours, or overnight.

3. Set the oven rack in the middle position. Preheat the oven to 325°F. Line a 14 by 16-inch baking sheet with a silicone liner or aluminum foil, shiny side up. Coat the foil with vegetable oil spray. Prepare two baking sheets, if desired.

4. Divide the chilled dough into four portions. Working with one section at a time, and keeping the remaining dough refrigerated, roll out the dough to a thickness of ¼ inch between two pieces of lightly floured wax paper. Cut out cookies with a 2½-inch round cookie cutter, dipped in flour. Place the cookies 2 inches apart on the prepared baking sheets, no more than 12 cookies per sheet. Bake the cookies for 18 to 20 minutes. Slide the foil or the silicone liner with the baked cookies onto a wire rack to cool. Remove the cooled cookies with a metal spatula and transfer to a second wire rack. Repeat with the remaining dough. Store the cookies, between sheets of wax paper, in a covered tin.

Yield: 2 to 2½ dozen cookies

HOW TO MELT CHOCOLATE

In the microwave: Cut the chocolate into shards with a sharp knife. Place the chocolate in a heatproof glass bowl. Do not cover. Microwave on low for 25 seconds and check the progress. Repeat as needed. Two or three 25-second intervals are usually enough to melt the chocolate. Stir after each interval. Allow the chocolate to cool before using. *This is our preferred method.*

On the stovetop: For this traditional method, place the shards of chocolate in the top of a double boiler over gently simmering water. When the chocolate appears to be melted, stir with a heat-proof spatula and remove it from the heat. It is important that no water touches the chocolate.

Fran's Sour Cream Espresso Brownies

How could we not like this recipe for brownies with sour cream in the batter and sour cream in the frosting? This recipe came from the manuscript cookbook of Fran Da Costa of Watertown, Massachusetts. We added the espresso powder to enhance the flavor of the brownies.

BROWNIES

¼ cup instant espresso powder

¼ cup water

2 cups flour

1 teaspoon baking soda

½ teaspoon salt

¼ cup American natural nonalkalized cocoa powder

1 cup granulated sugar

1 cup firmly packed brown sugar

1 cup (2 sticks) unsalted butter, melted

2 eggs

1 cup sour cream

1 teaspoon vanilla extract

FROSTING

4 cups confectioners' sugar, sifted

⅛ teaspoon salt

¼ cup American natural nonalkalized cocoa powder, sifted

6 tablespoons instant espresso powder

½ cup (1 stick) unsalted butter, at room temperature

½ cup sour cream

1 cup walnuts, toasted and coarsely chopped

1. Set the oven rack in the middle position. Preheat the oven to 350°F. Line the bottom and the sides of a 9 by 13 by 2-inch metal pan with aluminum foil, shiny side up. Coat the foil with vegetable oil spray.

2. To make the brownies: Dissolve the instant espresso powder in the water and set aside. Add the flour, baking soda, salt, and cocoa to a bowl and whisk to combine. Set aside.

3. Add the sugars to the bowl of a stand mixer fitted with the paddle attachment and mix. Add the butter to the sugar mixture and cream. Add the eggs one at a time, and combine. Add the sour cream and vanilla and continue beating until combined. Add the dry ingredients to the creamed mixture in three additions. Add the dissolved espresso and incorporate.

4. Pour the batter into the prepared pan and smooth with an offset spatula. Bake the brownies for 45 minutes, or until a metal tester inserted into the center comes out clean. The sides of the brownies will pull away slightly from the sides of the pan when done. Transfer the pan of brownies to a wire rack and cool for 15 minutes before frosting.

5. To make the frosting: Add the confectioners' sugar, salt, cocoa, and espresso powder to a bowl and whisk to combine. Set aside. Add the butter and sour cream to the bowl of the stand mixer fitted with the whisk attachment and whisk to combine. Add the sugar-cocoa-espresso mixture to the sour cream-and-butter mixture in three additions and whisk together. Transfer the frosting to a container or bowl and place in refrigerator until the brownies have cooled for 15 minutes. *The brownies should still be warm before spreading the frosting on top.* Using an offset spatula, spread the frosting on the warm brownies. Sprinkle the walnuts on top of the frosting. Gently press the walnuts into the frosting with the palm of your hand.

6. Allow the frosted brownies to cool for another 15 minutes, then place in the refrigerator to continue cooling. Remove the cooled brownies from the refrigerator. Carefully remove the brownies from the pan, lifting them by the foil edges. Tilt the brownies at an angle and remove the foil. Place the brownies on a cutting board and cut into 2¼-inch squares. There will be a discernable thick layer of frosting on top of the brownies. Any leftover brownies should be stored, loosely covered with wax paper, in the refrigerator.

Yield: about 2 dozen squares

Gloria's "Glorious" Chocolate Pound Cake

Our friend Sue Truax from Bellevue, Nebraska, is the Queen of Chocolate Cakes. A talented writer, she has dedicated herself to preserving the recipes and stories of her family's culinary legacy. This is her mother Gloria Schleiger Story's fabulous chocolate pound cake that always vanished quickly at family gatherings. Sue told us that Gloria's cake is even better the day after it is baked. We added the instant espresso powder to enhance the flavor of the chocolate, but this is a chocolate cake, through and through.

CAKE

3 cups flour

½ cup American natural nonalkalized cocoa powder

1 teaspoon instant espresso powder

½ teaspoon baking powder

1 teaspoon salt

1½ cups (3 sticks) unsalted butter, at room temperature

2½ cups granulated sugar

5 eggs

1 teaspoon vanilla extract

1 cup milk, at room temperature

CHOCOLATE GLAZE

1 cup confectioners' sugar

1 teaspoon instant espresso powder

Pinch of salt

½ teaspoon vanilla extract

3 to 4 tablespoons cold water

¼ cup chocolate chips, melted and cooled to warm

1 tablespoon unsalted butter, melted and cooled to warm

Chocolate perles or chocolate chips (optional)

1. Set the oven rack in the middle position. Preheat the oven to 325°F. Cut out a parchment paper circle to fit the bottom of a 10-inch tube pan. Coat the pan with vegetable oil spray. Place the parchment circle on the bottom of the pan. Dust the pan with flour and tap the pan to remove the excess flour.

2. Add the flour, cocoa, espresso powder, baking powder, and salt to a bowl and whisk to combine. Set aside. Add the butter to the bowl of a stand mixer fitted with the paddle attachment and cream until light and fluffy. Gradually beat in the granulated sugar.

3. With the mixer running, add the eggs one at a time. Add the vanilla and continue to beat. Add the dry ingredients and milk to the creamed mixture alternately in three additions, and beat until completely incorporated. Pour the batter into the prepared pan and place in the oven. Bake for 1 hour and 15 minutes, or until a metal tester inserted into the cake comes out clean and the cake pulls away from the edges of the pan. Remove the cake from the oven, place upright on a wire rack, and let cool for 20 minutes. Go around the edges of the pan and tube with a thin, sharp knife to loosen the cake from the pan, and remove. Then flip the cake onto the rack, right side up. Allow the cake to cool completely on the rack before glazing.

4. To make the chocolate glaze: Sift the confectioners' sugar, espresso powder, and salt into a small bowl. Add 2 tablespoons of the cold water gradually, whisking until the glaze is the desired consistency. Add the vanilla and melted chocolate and whisk to combine. Add the remaining water to glaze, 1 teaspoon at a time, if needed. Add the melted butter and continue to whisk until the glaze is glossy. Slip a sheet of wax paper under the wire

rack with the cake to catch drips. Using a teaspoon or fork, drizzle the glaze over the top of the cake. Allow the glaze to drip down the sides. Sprinkle chocolate perles or chocolate chips on top of the glaze, pressing down gently with your hand to secure the perles or chips to the glaze. When the glaze has set, store the cake, loosely covered with wax paper, at room temperature.

Yield: one 10-inch tube cake; 14 to 16 slices

SWEET TIPS: Gloria's "Glorious" Chocolate Pound Cake can be frozen. Remove the cake from the freezer and allow to come to room temperature before serving.

• See page 147, "How to Melt Butter in a Micro-wave Oven."

Jack's Chocolate Walnut Caramel Tart

We've known award-winning caterer Jack Milan for more than thirty years, and he's generously shared baking tips and recipes. This is an outstanding tart because it contains so many of the elements we love—chocolate, walnuts, and caramel. This tart makes a beautiful presentation, especially when it is drizzled with rich melted chocolate. We suggest you make it early in the day.

CRUST

Unbaked crust for a single-crust pie (page 154)

FILLING

¾ cup sugar

⅛ teaspoon salt

¼ cup water

⅓ cup plus 1 tablespoon milk

½ cup plus 3 tablespoons (1 stick plus
    3 tablespoons) unsalted butter, cut into
    11 slices, at room temperature

¼ cup honey

2 cups walnuts, toasted and coarsely chopped

CHOCOLATE TOPPING

2 ounces bittersweet chocolate

2 tablespoons unsalted butter, at room
    temperature

1. Coat a 9-inch tart pan with a removable bottom with vegetable oil spray. Line the bottom of the tart pan with a parchment paper circle.

2. Roll out the disk of pie dough between two sheets of floured wax paper or parchment paper until it is 2 inches wider than the diameter across the top of the tart pan—11 inches.

3. Remove the top piece of wax paper and fold the rolled crust in half and then in quarters. Place the folded dough into the bottom quarter of the tart pan. Carefully unfold the dough, and let it relax into the tart pan. Be sure that the dough on the sides of the pan is at least ³⁄₁₆ inch thick. Trim the excess dough from the rim with a sharp knife. Chill the tart crust while preparing the filling.

4. *Have a bowl of ice water handy when working with hot caramel. Have an additional small bowl of water and a pastry brush nearby to brush down sugar crystals from the sides of the saucepan.* To make the filling: Add the sugar, salt, and water to a heavy-bottomed 2-quart saucepan. Stir the ingredients with a wooden spoon to combine. Place the saucepan over medium heat. Using the wooden spoon, stir until the sugar has dissolved and the mixture comes to a boil. Wash down any sugar crystals

Jack's Chocolate Walnut Caramel Tart

Jack's Chocolate Walnut Caramel Tart

clinging to the sides of the pan with a pastry brush dipped in cold water. Increase the heat to medium-high and let boil without stirring. When the mixture starts to color, swirl the pan occasionally, until the syrup caramelizes to a golden butterscotch color, 4 to 6 minutes.

5. Remove the pan from the heat and add the milk slowly. *Be very careful, as it will give off a lot of steam, and it will bubble rapidly and rise in the pan.* When the bubbles subside, add the butter slowly. Using a wooden spoon, stir the butter into the hot mixture until dissolved. Return the pan to the heat and adjust the heat to low so that this mixture *barely* simmers, and cook, stirring occasionally with the wooden spoon, for 15 minutes. *Do not leave the pan unattended.* Do not be concerned if the mixture appears to seize. Any curdling will be rectified in the baking process. After 15 minutes, turn off the heat, remove the pan from the stove, and stir in the honey and walnuts. The mixture will still be a little loose. Carefully transfer the hot filling to a heatproof bowl. Cool to room temperature.

6. Set the oven rack in the middle position. Preheat the oven to 475°F. To prevent spills in the oven, prepare an aluminum foil-covered heavy rimmed baking sheet on which to place the un-baked *filled* pie.

7. Add the filling to the prepared tart shell. Place on the lined baking sheet and bake for about 20 minutes, until the tart is a golden brown. Remove the tart carefully from the oven, still on the baking sheet, and place on a wire rack to cool completely. Use a heatproof spatula to smooth any clumps of filling on the surface of the tart. Place the cooled tart in the refrigerator. The tart filling may appear loose, but it will firm up after being refrigerated.

8. To make the chocolate topping: Put the chocolate and butter in a glass bowl, cover with plastic wrap, and place in the microwave oven. Heat in 20-second increments twice, until melted. Remove from the microwave oven, stir to combine, and drizzle over the top of the cooled tart. Store the tart in the refrigerator until ready to serve. Serve chilled directly from the refrigerator. Store any leftover tart, covered with plastic wrap, in the refrigerator.

Yield: one 9-inch tart; 12 slices

SWEET TIP: Any leftover chocolate topping can be placed in a glass bowl, covered with plastic wrap, reheated in the microwave for 10 to 20 seconds, and served with ice cream.

Julia's Chocolate Coconut Bars

When we were on the book tour for Heirloom Cooking, *we appeared on the Fox Network, in Detroit, Michigan. It was a hilarious segment with Marilynn chasing the anchor around a table trying to get him to taste her Sweet Potato Salad. They had to bring the meteorologist on the set to calm everyone down. The cameras were bobbing up and down because the camera operators were laughing so hard. Viewers e-mailed the station asking if we could be on daily. A viewer by the name of Olga Greevsky wrote to the station offering us her late mother-in-law's handwritten manuscript recipes. We tried this recipe for Coconut Bars and added a chocolate topping, really more of a ganache, and it turned out to be a real winner.*

DOUGH

1 cup flour

¼ cup confectioners' sugar

⅛ teaspoon salt

½ cup (1 stick) cold unsalted butter, cut into
    ½-inch dice

FILLING

2 tablespoons flour

½ teaspoon baking powder

⅛ teaspoon salt

1 cup walnuts, toasted and coarsely chopped

½ cup sweetened coconut, shredded

2 eggs, beaten

1½ cups firmly packed brown sugar

1 teaspoon vanilla extract

TOPPING

¼ cup heavy cream

½ cup dark chocolate chips

Pinch of salt

½ teaspoon vanilla extract

1. Set the oven rack in the middle position. Preheat the oven to 350°F. Cover the bottom and sides of an 8 by 8 by 2-inch pan with aluminum foil, shiny side up. Coat the foil with butter or vegetable oil spray.

2. To make the pastry: Add the flour, confectioners' sugar, and salt to the bowl of a food processor fitted with the metal blade and pulse to mix. Add the butter and process until the butter forms small pea-size particles. Remove the dough from the bowl of the food processor and gently form into a ball. Pat the dough into the bottom of the prepared pan with your fingers until the bottom is evenly covered.

3. To make the filling: Add the flour, baking powder, salt, walnuts, and coconut to a bowl, and whisk so that the walnuts are coated with the dry ingredients. Set aside.

4. Add the eggs and brown sugar to the bowl of the stand mixer fitted with the paddle attachment and mix to combine. Add the vanilla and mix in. Add the flour-walnut-coconut mixture to the egg-sugar mixture in three additions and continue beating until the filling comes together. Pour the filling into the dough-lined pan and smooth the top with an offset spatula. Bake for 40 to 45 minutes, or until a metal tester inserted into the filling comes out clean. Remove the pan from the oven and place on a wire rack. Allow to cool for 30 minutes. Place the pan in the refrigerator for 1 hour, or until firm.

5. To make the topping: Heat the cream in a heavy saucepan over medium heat until bubbles form around the edges. Remove from the heat, add the chocolate chips, and let stand for 5 minutes. Stir with a wooden spoon to combine. Stir in the salt and vanilla. Set aside to cool until thickened. Remove the pan with the bars from the refrigerator and pour the topping over the filling. Spread the filling over the top of the bars with an offset spatula. Return the pan to the refrigerator until the topping is firm. Remove the bars from the pan by lifting the foil. Remove the bars from the foil, and cut into squares with a wide-bladed knife while still cold. Store the bars, between sheets of wax paper, in a covered tin in the refrigerator; the chocolate topping tends to soften at room temperature.

Yield: sixteen 2-inch squares

SWEET TIP: Pulse the coconut in a food processor to reduce the length of the flakes. This will make cutting the squares easier.

SWEET TOUCH: Toasted coarsely chopped pecans or slivered almonds can be used instead of the walnuts.

Mocha Truffle Tart

This is one of the recipes that everyone seems to ask us to bring when we receive an invitation to a dinner party. We've been making it for more than forty years. We like the fact that we can make the tart shell ahead, and make the filling the same day as the tart is to be served. The filling is basically a chocolate ganache. Whenever we make this tart, wonderful memories from the 1960s and 1970s, when we began making it, add a bit of sweetness.

CHOCOLATE TART SHELL

1 teaspoon vanilla extract

¼ cup ice water, less 1 teaspoon

2 cups flour

½ cup American natural nonalkalized cocoa
      powder

3 tablespoons sugar

¼ teaspoon salt

1 cup (2 sticks) cold unsalted butter, cut into
      16 slices

FILLING

8 ounces heavy cream

2 teaspoons instant espresso powder

10 ounces bittersweet chocolate

1 teaspoon vanilla extract

Pinch of salt

GARNISH

Sweetened whipped cream

Chocolate coffee beans

1. Coat a 9-inch tart pan with a removable bottom with vegetable oil spray. Line the bottom of the tart pan with a parchment paper circle.

2. To make the chocolate tart shell: Add the vanilla to a ¼-cup measuring cup, then add enough ice water to fill the cup, and set aside. Place the flour, cocoa, sugar, and salt in the bowl of a food processor fitted with a metal blade and pulse three times to mix. Add the butter and pulse until crumbly. Add the vanilla and ice water and pulse until the mixture comes together.

3. Remove the dough from the bowl of the processor, divide it in half, and shape each half into a disk. Unless your kitchen is very warm, you don't have to chill the dough before rolling it out. Reserve the second disk of dough in the refrigerator or freezer for another chocolate pie shell.

4. Roll out the disk of dough between two sheets of floured wax paper or parchment paper until it is 2 inches wider than the diameter across top of the tart pan—11 inches.

5. Set the oven rack in the middle position. Preheat the oven to 400°F.

6. Fold the rolled crust in half, and then in quarters. Place the folded dough into the bottom quarter of the tart pan. Carefully unfold the dough and let it relax into the tart pan. Trim the excess dough from the rim with a sharp knife. Prick the bottom of the tart shell with a fork to prevent the pastry from bubbling during baking. Place a piece of foil coated with vegetable oil spray, coated side down, on top of the tart shell, fitting it loosely into the bottom and sides of the pan, and gently press it down. Bake for 20 minutes.

7. Remove the foil carefully. Prick any existing bubbles in the tart shell. Return the shell to the oven and continue baking. Cover loosely with foil. The tart shell is done when it pulls away slightly from the sides of the pan. This will take at least 5 to 10 minutes. Cool the tart shell on a wire rack before adding the filling.

8. To make the filling: To a heavy-bottomed

saucepan, add the cream and instant espresso powder and whisk to combine. Scald the mixture over low to medium heat, mixing with a wooden spoon, until small bubbles form around the edges of the pan. Remove the pan from the heat and add the chocolate. Allow to sit for 5 minutes, or until the chocolate melts into the cream mixture. Add the vanilla and salt and continue to slowly stir until completely combined. Strain the filling over the cooled tart shell to minimize bubbles forming on the top. Allow the tart to cool to room temperature. When cool, place in the refrigerator until ready to decorate.

9. Decorate the tart with rosettes of whipped cream and chocolate coffee beans. Refrigerate the tart until 10 minutes before serving. Store any leftover tart, loosely covered with wax paper, in the refrigerator.

Yield: one 9-inch tart; 8 slices

Mrs. Finkelstein's Marble Cake

We were given this recipe by our friend Anne Marie Geldart, and when we asked her who Mrs. Finkelstein was, she said she didn't know. She received the recipe from her mother, and her mother didn't know. We have not solved the mystery of Mrs. Finkelstein, but whoever she is, she sure makes a great cake!

3 cups flour

½ teaspoon salt

2½ teaspoons baking powder

4 eggs, separated

1 cup (2 sticks) unsalted butter, at room
    temperature

1¾ cups sugar

1 teaspoon vanilla extract

1 cup milk

1 cup chocolate syrup

2 ounces milk chocolate, chopped into small
    pieces

¼ cup walnuts, toasted and coarsely
    chopped

1. Set the oven rack in the middle position. Preheat the oven to 350°F. Coat a 10-inch tube pan with vegetable oil spray or butter. Dust the pan with flour and tap the pan to remove the excess flour.

2. Add the flour, salt, and baking powder to a bowl and whisk to combine. Set aside.

3. Add the egg whites to the bowl of a stand mixer fitted with the whisk attachment and whip until they form soft peaks. Set aside. If you don't have a second mixer bowl, transfer the egg whites to another bowl and set aside. The cake comes together quickly, so the beaten egg whites will not have time to deflate.

4. Add the butter and sugar to the bowl of the stand mixer fitted with the paddle attachment and cream until combined. Add the egg yolks one at a time, and combine. Add the vanilla and beat in.

5. Add the dry ingredients alternately with the milk to the creamed mixture and combine. Fold in the egg whites, and spoon half of the batter into the prepared pan. Gently shake the half-filled pan to evenly distribute the batter. Add the chocolate syrup to the batter remaining in the mixer bowl and fold in to combine.

6. Spoon the chocolate batter over the vanilla batter in the pan and smooth the batter with a spatula. *Do not mix the batters.* Sprinkle the chopped chocolate and chopped walnuts over the top of the batter. Place the pan in the oven and bake for 60 to 65 minutes, or until a metal tester inserted into the cake comes out clean.

7. Transfer the cake to a wire rack and cool for 25 minutes. Run a butter knife gently around the edges and tube of the pan and invert the cake onto a second rack. Turn the cake right side up onto the first rack. Allow the cake to cool completely before slicing. Any leftover cake can be stored, covered with wax paper, at room temperature, or stored in a cake keeper.

Yield: one 10-inch tube cake; 16 slices

SWEET TIP: We suggest that you treat cake batters gently when using egg whites as part of the leavening so that the air from the beaten egg whites in the batters doesn't deflate. That's why we gently shake the pan filled with batter rather than tap it on the counter to remove air bubbles.

Mrs. Finkelstein's Marble Cake

Palma Snarskis's Cranberry, White Chocolate, and Walnut Squares

Palma Snarskis's Cranberry, White Chocolate, and Walnut Squares

Palma Snarskis and Birute (Ruth) Kascukas were good friends for many years, and Palma baked these cranberry and walnut squares to bring to the gathering after Birute's funeral in 2008. Birute died just days after her fiftieth wedding anniversary. We added the white chocolate chips for a little extra richness. These are simple to make and are good to serve when you want to add a little sweetness to life.

2 cups flour

1 teaspoon salt

2½ cups dried cranberries (can be chopped)

1 cup white chocolate chips

1 cup walnuts, toasted and coarsely chopped

2 cups sugar

⅔ cup (10⅔ tablespoons) unsalted butter, melted and cooled

4 eggs

2 teaspoons vanilla extract or vanilla paste

1. Set the oven rack in the middle position. Preheat the oven to 350°F. Cover the bottom and sides of a 9 by 13 by 2-inch metal pan with aluminum foil, shiny side up. Coat the foil with butter or vegetable oil spray.

2. In a bowl, whisk together the flour, salt, cranberries, white chocolate chips, and walnuts. Set aside.

3. Add the sugar and butter to the bowl of a stand mixer fitted with the paddle attachment and mix until combined. Add the eggs one at a time, beating well after each addition. Add the vanilla and combine. Add the dry ingredients in three additions to the butter-sugar mixture, beating slowly until thoroughly combined.

4. Turn the batter into the prepared pan and distribute evenly, then smooth the top with an offset spatula. Bake for 45 minutes, or until the top is golden brown and a metal tester inserted into the middle comes out clean.

5. Transfer the pan to a wire rack and allow to cool. Flip the cooled bars from the pan in one piece and place on a cutting board or rimless metal cookie sheet. Remove the foil and flip onto another cutting board. Cut into 2¼-inch bars with a wide-bladed knife. Place the bars in a covered tin between sheets of wax paper. The bars can be successfully frozen and served at a later date.

Yield: about twenty-four 2¼-inch bars

SWEET TIPS: Alternatively, the cranberries can be placed in the bowl of the food processor fitted with the metal blade and pulsed a few times to chop.

• Coat the offset spatula and wide-bladed knife with vegetable spray before using.

• The recipe can be cut in half and baked in an 8 by 8 by 2-inch metal pan. The baker should check the bars at 40 minutes to be sure they aren't browning too quickly. If they are, cover the bars with a piece of foil, shiny side up. The bars are done when a metal tester inserted into the center comes out clean, about 45 minutes.

Yield: about sixteen 2-inch bars

Shirley Broner's Fudge Squares
(Chocolate Tea Brownies)

Our friend Cynthia Broner gave us her mother's recipe for "Fudge Squares" a month after her mother died. It is a fitting testimonial to her mother, Shirley Broner, an extraordinary woman who served as a Navy WAVE during World War II, that her recipe—often made as an after-school treat for Cynthia and her sisters—be preserved and handed down. We discovered that these brownies are thin and dainty, so we renamed them "Tea Brownies." This is a simple recipe whipped up in a saucepan, and the Broner girls would compete for who got to lick the pan. We used pecans instead of walnuts, but the recipe lends itself to both nuts.

½ cup (1 stick) unsalted butter, cut into 1-inch
    slices, at room temperature
2 ounces bitter chocolate, cut into shards
1 cup sugar
¼ teaspoon salt
1 teaspoon vanilla extract
2 eggs, beaten
½ cup flour
¼ cup pecans or walnuts, toasted and coarsely
    chopped

1. Set the oven rack in the middle position. Preheat the oven to 350°F. Line the bottom and four sides of an 8 by 8 by 2-inch metal pan with aluminum foil, shiny side up. Coat the foil with vegetable oil spray.

2. Melt the butter in a 2-quart heavy-bottomed saucepan over low heat, stirring with a wooden spoon. When the butter has melted, add the chocolate and mix until it has melted. Remove the pan from the heat, add the sugar, salt, and vanilla, and whisk to combine. Add the beaten eggs and whisk in quickly. Add the flour and continue whisking to combine. Fold the nuts into the batter.

3. Pour the batter into the prepared pan and bake for 25 minutes, or until a metal tester inserted into the brownies comes out clean. Transfer the brownies to a wire rack to cool for 45 minutes. Remove the cooled brownies from the pan with the foil and place on a cutting board. Remove the foil from the brownies and cut into 2-inch squares. The brownies can be covered with wax paper and stored at room temperature.

Yield: 16 squares

Sue's Buttermilk Chocolate Cake

This recipe came from two sources—Sue Truax from Bellevue, Nebraska, and Big Mama, Ethel Johnson Geer, a true Southern lady from Ashburn, Georgia. We combined and adapted the two recipes by adding half butter and half oil and making it in a stand mixer, rather than with a hand mixer. Either way, this is a great cake, and the Chocolate Butter Icing is the closest you can come to a real buttercream without using eggs.

CAKE

2½ cups flour

2 teaspoons baking soda

½ teaspoon salt

½ cup natural nonalkalized American cocoa powder

½ cup (1 stick) unsalted butter, at room temperature

½ cup vegetable oil

2 cups granulated sugar

2 eggs

2 teaspoons vanilla extract

1 cup buttermilk

1 cup boiling water

CHOCOLATE BUTTER ICING

6 tablespoons (¾ stick) unsalted butter, at room temperature

2 cups confectioners' sugar

6 tablespoons natural nonalcalized American cocoa powder

Pinch of salt

1 teaspoon vanilla extract

3 tablespoons milk

1. Set the oven rack in the middle position. Preheat the oven to 350°F. Line a 9 by 13-inch metal baking pan with aluminum foil, running the foil up the four sides of the pan. Coat the pan with vegetable oil spray.

2. To make the cake: Add the flour, baking soda, salt, and cocoa to a bowl and whisk to combine. Set aside.

3. Add the butter, oil, and granulated sugar to the bowl of a stand mixer fitted with the paddle attachment and cream until light and fluffy. With the mixer running, add the eggs one at a time, and continue to beat. Add the vanilla to the buttermilk in a glass measuring cup.

4. Add the dry ingredients and the vanilla-buttermilk mixture alternately to the creamed mixture in three additions and beat until combined. Add the boiling water and continue to beat until completely incorporated. Pour the batter into the prepared pan and bake for 45 minutes, or until a metal tester inserted into the middle of the cake comes out clean. Transfer the cake to a wire rack to cool. The cake will pull away slightly from the edges as it cools. When cake has completely cooled, it can be served directly from the pan, or it can be inverted and flipped onto a serving plate and then iced. If flipping the cake, go around the edges of the pan with a sharp knife, if necessary, to loosen the cake before flipping.

5. To make the chocolate butter icing: Add the butter to the bowl of the stand mixer fitted with the paddle attachment. In another bowl, sift together the confectioners' sugar, cocoa, and salt, then add to the butter. Add the vanilla and mix in. Add 2 tablespoons of the milk *gradually*, beating until the icing is at the desired consistency. Add the remaining 1 tablespoon milk to the icing, if needed. Using a spatula, add the icing to the top of the cake. Using an *offset* spatula, smooth the icing until

just the top of the cake is covered. When the icing has set, store the cake, loosely covered with wax paper, in the refrigerator.

Yield: 1 dozen 3-inch squares

SWEET TIPS: It is better to ice the cake after removing it from the pan.

- There will be just enough icing to cover the top of the cake.

HOW TO SUBSTITUTE WHOLE MILK FOR BUTTERMILK

Buttermilk, or whole milk soured with a tablespoon of lemon juice or apple cider vinegar, can be used interchangeably in baking. Some buttermilk has a small percentage of butterfat, but some is cultured skim milk. Using the buttermilk with the butterfat will result in a slightly richer taste. To sour whole milk, add 1 tablespoon of lemon juice or apple cider vinegar to whole milk and allow to stand for 15 minutes before using.

10 Something Savory

THE RECIPES

Cheddar Poppy Seed Biscotti

Aunt Grace's Rhubarb-Walnut Conserve

Blue Cheese and Pear Tart

Caraway Seed Cookies

Curried Cashew Rounds

Sun-Dried Tomato Parmesan Cocktail Crackers

Savory Cornmeal Parmesan Biscotti

Vidalia Onion Marmalade

Growing up in the middle of the twentieth century in a small
New England town, we weren't exposed to what most sophisticated diners would call "savories." We were familiar with the savory stews,
roasts, and soups that comprised the main courses of our home-cooked
meals, but the only time we found ourselves eating anything that could be
remotely considered a savory were the bologna roll-ups, filled with potato
salad, provided by our distant cousin Gertie Fisher, at family circle events.
These cold-cut cornucopias, however, were called appetizers or *hors
d'oeuvres,* if you wanted to talk fancy. We would also have included little
cocktail franks and sweet-and-sour meatballs with their separate bowl of dipping sauce in this category, but it would be years until we tasted mini quiches
or puff pastry triangles filled with cheese and spinach.

During the 1960s and 1970s, we were beginning to experience the presentation of the "cheese plate" or sometimes the "fruit and cheese" plate at the
houses of more sophisticated friends. When we each moved into our own
apartments in Cambridge, Massachusetts, for the first time, we had the chance
to experiment with the savories we had tried at the homes of the well traveled or in restaurants. The first book Marilynn bought when she moved to

Cambridge was *The Book of Cheese.* This was pretty exciting for someone whose idea of cheese had been cottage or cream, American or cheddar. In our sheltered youth, Swiss and Gouda cheese had been occasionally encountered, but seemed exotic. We looked with awe at the ads on 1950s television at the unbelievable culinary combinations that could be achieved with Velveeta and Ritz crackers. At an iconic Valentine's Party in the 1970s, we served canned smoked oysters from a gift basket our father had received for the holidays from S.S. Pierce, Boston's answer to Dean & Deluca. These, and our lavish presentations of cheese and fruit, were the beginning of our relationship with savories.

It wasn't until we visited a bakery in the central part of Massachusetts that we finally tasted delicate, but piquant, cheese crackers in all manner of shapes—hearts, clubs, diamonds, and spades—that were not from a cardboard box. We were transfixed by the poppy- and sesame-seed–encrusted crackers. We ended up buying some of each and freezing them when we arrived home so that we could examine and taste them in wonder at our leisure.

And then we had a culinary epiphany when we read the recipe and baked the Peppery Cheese Coins created by our friend, pastry chef and cookbook author Nick Malgieri. They were even better than the cheese crackers we had tasted in that now-closed bakery.

We, ourselves, began to experiment with savories by coming up with recipes for Sun-Dried Tomato Parmesan Cocktail Crackers, Curried Cashew Rounds, Cheddar Poppy Seed Biscotti, and Savory Cornmeal Parmesan Biscotti.

We tried using cornmeal in some of our savory

biscotti for crunch, and we found a handwritten recipe for Caraway Seed Cookies that proved satisfying. We even created and baked a Blue Cheese and Pear Tart made with browned butter to serve along with our cheese and fruit plates.

We realized we had grown up when we served white wine with our savory baked treats, and we found that fresh figs, Champagne grapes, and ripe pears complemented the selection of cheeses that we served at our gatherings. Suddenly, the world became our smoked oyster. We invite you to join us in the adventure of discovering and baking savories.

Quick Tips

- Chill unbaked savory dough before slicing or shaping, if necessary.
- Add poppy seeds, sesame seeds, dill, rosemary, thyme, or cayenne pepper to savory dough.
- Garnish the tops of unbaked savories with a few grains of sea salt, cracked black pepper, or nuts.
- Use leftover Blue Cheese or Cheddar Cheese Piecrust to make savory crackers in different shapes, and sprinkle them with poppy seeds, sesame seeds, or pine nuts.
- Store baked savories made with cheese between sheets of wax paper, in covered tins in the refrigerator.

Cheddar Poppy Seed Biscotti

Like all twice-baked cookies or crackers, these Cheddar Poppy Seed Biscotti take some time, but the results are worth it. It's nice to have some of these savory biscotti available when guests drop by. They have a crunch to them, and they're not too spicy. They're great to serve with white wine or as part of a cheese plate. Cheddar Poppy Seed Biscotti also make a nice hostess gift at the holidays.

2 cups flour

1 teaspoon baking powder

½ teaspoon salt

¾ teaspoon black pepper

1 teaspoon paprika

2 tablespoons poppy seeds

1 cup grated extra-sharp cheddar cheese
    (about 4 ounces before grating)

½ cup (1 stick) unsalted butter, at room
    temperature

1 tablespoon sugar

3 eggs

1. Set the oven rack in the middle position. Preheat the oven to 350°F. Line two 14 by 16-inch baking sheets with a silicone liner or aluminum foil, shiny side up. Coat the foil with vegetable oil spray.

2. Add the flour, baking powder, salt, black pepper, paprika, poppy seeds, and cheddar cheese to a bowl and whisk to combine. Set aside.

3. In the bowl of a stand mixer fitted with the paddle attachment, cream the butter and sugar. Add the eggs one at time, and continue beating until combined. Add the dry ingredients in three additions to the creamed mixture and beat until combined and a soft dough comes together.

4. Place the dough in a covered freezer-proof container or in a sealed plastic bag, and chill in the freezer for at least 1 hour, or until the dough has firmed up. Remove the dough from the freezer when firm and, using a spatula, divide the dough into two portions. Place the portions on one of the prepared baking sheets.

5. Wearing disposable gloves, shape the dough into two rolls each measuring 8 inches long, and then *flatten* to 9 inches long and ¾ inches high. Alternatively, dip your fingers in a little cold water and form the loaves. Bake for 30 minutes, or until the loaves are golden brown and a tester inserted into the center of each loaf comes out dry. Transfer the baking sheet to a wire rack and cool the loaves for 15 minutes.

6. Transfer one loaf at a time from the baking sheet to a cutting board. Using a serrated knife, cut the loaf into diagonal slices about ½ inch wide. Repeat with the remaining loaf. Place the biscotti slices, cut side down, on the baking sheet and return to the oven for 10 minutes. Remove from the oven, turn the biscotti over (the second cut side will be up), and return to the oven for another 10 minutes. Slide the foil or the silicone liner with the baked biscotti onto a wire rack to cool. Remove the cooled biscotti with a metal spatula and transfer to second wire rack. Repeat with other loaf. Store the biscotti in a covered tin. Biscotti should keep crisp for a week. Biscotti also freeze well.

Yield: about 3 dozen biscotti

Aunt Grace's Rhubarb-Walnut Conserve

Aunt Grace's Rhubarb-Walnut Conserve

This recipe for rhubarb conserve came from Sue Truax's Aunt Grace, who was a first-generation descendent of the Czar's Germans, from Norka, Russia. This conserve is very much like a jam made from the tenderest stalks of rhubarb. We cut this recipe in half to make a smaller amount of the gingery, crunchy conserve. We suggest that you keep a bowl of ice and water close at hand when making and pouring the conserve into jars.

2 pounds rhubarb, cut into ½-inch pieces
   (8 cups)
4½ cups sugar
Juice, pulp, and grated zest of 1 large orange
Juice, pulp, and grated zest of 1 lemon
¾ cup golden raisins
1 cup walnuts, toasted and coarsely chopped
1 teaspoon salt
1½ teaspoons ground ginger

1. Add the rhubarb, sugar, and orange and lemon juices, pulps, and zests to a large nonreactive glass or metal bowl. Do not use an enameled bowl. Mix the ingredients, cover with plastic wrap, and store in the refrigerator overnight.

2. The next day, remove the bowl with the rhubarb mixture from the refrigerator and stir. Add the contents of the bowl to a large, heavy Dutch oven. Add the raisins and stir to combine. Bring the mixture to a boil, stirring with a wooden spoon, and continue to boil for 10 minutes, stirring to prevent the mixture from sticking to the bottom of the Dutch oven. Add the walnuts and boil, stirring, for another 10 minutes. Add the salt and ground ginger to the hot mixture and stir to combine. Check the temperature of the conserve with a candy thermometer; it should register 220°F. Re-move the Dutch oven from the heat and place on a cool surface of the stovetop. Allow to cool to room temperature. The conserve will thicken as it cools.

3. Spoon the cooled conserve into clean glass containers. Cover, label, and refrigerate for up to 2 weeks. The conserve can be frozen for 2 months.

Yield: 5¼ cups conserve

SWEET TOUCHES: Aunt Grace's Rhubarb-Walnut Conserve is wonderful on homemade bread.
• The conserve is also good on top of vanilla ice cream or sandwiched between Graham Shingles (see page 93).

Blue Cheese and Pear Tart

This is an unusual tart because it is both savory and sweet. Serve this golden tart as a first course, a luncheon dish, or a dessert. It is also perfect to serve with a cheese and fruit plate. There is blue cheese in both the crust and in the filling, and this is a good recipe for learning to make browned butter that can be used in other recipes.

BLUE CHEESE CRUST

2½ cups flour

2 tablespoons sugar

¼ teaspoon salt

1 cup (2 sticks) cold unsalted butter, cut into
⠀⠀½-inch dice

2 ounces cold blue cheese, cut into ½-inch
⠀⠀pieces

¼ cup ice water

FILLING

½ cup (1 stick) unsalted butter, at room
⠀⠀temperature

¼ cup flour

¼ cup sugar

⅛ teaspoon salt

2 eggs

2 teaspoons Poire Williams liqueur or 1
⠀⠀teaspoon vanilla extract

3 firm pears, peeled, cored, and cut
⠀⠀lengthwise into ½-inch slices

1 ounce blue cheese, crumbled, at
⠀⠀room-temperature

1. Coat a 9-inch tart pan with a removable bottom with vegetable oil spray. Line the bottom of the tart pan with a parchment paper circle.

2. To make the blue cheese crust: Put the flour, sugar, and salt in the bowl of a food processor

fitted with the metal blade and pulse three times to mix. Add the butter and blue cheese and pulse until crumbly. Add the ice water and pulse until the mixture comes together.

3. Remove the dough from the bowl of the processor, divide in half, and shape each half into a disk. Unless your kitchen is very warm, you don't have to chill the dough before rolling it out. This recipe will make two piecrusts. Roll out one of the disks into a circle eleven inches in diameter and ³⁄₁₆ inch thick. Fit into the prepared tart pan and trim the top edge. Store the other half of the dough in the refrigerator or freezer for another use. It can be used to make Blue Cheese Crackers, page 282.

4. To make the browned butter for the filling: Add the butter to a 9- or 10-inch heavy frying pan and stir with a wooden spoon over medium heat for 1½ to 2 minutes, or until the butter is bubbling and foamy. Stop using the wooden spoon, but continue to move the butter around by swirling the pan until the butter is golden brown. Do not allow the butter to darken or burn. *Be patient, this will take a few minutes. If the butter starts to "spit" out of the pan, turn the heat down slightly.* Strain the browned butter into a glass bowl; there may be some brown spots left in the butter, but this will improve the flavor. Set aside.

5. Set the oven rack in the middle position. Preheat the oven to 375°F. Cover a 14 by 16-inch baking sheet with aluminum foil, shiny side up. Coat the foil with vegetable oil spray.

6. Whisk together the flour, sugar, salt, eggs, and Poire Williams liqueur in a bowl. *Slowly* add the browned butter and whisk to combine. Set aside. Arrange the pear slices in a circular pattern on top of the tart shell. Sprinkle the blue cheese over the pears. When arranging the pear slices, al-

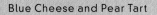
Blue Cheese and Pear Tart

low room for the browned butter filling. Carefully pour the browned butter filling over the pears and blue cheese.

7. Place the tart on the foil-covered baking sheet to prevent spills in the oven. Bake the tart for 1 hour, or until the filling is bubbling and the crust is golden brown. Check for doneness after 45 minutes and in 5-minute increments thereafter. If the crust is browning too quickly, tent with foil. Remove the tart from the oven and place on the stovetop. Carefully remove the tart from the foil-covered baking sheet and place on a wire rack to cool. When cool enough to handle, remove from the tart pan and transfer to a serving platter. Serve warm or at room temperature. *Do not leave the tart out of the refrigerator for long periods of time because it contains an egg custard.* Store any leftover tart, covered with plastic wrap, in the refrigerator.

Yield: one 9-inch tart; 8 to 10 slices

SWEET TIP: Other cheeses can be substituted for the blue cheese, such as cheddar or Gruyère.

Caraway Seed Cookies

We found this handwritten recipe on a page from a fragile manuscript cookbook. It is the only recipe for a cookie using caraway seeds that we've ever found. When we baked the seed cookies, we found that they were moist and rich yet still crisp. Although the recipe calls for sugar, the addition of caraway seeds elevates these cookies to another level. They pair well with cheese and wine, but they can also be enjoyed with a cup of tea.

2¾ cups flour

1 teaspoon baking soda

¼ teaspoon salt

1 tablespoon caraway seeds

1 cup (2 sticks) unsalted butter, at room
temperature

1½ cups sugar

1 cup milk

1. Set the oven rack in the middle position. Preheat the oven to 350°F. Line a 14 by 16-inch baking sheet with a silicone liner or aluminum foil, shiny side up. Coat the foil with vegetable oil spray.

2. Place the flour, baking soda, salt, and caraway seeds in a bowl and whisk to combine. Set aside. Add the butter and sugar to the bowl of a stand mixer fitted with the paddle attachment and cream until smooth. Add the dry ingredients and milk alternately to the creamed mixture in two additions and continue to mix until the dough comes together.

3. Drop the dough by rounded teaspoons onto the prepared baking sheet, 12 cookies per sheet. Place in the oven and bake for 20 minutes. Slide the foil or the silicone liner with the baked cookies onto a wire rack to cool for 5 minutes. Remove the cooled cookies with a metal spatula and transfer to a second wire rack. The cookies will firm up as they cool. Store the cookies, between sheets of wax paper, in a covered tin.

Yield: 5 dozen cookies

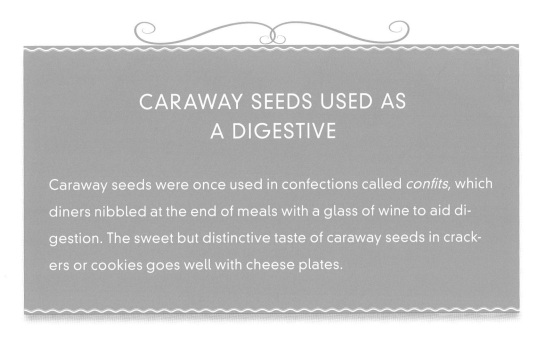

CARAWAY SEEDS USED AS A DIGESTIVE

Caraway seeds were once used in confections called *confits*, which diners nibbled at the end of meals with a glass of wine to aid digestion. The sweet but distinctive taste of caraway seeds in crackers or cookies goes well with cheese plates.

Curried Cashew Rounds

Curried Cashew Rounds

We made these savory crackers because we wanted to try baking one using curry and cashews. We've always found cashews a bit exotic because of their texture and flavor, and the cheddar cheese seems to balance the spiciness of the curry. We found that our guests enjoyed these salty crackers with both beer and white wine, so we started giving them as hostess gifts. They are simple to make, and we love the way our kitchen smells when these crackers are baking. They remind us of the dark spicy aromas of the Indian restaurants we used to visit when we first moved to Cambridge. The amount of curry powder can be adjusted for a stronger curry flavor.

1 cup flour
½ teaspoon salt
½ teaspoon coarsely ground black pepper
2 teaspoons curry powder
4 ounces extra-sharp cheddar cheese
½ cup (1 stick) cold unsalted butter, cut into
    8 slices
1 cup cashews, toasted and coarsely chopped
36 whole cashews

1. Add the flour, salt, pepper, and curry powder to a bowl and whisk to combine. Set aside. Add the cheddar cheese and butter to the bowl of a food processor fitted with the metal blade and pulse five or six times to combine. Add the dry ingredients and pulse until the mixture forms a ball.

2. Remove the dough from the bowl of the food processor. Add the chopped cashews to the dough, and wearing disposable gloves, if desired, work the nuts into the dough. Divide the dough in half, wrap each half in wax paper or plastic wrap, and refrigerate until firm, about 2 hours.

3. Set the oven rack in the middle position. Preheat the oven to 350°F. Line three 14 by 16-inch baking sheets with silicone liners or aluminum foil, shiny side up. Coat the foil with vegetable oil spray.

4. Remove half of the dough from the refrigerator. Scoop out 1 teaspoon of the dough and form into ball 1¼ inches in diameter. Continue making balls with the rest of the dough. If the dough becomes too soft to work with, place it back in the refrigerator to firm up. Cut a 4 by 4-inch square of wax paper. Place the wax paper square on top of each ball and press gently with the bottom of a glass to flatten. Place a whole cashew in the center of each cracker. Repeat with the remaining half of the dough. Do not place more than 12 crackers on a baking sheet. Bake for 15 minutes. The crackers will be a pale yellow and slightly brown around the edges and bottoms. Slide the foil or the silicone liner with the baked crackers onto a wire rack to cool. Remove the cooled crackers with a metal spatula and transfer to a second wire rack. Store the crackers, between sheets of wax paper, in a covered tin.

Yield: 3 dozen 1¼-inch crackers

SWEET TIP: Do not add salt if using salted cashews.

Sun-Dried Tomato Parmesan Cocktail Crackers

These rosy-hued crackers came about because we discovered a package of sun-dried tomatoes on our pantry shelf, and we found we had a wedge of Parmesan cheese in our refrigerator. This is one of those recipes that comes together from bits and pieces, and then becomes a staple. The red color of these salty crackers makes them perfect for holiday gatherings. These rich crumbly crackers would also be appropriate for Valentine's Day.

1 cup flour, plus 3 tablespoons

½ teaspoon kosher salt

½ teaspoon coarsely ground black pepper

⅛ teaspoon cayenne pepper

⅓ cup sun-dried tomatoes, firmly packed

½ cup (1 stick) cold unsalted butter, cut in
    8 slices

1 cup grated Parmesan cheese (about
    4 ounces before grating)

3 tablespoons cold water

1. Add the flour, salt, black pepper, and cayenne to a small bowl and whisk to combine. Set aside. Add the sun-dried tomatoes, butter, and Parmesan cheese to the bowl of a food processor fitted with the metal blade and pulse three or four times. Add the dry ingredients and pulse to combine. Add the water and pulse until a soft dough forms.

2. Remove the dough from the processor. Using your hands, or wearing disposable gloves, form the dough into a log 12½ inches long by 1½ inches wide. Cover the log with wax paper or plastic wrap and chill in the refrigerator for about 2 hours, or until the log is firm enough to slice into disks.

3. Set the oven rack in the middle position. Preheat the oven to 350°F. Line three 14 by 16-inch baking sheets with silicone liners or aluminum foil, shiny side up. Coat the foil with vegetable oil spray.

4. Cut the chilled dough into ¼-inch slices. Place the slices on the prepared baking sheets, no more than 16 crackers per sheet. Bake for 15 minutes. The rose-colored crackers will be lightly brown around the edges. Slide the foil or the silicone liner with the baked crackers onto a wire rack to cool. Remove the cooled crackers with a metal spatula and transfer to a second wire rack. The crackers will firm up a bit on cooling. Repeat with remaining dough. Store the crackers, between sheets of wax paper, in a covered tin.

Yield: 42 crackers

SWEET TIP: Because the dough for these crackers is red in color, they will never fully brown when baked.

Savory Blue Cheese Crackers and
Savory Cheddar Cheese Crackers
from leftover piecrust

BEING CREATIVE WITH LEFTOVER PIECRUST

We've always been excited about working with leftover scraps of piecrust, ever since the days when we made jam tarts with our mother at the kitchen table on Sea Foam Avenue. There always seemed to be such a joyful sense of adventure in deciding and making unexpected treats with these bits and pieces of dough that were too good to discard.

When we were testing the Blue Cheese and Pear Tart and the Cheddar Crumble Apple Pie with Cheddar Cheese Crust, Sheila decided to make savory crackers from the scraps of both types of dough. She put together the scraps of dough from the tart and the pie, wrapped them separately in plastic wrap, and chilled them in the refrigerator until they were cold enough to roll out between 2 sheets of lightly floured wax paper.

We found that rolling out the dough ¼ inch thick made it easy to work with. After cutting out the "crackers," we placed them on a 14 by 16-inch baking sheet covered with a silicone liner or aluminum foil, shiny side up. We coated the foil with vegetable oil spray.

We set the oven rack in the middle position and preheated the oven to 350°F.

We chose pine nuts, pecan halves, or coarsely chopped walnuts, and toasted the nuts to bring out their flavor. We also added poppy seeds or sesame seeds to the dough, or sprinkled them on top.

We chose round, square, triangular, or any unusual-shaped cookie cutters to shape our crackers.

We baked the crackers for 15 to 17 minutes, or until they were a light golden color. Slide the foil or the silicone liner with the baked crackers onto a wire rack to cool. Remove the cooled crackers with a metal spatula and transfer to a second wire rack. We stored them separately, between sheets of wax paper, in covered tins.

CRACKER FACTS

• Your crackers might be a little crisper because the dough scraps have been handled more.

• This is also good for using up an extra piecrust when making two piecrusts at once and using only one for a bottom crust or one for a top crust.

Savory Cornmeal Parmesan Biscotti

This is one of those recipes that came about because we love the taste of Parmesan cheese and the crunch of cornmeal. We firmly believe that not all biscotti have to be sweet. These biscotti are wonderful with a cheese and fruit plate, and can make an unusual addition to the holiday breadbasket. Nice, too, with a bowl of hot soup.

2 cups flour

½ cup cornmeal

1 teaspoon baking powder

1 teaspoon salt

1 teaspoon coarsely ground black pepper

½ teaspoon cayenne pepper

1 cup dried cranberries (optional)

½ cup (1 stick) unsalted butter, at room
    temperature

¼ cup sugar

3 eggs

1 cup grated Parmesan cheese
    (about 4 ounces before grating)

½ cup pine nuts, toasted

1. Set the oven rack in the middle position. Preheat the oven to 350°F. Line two 14 by 16-inch baking sheets with silicone liners or aluminum foil, shiny side up. Coat the foil with vegetable oil spray.

2. Add the flour, cornmeal, baking powder, salt, black pepper, cayenne, and cranberries, if using, to a bowl and whisk to combine. Set aside.

3. In the bowl of a stand mixer fitted with the paddle attachment, cream the butter and sugar. Add the eggs one at a time, and continue beating until completely incorporated. Add the dry ingredients, Parmesan cheese, and toasted pine nuts to the creamed mixture in three additions, and beat until combined and firm dough comes together. Turn off mixer.

4. Remove the dough from the mixing bowl and, using a knife or spatula, divide the dough in half on a silicone-lined baking sheet. Shape the dough into 2 loaves measuring 11½ inches long by 2½ inches wide and about ½ inch high. Dip your hands in cold water, or wear disposable gloves, when forming the loaves.

5. Place the baking sheet in oven and bake for about 25 minutes, or until the loaves are golden brown and a metal tester inserted into the center of each loaf comes out dry. Transfer the baking sheet to a wire rack and cool the loaves for 10 minutes.

6. Transfer one cooled loaf at a time from the baking sheet to a cutting board. Using a long serrated knife, cut the loaf into diagonal slices ½ inch thick. Repeat with the remaining loaf. Divide the biscotti slices cut side down, between *two baking sheets*. Return one sheet to the oven for 12 minutes. Remove the pan from the oven, turn the biscotti over (the second cut side will be up), and return to the oven for another 12 minutes, depending on how crisp you want the biscotti. *Do not let the biscotti burn.* Slide the foil or the silicone liner with the baked biscotti onto a wire rack to cool. Remove the cooled biscotti with a metal spatula and transfer to a second wire rack. Repeat with the remaining sheet of biscotti if not enough room for all slices on one sheet. Store the biscotti, between sheets of wax paper, in a covered tin. Biscotti stay crisp for a week.

Yield: about 32 biscotti

SWEET TIP: Toast pine nuts in a 350°F. oven for *3 minutes* on each side. Check carefully that they do not burn.

Vidalia Onion Marmalade

This sweet-and-sour marmalade goes well with our Salt and Pepper Potato Bread and the Orange Pecan Yeast Bread. We make it when Vidalia onions are in season. Because the sugar level of Vidalia onions is higher than that of other onions, we can't guarantee that the marmalade will taste the same if Vidalia onions aren't used. We also like to serve this marmalade with savory dishes such as brisket or glazed corned beef. Slicing the onions in a food processor achieves the desired size. Adding the butter at the end balances the flavor of the Vidalia Onion Marmalade.

¼ cup olive oil

8 cups thinly sliced Vidalia onions
    (about 2 pounds)

1 teaspoon black pepper

½ teaspoon kosher salt

¼ cup honey

½ cup plus 2 tablespoons apple cider vinegar

1 cup golden raisins

¼ cup firmly packed brown sugar

¼ cup dry sherry

2 tablespoons unsalted butter

1. Heat the olive oil in a large Dutch oven over medium heat. Add the Vidalia onions and black pepper and cook over medium-high heat, stirring with a wooden spoon, until the onions begin to wilt, 3 to 4 minutes.

2. Add the salt and continue to cook, stirring, until the onions become translucent, about 3 minutes. Add the honey and vinegar and continue cooking for 2 minutes. Turn off the heat and add the golden raisins, brown sugar, and sherry. Turn the heat back on to medium-high and continue to cook, stirring with a wooden spoon, for 12 to 15 minutes, or until the liquid has evaporated; turn the heat to high if necessary. The onions will turn lightly brown.

3. Turn off the heat, add the butter and stir. Cool completely and place in nonreactive glass containers. The onion marmalade should be covered, and can be stored in the refrigerator for 2 weeks, or transferred to freezer containers and frozen for 2 months.

Yield: 4 cups marmalade

SWEET TIPS: One pound of Vidalia onions equals 4 cups sliced onions.

- It's easier to work with large onions.
- This recipe can be cut in half.

SOURCES

Ingredients and Equipment, Collectible Cookbooks

King Arthur Flour
www.kingarthurflour.com
The Baker's Catalog
Tel. 800-827-6836
www.bakerscatalogue.com
Grains, ingredients, equipment

Bob's Red Mill
Tel. 800-349-2173
www.bobsredmill.com
Grains, gluten-free flours and ingredients

Christina's Homemade Ice Cream,
Spice & Specialty Foods
1255 Cambridge Street
Cambridge, MA 02139
Tel. 617-492-7021
Baking supplies, grains, spices, flours

Fancy Flours
Tel. 406-587-0118
www.fancyflours.com
Baking supplies, cupcake liners, food styling
(edible art)

Fantes
Tel. 888-44-FANTE
mail@fantes.com
www.fantes.com
Baking supplies, equipment, food molds

Fat Daddios
Tel. 866-418-9001
info@fatdaddios
www.fatdaddios.com
Baking equipment, food molds

Formaggio Kitchen
244 Huron Avenue
Cambridge, MA 02138
Tel. 888-212-3224
Specialty foods, baking supplies

JB Prince
Tel. 800-473-0577
www.jbprince.com
Baking equipment, food molds,
books on baking

Kalustyan's
Tel. 800-352-3451
www.kalustyans.com
Spices, specialty foods

KitchenWares by Blackstone's
Tel. 857-366-4237
info@kitchenwaresboston.com
Baking equipment, specialty foods, books

Nielsen-Massey Vanillas Inc.
Tel. 800-525-PURE (7873)
info@nielsenmassey.com
Baking supplies, extracts, spices

Nordic Ware
Tel. 877-466-7342
www.nordicware.com
Baking equipment

Penzeys' Spices
Tel. 800-741-7787
www.penzeys.com
Spices, extracts

Trader Joe's
www.traderjoes.com
Baking supplies

Sparrow Enterprises
Tel. 617-569-3900
www.chocolatebysparrow.com
info@sparrowfoods.com
Chocolate, baking supplies
Chocolate perles (chocolate pearls)
Jimmies (chocolate vermicelli)

Sur la Table
Tel. 800-243-0852
www.surlatable.com
Baking supplies, equipment

Whole Foods Market
www.wholefoodsmarket.com
Baking Supplies

Williams-Sonoma Marketplace
Tel. 877-812-6235
www.williams-sonoma.com
Baking supplies, equipment

Zabar's
Tel. 800-697-6301
www.zabars.com
Specialty Foods, baking equipment

Cookbooks

Bonnie Slotnick Cookbooks
28 East Second Street (Bowery/Second Avenue)
New York, NY 10003
Tel. 212-989-8962
bonnieslotnickbooks@earthlink.net
www.bonnieslotnickcookbooks.com
Out of Print Cookbooks
Ephemera

Rabelais: Fine Books on Food & Drink
Don & Samantha Lindgren
2 Main Street, 18-214
Biddeford, Maine 04005
Tel: 207-602-6246

INDEX